LOBBYING
AND
GOVERNMENT
RELATIONS

Recent Titles from Quorum Books

Computer Simulation in Business Decision Making: A Guide for Managers, Planners, and MIS Professionals
Roy L. Nersesian

A Stakeholder Approach to Corporate Governance: Managing in a Dynamic Environment
Abbass F. Alkhafaji

The Impact of Intergovernmental Grants on the Aggregate Public Sector
Daniel P. Schwallie

Managing Employee Rights and Responsibilities
Chimezie A. B. Osigweh, Yg., editor

The Coming Crisis in Accounting
Ahmed Belkaoui

Managing Human Service Organizations
Lynn E. Miller, editor

Behavioral Accounting: The Research and Practical Issues
Ahmed Belkaoui

Personnel Policies and Procedures for Health Care Facilities: A Manager's Manual and Guide
Eugene P. Buccini and Charles P. Mullaney

Designing the Cost-Effective Office: A Guide for Facilities Planners and Managers
Jack M. Fredrickson

Evolution of United States Budgeting: Changing Fiscal and Financial Concepts
Annette E. Meyer

The Employment Contract: Rights and Duties of Employers and Employees
Warren Freedman

ERRATA

On page 201, the Committee for Survival of a Free Congress should be listed as "conservative."

On page 202, the sixth organization listed should read, National Conference of State Legislatures.

LOBBYING AND GOVERNMENT RELATIONS

A Guide for Executives

CHARLES S. MACK

Foreword by
RICHARD A. EDWARDS

Q

QUORUM BOOKS

New York • Westport, Connecticut • London

Library of Congress Cataloging-in-Publication Data

Mack, Charles S.
    Lobbying and government relations.

    Bibliography: p.
    Includes index.
    1. Lobbying—United States.   2. Business and
politics—United States.   I. Title.
JK1118.M28   1989   324'.4'0973   88–35730
ISBN 0–89930–390–0 (lib. bdg. : alk. paper)

British Library Cataloguing in Publication Data is available.

Library of Congress Catalog Card Number: 88–35730
ISBN: 0–89930–390–0

First published in 1989 by Quorum Books

Greenwood Press, Inc.
88 Post Road West, Westport, Connecticut   06881

Printed in the United States of America

The paper used in this book complies with the
Permanent Paper Standard issued by the National
Information Standards Organization (Z39.48–1984).

10 9 8 7 6 5 4 3 2 1

Copyright Acknowledgments

The author and publisher gratefully acknowledge permission to reprint material
from the following copyrighted sources.

Guidelines for Professional Conduct. Washington, D.C.: American League of
Lobbyists, September 1987.

A Statement of Ethical Guidelines for Business Public Affairs Professionals.
Washington, D.C.: Public Affairs Council, May 1979.

Guidelines for the Operation of a Business-Employee Political Action Committee.
Washington, D.C.: Public Affairs Council, September 1986.

To Alice,
the bringer of joy

Contents

Foreword

Richard A. Edwards

In his book entitled *Management: Tasks, Responsibilities, Practices* (New York: Harper & Row, 1974), Peter F. Drucker wrote: "Few relationships are as critical to the business enterprise itself as the relationship to government," adding that such a relationship "urgently needs rethinking, reappraisal, and restructuring." Those needs have grown in the intervening years, deregulation and regulatory reform to the contrary notwithstanding.

During the eight years of the Ronald Reagan presidency, several major corporations reduced their external relations staffs, which included the release of many individuals who had been charged with lobbying responsibilities. The apparent reason for this phenomenon was the administration's favorable attitudes toward business. A new administration may signal the need for an expert lobbying staff to return. This book will provide expert guidance as to both the content and structure of such new or restored programs.

Charles Mack has, in this book, made a significant contribution to an improved understanding of the keystone of business-government relations, namely lobbying. For four reasons, this book deserves careful reading and thoughtful consideration by students and teachers as both novice and experienced practitioners of business-government relations.

First, and most importantly, the book is the product of the author's quarter-century of experience in leadership roles in national and state trade associations, major corporations, and the political process. Unfortunately, much of the literature in this field has been written by individuals with no managerial experience, those who rely upon interviews and questionnaires as a most unreliable substitute for actual experience.

Charles Mack, by contrast, is well known to virtually all business-government relations practitioners. He played an active leadership role in the Public

Affairs Committee of the National Society of State Legislators and, when that society was merged with two other organizations to form the National Conference of State Legislatures, he assisted in the creation of the conference's premier corporate support group, the State Governmental Affairs Council.

Second, the author writes in an extraordinarily clear and direct manner without any of the obfuscatory jargon—e.g., prisoner's dilemma, linear functions, cognitive restraints, multiple hypotheses, performance ambiguity—so frequently encountered in managerial theory literature.

Third, the author has drawn upon his extensive experience to provide the reader with numerous specific examples of the conceptual points he offers. These include, for example, the reasons that groups lobby (Chapter 1), the goals of issue research (Chapter 2), the types of lobbying strategies (Chapter 3), a model government relations program (Chapter 4), and so on throughout the book.

Fourth, this book provides an excellent and totally defensible rationale for lobbying, including its role in a pluralistic society and the manner in which ethical constraints should be observed.

The principal merit of this excellent book is its systematic focus on the lobbying concept, function, and administration. In my forty-eight years as a student, teacher, and practitioner of business-government relations, I do not recall encountering a more useful and accurate treatment of lobbying. Indeed, I believe this book will be recognized as the definitive work on that subject.

Richard A. Edwards is former Senior Vice President, Government and Industry Relations, Metropolitan Life Insurance Company, and Frederick R. Kappel Professor of Business-Government Relations, University of Minnesota.

Preface

This book is about the communications of the people in a pluralistic society as they exercise their First Amendment rights to assure that their elected representatives and other government officials are responsive to their democratically expressed wants and needs.

Someone else, with a different point of view, might say that this book is about the ultra-sophisticated techniques of persuasion employed by the special interests to manipulate legislators and other government officials into doing their bidding, whether the public interest is served or not.

In other words, this book is about lobbying—one of the most controversial exercises of constitutional rights, but also one of the most important.

Lobbying has generally meant the efforts of individuals and the interest groups they usually represent to influence legislation or the regulatory actions of governments. This book goes beyond this traditional description to delve into the newer arts, skills, and technologies that have taken modern lobbying well beyond the personal salesmanship of persuasive advocates.

As far back as the early 1970s when I was teaching a course on government relations at West Point, I have searched for a comprehensive description of the subject from the viewpoint of a manager and practitioner. Although many books have been published on various aspects of government relations—political finance, grass-roots programs, and issue management particularly—there has been no satisfactory work that covers the field as a whole from an "insider's" perspective.

The result was my decision to write such a book, based on more than a quarter-century of personal experience in politics, lobbying, consulting, corporate-government relations, and trade association management.

The work is intended as a guide and resource for five audiences:

- Corporate executives with a need to start, reassess, or revitalize government relations programs in their companies.

- Executives and leaders of trade associations, labor unions, public interest groups, and other organizations with a similar need.

- Government officials, including legislators and their staffs, with an interest in exploring how the private sector approaches government relations.

- Civic and community leaders wishing to learn how the lobbying process operates.

- Political science students, both graduate and undergraduate, with a need for a practical book on the lobbying arts to supplement the many scholarly works on issue group analysis.

No book of this kind can be prepared without considerable help, and I have had more than my share—particularly from the excellent staff of the Public Affairs Council. My particular gratitude goes to Leslie Swift-Rosenzweig, executive director of the Council's Foundation for Public Affairs, for her impressive knowledge of source materials and unfailing graciousness in providing me with access to them. Peter Kennerdell and Wes Pederson of the Council staff also provided helpful advice and assistance.

Raymond L. Hoewing, the Council's able president, and his distinguished predecessor, Richard A. Armstrong, provided numerous analytical comments that improved the manuscript substantially—as did the excellent suggestions of Stevenson T. Walker, director of government relations for the Reynolds Metals Company.

My especial gratitude must go to Richard A. Edwards, former senior vice president of the Metropolitan Life Insurance Company and, until his recent retirement, Kappel Professor of Business-Government Relations at the University of Minnesota, not only for the generous foreword he contributed but also for his suggestions and support throughout this project.

My wife, Alice Barrett Mack, was a constant source of loving encouragement and editorial advice. The book could not have been written without her.

Others, far too numerous to mention by name, provided substantial information and advice on various subjects for which I am most grateful.

Of course, the author alone is fully responsible for any errors of fact or judgment that the book may contain.

A request to the reader: Because the field of government relations is evolving so rapidly, I would be grateful for any information about program innovations and developments that could be incorporated into future editions.

We are all creatures of our experiences. Mine are the product of a career spent in political activity and the service of business organizations. Those experiences are reflected in these pages. However, this book is not about policy or philosophy, but about process.

The government relations techniques used by business are also available to the AFL-CIO, the Sierra Club, the Consumer Federation, and Common Cause. This book is offered to each of them, and all the other interests striving within this American republic.

Charles S. Mack

1

Introduction: What is Government Relations?

Congress shall make no law respecting establishment of religion, or prohibiting the free exercise thereof; or abridging the freedom of speech, or of the press, or the right of the people peaceably to assemble, and to petition the Government for a redress of grievances.

The First Amendment to the U.S. Constitution

THE ORIGINS OF LOBBYING

The interaction between the government and the governed has been the subject of continuing analysis and controversy since the invention of government itself. The Greek philosophers spent considerable time discussing the nature of the governed and government. Much of both the Old and the New Testaments of the Bible is devoted to the subject. The flight from Egypt was, after all, an escape from a tyrannical ruler. The crucifixion was the result of a Roman bureaucrat's decision to rid himself of a troublesome preacher.

Our preoccupation with governance is, perhaps, the second most popular topic of human discourse. Virtually all of what we consider news relates, one way or another, to the subject. Although we like to believe that government should not be above the law, we sometimes forget that there was no body of law until the first code was proclaimed by a political ruler, Hammurabi. Long before there was law, there was government, beginning at the tribal level. And where there was government, undoubtedly there were politics and lobbying.

These three processes—government, politics, and lobbying—are so interrelated that it is not always easy to distinguish among them:

Government is the exercise of sovereign authority in ruling a society or nation.

Politics is the pursuit of governmental power.

Lobbying is the process of influencing public and governmental policy.

Lobbying involves the advocacy, either by individuals or by groups, of a point of view—the expression of an interest that is affected, actually or potentially, by the affairs of government. *Issues* are public policy proposals; the word implies a topic of contention, and indeed lobbying commonly involves an adversarial and competitive process between different interests. *Interest groups* are organizations comprised of individuals or enterprises with shared points of view on issues. The proliferation of organized interest groups has typified American democracy since the founding of the republic.

Government, politics, and lobbying will exist in any human society. What distinguishes democratic societies is the relative freedom and openness accorded all three processes. It is not that politics and lobbying do not exist where freedom is restricted, but that where they cannot operate openly they will operate secretly, and sometimes violently.

For example, Solidarity, the Polish trade union movement, is essentially the fight of workers to organize themselves that they may better affect the policies of government and employers; to become, in other words, an accepted interest group.

There are also examples of a different kind. The African National Congress is embarked on a campaign to alter the politics and policies of the South African government. The Irish Republican Army pursues its goal of driving out the British and unifying both parts of Ireland. The Palestine Liberation Organization seeks to create a new state atop the territory of another nation, Israel. All three groups are restricted in various ways in their ability to advance their policies openly. All utilize means that are sometimes political, sometimes violent.

One need not necessarily sympathize with these causes to understand that each illustrates the oft-quoted dictum of the German military strategist, Karl von Clausewitz: "War is not merely a political act, but also a political instrument, a continuation of political relations, a carrying out of the same by other means." Another military strategist, Mao Tse-Tung, echoed the concept a century later: "War cannot be divorced from politics for a single moment."

The American Revolution was just such "a political act" as, later, was the secession of the South and the Civil War that resulted.

A movement that feels strongly enough about its cause and that is prohibited from advancing it openly and legitimately will resort first to illegal protest and ultimately to violence. Whether such a movement is a political organization or an interest group is unimportant.

We have seen this principle at work even in modern-day America. Twenty years afterward, many Americans celebrate the success that the civil rights movement achieved through non-violent (though often illegal) protests. We prefer to forget the memory of soldiers patrolling the streets of the nation's capital and other cities in the wake of the violence that swept across the country. The stability of the system was preserved because the country adjusted its official values, altered its laws and ultimately much of its people's behavior to accommodate a political cause that had been unsuccessful through traditional lobbying in its efforts to change federal, state, and local laws. Had that accommodation not occurred, had that cause not been legitimatized, it would have been the riots in Watts and not the march on Selma that we remember today.

It is this openness and the ability to accommodate diverse needs that is fundamental to democracy. The freedom of groups to lobby, to attempt to reshape unwelcome public policies, is among the greatest strengths of the American political system.

GOVERNMENTS LOBBYING GOVERNMENTS

Lobbying is not limited to the efforts of political or interest groups to affect government. The fact is that governments also lobby each other:

New York City lobbies the state legislature for changes in mass transit laws.

Wisconsin lobbies the federal government for more financial aid.

Canada lobbies the U.S. Congress for action on acid rain.

American officials return the favor by lobbying the Canadian parliament for changes in foreign ownership laws.

Israel and Egypt lobby foreign legislatures for political support and new armaments.

Indeed, between sovereign powers, it is sometimes difficult to tell where diplomacy ends and lobbying begins.

Lobbying is also prevalent within governments. Probably the most active lobbyists of the U.S. Congress are officials of the White House and the departments and agencies of the executive branch—notwithstanding nominal legal prohibitions against the practice.

Intramural lobbying is certainly not restricted to democracies. In a totalitarian or single-party state, the absence of competing electoral forces makes it all the more certain that economic and social interests will try to influence government policies through informal, personal approaches—i.e., lobbying.

In the Soviet Union, for example, where the line between the public and private sectors is officially non-existent, the amount of lobbying going on within the Kremlin walls among ministries seeking to shape each other's policies must surely be prodigious. Of course, the biggest single influencer of public policies in the USSR is the Communist Party.

The world's largest lobby is undoubtedly the Vatican, which seeks to influence social and sometimes economic policies in governments all across the globe.

LOBBYING AND GOVERNMENT RELATIONS

The focus of this book, however, is the United States, particularly the government relations activities of private-sector interests.

To most Americans, the world "lobbying" is a more familiar term than "government relations." Traditional lobbying is still the core activity of government relations, but only one of its components. What is lobbying? What is government relations? How do they differ?

Government relations is the application of one or more communications techniques by individuals or institutions to affect the decisions of government—at the local, state, national, or international levels, or some combination of them.

As used in this book, *lobbying* means the practice of the various forms of government relations, which include:

• Campaigns to mobilize constituents at the "grass-roots."
• Political fund-raising and contributions programs.
• A variety of communications technologies and techniques.
• Alliances with trade associations and with other groups with their own agendas.

All these are the media of modern lobbying. The term *direct lobbying* is used in this book to describe the traditional form of personal persuasion—still a mainstay of government relations—and to distinguish it from the other techniques used today.

These techniques, taken together, comprise the art form called government relations. Explaining how each of these tools operates and meshes with the others as part of a comprehensive government relations program is the primary purpose of this book.

Many of the techniques of government relations have been adapted from innovations, first of marketing and then of politics. Stimulated by intense competition to develop new products, new approaches to market research, and new ways to persuade and sell, consumer marketers have blazed a trail that political marketers have since been applying to electoral competition. From there, it has been a simple step to adapt these approaches to legislative and regulatory advocacy.

Marketing, politics, and lobbying share a common characteristic, the need to persuade in order to sell. Whether the sale be that of a product or service, a candidate, or a public policy, each of the three fields has become ever more sophisticated in its sales approach. Marketing, spurred by economic incentive, generally has taken the lead in technical innovation. Politics and lobbying have tended to borrow these innovations freely if not yet totally.

Government relations applies marketing and political techniques to the objectives of lobbying, a set of skills typically utilized by the private sector to affect the policies and actions of the public sector.

LOBBYING'S IMAGE

Its importance and prevalence notwithstanding, government relations in America has never been the most popular form of human endeavor. To call someone an "influence peddler" is to damn him as one operating in the gray reaches of the law and business ethics. Nor are the connotations of the word "lobbyist" significantly better. The Thomas Nast cartoons of the nineteenth century, showing overweight, cigar-smoking railroad lobbyists trading bags of money to legislators in return for their votes, are still part of the folklore of lobbying, often reproduced in history books for the edification of our youth.

The historic image has valid elements. Direct lobbying *has* had its excesses. Its coupling with political finance has often raised hackles among Americans, a people whose populist streak is never far below the surface of the national character.

Lobbyists share a gallows humor about the image of their trade. "Lobbyists are buried in unmarked graves," said one. "It spares their families the pain of seeing the tombstones desecrated."

"My mother sleeps better not knowing that I'm a lobbyist," states another. "She thinks I'm in prison."

With such an image, many organizations shun the use of the word, preferring instead such euphemisms as "advocacy," "policy representation," "policy marketing," "legislative communications," "public affairs," "government affairs," and of course, "government relations." (These terms all have different connotations but each expresses the organization of efforts to affect public policy. The exception is "public affairs," which, as used by most practitioners, covers not only government relations but also public relations, community relations, educational support, philanthropic programs, and the like.)

WHY GROUPS LOBBY

Organizations (and individuals) lobby public officials for any of several reasons:

1. *To gain benefits or relief unavailable in the private sector.* The consumer movement turned to government for actions to regulate what it considered unacceptable behavior by business. Labor unions and civil rights groups sought from government what they could not win in the private sector. Companies and their trade associations sometimes seek relief from unacceptable market conditions or onerous government regulations.

2. *To gain or retain an economic advantage.* Groups seek to gain or hold onto a privilege bestowed by law. Farm groups seek to extend and sometimes expand agricultural subsidies. Veterans' organizations press for improved benefits. Retirees fight any changes that they feel might weaken Social Security. Companies press for the elimination of restraints that hamper their ability to penetrate new markets.

3. *To gain relief or advantage at one level of government that has been denied at another.* Civil rights groups turned to Washington when they could not win the legislation they sought at the state and local levels. Some industries seek federal legislation pre-empting a diversity of state regulatory activities that they feel interfere with interstate marketing. Other industries prefer state regulation and oppose federal intervention. Consumer groups and some state and local officials argue for pre-emption that sets a floor but allows state and local governments to impose stricter standards above the floor.

4. *To create beneficial programs.* Educational institutions lobby for enactment of grant-in-aid programs for which they can then apply as new revenue sources. Defense contractors help persuade legislators to support new weapons systems that they can then bid to supply. Labor unions back public works programs that then become sources of new jobs for their members. Business groups support tax benefits that encourage capital formation and investment. Liberal groups press for other tax changes in order to redistribute income through new government social programs.

5. *To resolve public problems only governments can handle.* Whether for reasons of law or practice, there are problems that only governments can resolve. Different groups may have different ideas about how to deal with AIDS, but it is a public health problem that requires government action. Environmental issues like acid rain and atmospheric ozone depletion have ramifications that involve governments internationally as well as domestically. On issues as varied as international trade, school prayer, medical pollution of the coastlines, and police protection, government makes the key decisions, and in some cases the only ones.

Some people may look at these varied motivations to lobby and see selfishness and greed. Others see enlightened self-interest or even the public interest—perceived astoundingly often as the same thing. Some may see government as the court of first resort, others the last.

Groups lobby governments because government, and frequently only government, has the power to give them what they want.

THE DEMOCRATIC FUNCTION OF LOBBYING

Government relations performs three functions essential to the proper functioning of government and democracy:

1. Providing means for the resolution of conflicts, essential to the perpetuation of a democratic and mutually tolerant society.

2. Funneling important information, analysis, and opinion to government leaders to facilitate informed and balanced decision making.

3. Creating a system of checks and balances, comparable to that within our government, by which competition among interest groups keeps any one of them from attaining permanent power.

These concepts merit elaboration.

Conflicting Interests

Sorting out adversarial interests and points of view is a major function of government, and of elected legislators especially. Boiled down to its essentials, government relations is really only the organized expression of those interests and views.

Interests are inherently neither good nor evil. A basic tenet of elementary sociology is that every human being has multiple interests: jobs, families, hobbies, religions, social causes, civic concerns, taxpayer stakes, among innumerable others.

Differences arise between and among those interests, thereby creating issues. Some of those issues move into the public arena because of the size or number of interests affected. Those interests may already be organized. If not, and the impact of the issue is great enough, a new special interest may be formed, and a new organization established.

As individuals, the same proposal may affect our personal interests in different, possibly conflicting ways. Consider the following example:

Let us say that the county is considering a program to expand an airport near my home. I travel considerably and the airport now will be even more convenient since I can fly to more destinations on more airlines. New companies may be attracted to the area and this will increase the value of my home and perhaps provide new opportunities for my consulting business. Jobs will be created, which is good because my son is always looking for one.

However, the planes take off right over my home and the roar is very annoying. Sometimes the noise is so bad that it gets on my wife's nerves, and then our medical costs go up. Local taxes will rise to fund the costs of airport expansion and of road construction to get the additional passengers to the airport. All this construction will jeopardize the flop-eared jacknape, an endangered species I am committed to preserving.

As individual citizens, we sort out our own conflicting personal pressures all the time. But the personal conflicts pale into insignificance compared to the problems of the government officials who must somehow resolve the competing interests of: local citizens, homeowners and taxpayers; environmental groups; airlines now serving the airport who would like to keep out competing airlines wanting to come in; labor unions, the construction industry, and local merchants who want to see new jobs created; the state and federal agencies that regulate airports, to say nothing of local governments of the neighboring communities; and, of course, my son, my wife, and her physician.

All these interests will have something important to say on this issue—and they have every right to say it in every legitimate medium they can find and afford—to the legislators who must make the ultimate decision.

It is the job of the legislator to sort out all those competing, conflicting interests and decide what the public interest really is on this issue.

Information and Diversity

The public accepts lobbying because the system benefits from the expression of diverse views. No legislator, no government agency can possibly have all the information needed to make sound public policy decisions. But the affected interests do.

Dr. Richard A. Edwards, who recently retired from the Kappel Chair of Business-Government Relations at the University of Minnesota's School of Management, offers this perspective:

[L]obbyists serve essentially the same role in the legislative arenas that lawyers do in the judicial branch. Every point of view, on all public policy issues, is or can be provided by lobbyists to those responsible for the formulation of public policy, national and state. The reason is clear: Lobbyists have access to the information needed for the creation of regulatory and tax policy which is founded upon actuality rather than assumption. The conflict of opinion among lobbyists provides the legislators with a comprehensive spectrum of decisional options, a rationale in support of or opposition to each, and relevant factual data.[1]

In martialing their arguments, interest group advocates add value to the legislative process by bringing forth data, analyses, insights, and points of view that policymakers must have in order to make rational and fair decisions on the issues. Indeed, legislators frequently solicit information from interest groups and their representatives.

Checks and Balances

Because interest groups and their lobbyists generally play adversarial roles on particular issues, they tend to act as a rein on each other, preventing any single interest from getting too powerful for too long. Business groups compete with unions on labor issues. Union A fights tax benefits for industry; Union B supports them to the extent that they create new jobs for its members. Auto Company X favors mandatory air bags for safety; Auto Company Y opposes them. One environmental group opposes commercial nuclear power;

another group favors it because it is the principal alternative to petro-power, which may be damaging the ozone layer; both fight the efforts of some manufacturers to ease clean air and water regulations.

Thus each group tends to check the others while elected lawmakers sort out the substantive and political factors involved in public policy decision making. No one interest is allowed to dominate for very long. Cycles in public opinion, working through the political process, also keep interest group alliances of either the left or the right from gaining permanent ascendancy.

Moreover, the very debate between competing interests and competing lobbies contributes, win or lose, to acceptance of the process, just as it does in both law and electoral politics. Knowing that at least it has had its day in court and that there are other opportunities and other issues, each interest group accepts the validity of the legislative process, often accepting compromises that make the final decision acceptable, or at least palatable.

Thus, in our highly heterogeneous, pluralistic society, it is the breadth, skill, and comity of the interest groups that allow democratic policymaking to occur.

This is no small asset in a society as heterogeneous as ours. Groups vie for their points of view, struggling to prevail totally if they can or at the very least to gain as much of their position as circumstances permit. Yet, in the end the policymakers decide and the decision is accepted—without recourse to the strategies of Clausewitz—and rarely even to public protests.

Even in the advanced democracies of Western Europe, unpopular legislative decisions have often led to huge demonstrations and even general strikes. In still other countries, usually far less socially diverse than the United States, unpopular governmental decisions have commonly produced riots, military coups, and violent revolutions. Not so in the United States. The marches and sit-ins that accompanied the civil rights and Vietnam War protests are as violent as public controversies have gotten here in at least the past half-century.

Many factors work against violent refusals and protests in this country, but lobbying—the interaction of the legislative and lobbying processes to give each point of view its day in court—surely ranks high on the list.

It is the ability of the lobbies to express and represent their rival interests that allows those interests to tolerate each other, and democracy to function and perhaps even survive in America's diverse and constantly quarrelsome society.

Which brings us back once again to the problem of defining what government relations in America is really all about.

Government relations encompasses all the means used by the people, operating through their interest groups, to keep their governments responsive to social and economic demands. Government relations, together with the processes of free elections, is the lubricant which allows competing social and economic forces to contend within the democratic framework. Indeed, government relations is the complex of instruments used by interest groups to hold government accountable between elections.

Examining those diverse instruments is what this book is all about.

NOTE

1. Richard Edwards, "The Ethics of Lobbying." *Ethics: Easier Said Than Done*, Spring/Summer 1988, p. 106.

2

The External Environment: Issues Research

Facts are stubborn things; and whatever may be our wishes, our inclinations, or the dictates of our passions, they cannot alter the state of facts and evidence.

John Adams

Some years ago the comptroller of a large corporation was told by his company's public affairs officer about a new tax proposal being considered by a congressional committee. His immediate response: "Look, you better get yourself on the next plane to Washington and tell those damn politicians to kill that bill. It would cost us a fortune."

The financial executive's reaction was intuitive and emotional. He understood immediately that his company would be adversely affected if the tax proposal became law, and his reaction was also colored by his lack of affection for government. The political considerations were as irrelevant to him as his personal opinion would have been to the legislators; the small fact that they, not he, had the power to decide the issue was overlooked.

He also neglected to ask what the bill was really all about. What was its justification? Who would benefit from it, and how?

Too often in many organizations there is a strong reflex to act immediately on defensive issues without taking time to understand what may be really involved or at stake—substantively and also politically.

It is important to analyze issues in terms of their impact on the organization's needs. That requires a definition of those needs in terms of the dynamics of the public policy process: The needs of an interest group may produce a desire for change. This leads first to the development of issues and then to the creation of proposed governmental remedies that may well come at the expense of some other interest group.

NEEDS ANALYSIS

Organizations generally first become involved in government relations because of an internal need associated with a specific issue or group of issues. Later, if the needs and issues become chronic, the organization begins to explore the value of a long-range capability to deal with all relevant issues as they unfold.

There is an important distinction between needs and issues. *Needs* are internal to the organization or interest group. *Issues* are matters of public debate preceding governmental decision making. Issues flow from, and interact with, interest group needs.

For instance, a company may perceive an internal need because of the cost or burden created by an existing law or regulation. The internal need is translated into an external issue once the company takes steps to repeal or amend the governmental requirement.

The converse situation can also occur. The issue may produce an internal need, perhaps as a consequence of new, burdensome legislation arising out of another group's desire for change.

Internal needs can also become translated into positive opportunities to reduce costs, open up markets, or seek other advantages, by taking the initiative to seek new legislation or amendments to existing law.

Almost every issue involves change and confrontation. One group's changed economic or social circumstances may lead it to seek remedies in changed law. Since other groups are likely to prefer the status quo, they resist change; the result is confrontation. It generally falls to government to resolve the conflict, sometimes through the legislative process, sometimes through the judicial.

Defensive Needs

The most familiar governmental problems to businesses are the ones that add to costs and the difficulties of managing the organization. Some flow from existing laws or regulations; others from proposals for future action by government.

Such issues are often characterized by a complaint:

- Why do we have to put up with this unfair regulation?
- Why are they planning to impose this costly new tax?
- Why do we have to fill out all these cumbersome government forms?
- Why is the government planning to put us at a disadvantage with our competition or the unions?

• Why do we have to comply with these expensive safety, environmental and consumer requirements?

Non-business organizations have their own complaints, of course, such as:

• Why are companies allowed to engage in this or that unfair or unhealthy labor, environmental, or consumer practice?
• Why does the government permit or even authorize this social, educational, or cultural wrong?

In each case, the answer is usually that the law was made either when circumstances were different, or as the result of a conflict between two (or more) interests in which one side lost.

The more significant question is "What can be done about it?" The answer usually involves changing the law, and that means lobbying the lawmakers to do so. It is important to keep clearly in mind that any legislator can introduce a bill; getting it enacted is extraordinarily difficult, which is why the vast majority of legislative proposals are stillborn. To kill a bill, it need only be stopped at any one of the many hurdles it must overcome between introduction and final passage.

Marketing Opportunities

Nonetheless, interest groups of all kinds seek new legislation (or regulations) to effect change that they believe would have positive effects on their own internal needs. For example, a company or an industry that finds itself barred by law from entering a market may initiate proposals to revamp the law in order to expand its marketing opportunities.

The banking industry, for instance, has long been barred from operating across state lines and from diversifying into other financial activities. Relentless campaigns, some in Washington and some in the states, eventually have brought about a long series of changes, which are at least partly accomplishing the diversification goals of major banking companies. This has occurred only over the opposition of other financial interests, which have little desire to see potent new competitors enter their particular fields of business. Bankers prevailed over securities brokers in a major federal legislative battle in 1988, but lost to independent insurance brokers in the same contest.

At the end of Prohibition in 1933, to take another example, New York State was faced with the question of which kinds of retailers would be allowed to sell alcoholic beverages. Taking Solomon's sword against the contested infant, the legislature permitted alcoholic beverage stores to sell liquor and wine but forbade them to sell beer. Food retailers were allowed to sell beer but not wine and liquor. Ever since, food retailers have been struggling for the right to sell wine as well as beer. Liquor stores have tenaciously opposed not only this change but even a compromise that would let both kinds of retailers sell all alcoholic beverages.

As the examples illustrate, a bill or regulatory proposal to accomplish a change in the law very likely means goring someone else's ox. People and interests become accustomed to living and operating under sets of circumstances which may be altered by legislative or regulatory changes. Legislation that would benefit one set of businesses may be harmful to another. A consumer group that favors new labeling or advertising requirements runs up against the companies whose marketing practices would be regulated. Anti-smoking advocates take aim not only at cigarette manufacturers but also at the government price-support programs that encourage farmers to grow tobacco. An issue that is defensive to one group may be offensive to another—often literally.

Assessing Needs

The questions that produce a needs assessment are these:

1. What proposals are governmental policymakers considering that would increase business costs or restrict our operations, marketing, or profitability?
2. What changes in existing governmental requirements could lower our costs of doing business or decrease restrictions on our operations?
3. Are there changes down the road in the public environment that could significantly affect us for better or worse?
4. What legislative or regulatory changes would open up markets for products or services from which we are presently barred?
5. What changes would facilitate our achieving other or non-business objectives?

It is one thing to state needs, and quite another to satisfy them. For each need, there exists at least one real or potential issue. To be actionable, organizations must define their issues, at least internally, clearly and carefully.

Defining the Issues

Once needs have been stated, the next step is to list clearly all the issues that satisfy (or challenge) those needs.

An issue may be defined very broadly. For instance, "all legislation that would restrict the company from marketing its products." This is an appropriate and usable definition if the issues have potentially severe impacts on the company's basic business. Tobacco companies, faced with innumerable proposals to limit smoking, define their issues in such broad strokes. So did trading stamp companies when legislation arose all across the country to ban or highly regulate stamps.

Or, the issue may be specific: "Legislation to increase the minimum wage."

"Bills requiring a deposit on all beverage containers." "Proposals restricting the union's ability to organize."

The issue may also be stated in great detail: "Section 17 of S. 1234, to increase the sales tax to 9 percent on widgets retailing for more than $3,000."

Whether stated broadly or narrowly, it is important that the issue be set forth clearly and coherently, so that the organization can frame a workable position. The purpose, after all, is to have a definition on which a policy can be based and that is actionable. (If the bill is amended to raise the sales tax to only 8.5 percent on widgets selling for over $2,500, is it no longer of concern?) But at the other extreme, defining the issue as "all sales tax proposals" may be meaningless or unworkable.

RESEARCHING AND TRACKING CURRENT ISSUES

Researching issues involves three basic elements: (1) formulating the questions to get the necessary information, (2) knowing how and where to get the answers, and (3) analyzing and interpreting the results in the light of the organization's needs. The first two elements are discussed in the remainder of this chapter; the third is the subject of Chapter 3.

Issues research is important in order to develop sound positions and action plans, whether the issues be offensive or defensive, current or emerging. As in any other kind of managed activity, it is better to aim before firing. The aiming process in government relations means learning what is happening and why, what the impact is internally (on the company or among the organization's members), and also the significance externally—on friends, foes, and potential allies.

Time frame is the critical first consideration. If the issue is current, the kinds of information needed and the actions to be considered are wholly different than if the issue is still emerging or long term.

To develop sound intelligence on current issues, the government relations researcher will seek out answers to such questions as these:

What is this issue all about? What are the key bills or regulatory proposals? What are their provisions? What is their significance?

How, precisely, will it affect us?

Who are its governmental sponsors? What interest groups are their backers and allies, both actual and potential?

What is the rationale underlying the proposal, and what are the motivations of its supporters?

Who are the issue's opponents, both real and potential?

What are opponents' rationales and motivations?

Are there relevant government reports, academic studies, or other pertinent documentation on this issue?

What are the issue's prospects? Is it going anywhere?

What are the political implications of this issue? Is it part of some larger effort or movement? Does it relate to the fortunes of important interest groups, political leaders, or candidates?

What is the likely timetable for action—immediate, near future, or down the road? What is the issue's probable lifespan if action does not occur in the near term?

Will hearings be held? When? Who will testify? What are they likely to say?

As the issue moves along, what is its status at any given time? Are amendments being offered? What is their significance?

What are the long-term and strategic implications of this issue for our company or organization?

Are there timely steps that could be taken either to promote or forestall action on the issue?

The issues researcher must develop answers to these questions that are both accurate and actionable. Information and intelligence should be verified to the extent possible (not always feasible, though, particularly on political matters). Research also needs to be kept completely up-to-date. Once they start to move, issues can progress with speed. The political, legislative, or regulatory environments can also shift quickly.

Researchers get their information on issues from a large array of sources—some published, some public though unpublished, and some private. Information from private, or "back-channel," sources is usually political intelligence about issues and their background and prospects. It is gathered on a confidential basis by lobbyists in the course of their activities and is critical to the effectiveness of direct lobbying on specific issues (See Chapter 5, Direct Lobbying, for further discussion.)

Public Information Sources

Most of the information about issues is in the public domain, somewhere. However, information that is *public* is not at all the same as that which is *published*. Many of the essential facts about any issue are in print, but a great deal is not. The latter is almost always available, though, to researchers who know how to go about getting it. (The most valuable trait in an issues researcher is not so much in knowing the answers to questions as in knowing how to find them.)

Networking

Apart from published information sources, there are vast networks of individuals who can provide much of the information needed to understand an issue. These include:

Issue experts in the Congressional Research Service of the Library of Congress, and their counterparts in state legislative information services.

Staffs of individual legislators and legislative committees.

Government relations personnel and issue experts in other companies and organizations.

Personnel in executive and regulatory agencies.

Researchers with "think tanks" and academic institutions.

Policy research organizations including ideological, single-issue, and other "cause" groups.

Research staffs of national, state, and local Republican and Democratic committees (especially on political topics).

Trade association staffs, particularly including issue experts with such "umbrella" business groups as the Chamber of Commerce of the United States, the National Association of Manufacturers, the Business Roundtable, and their state and local counterparts.

The Conference Board and other business research groups.

Staffs of such non-business interest groups as labor unions (particularly the AFL-CIO at both national and state levels), environmental groups, consumer organizations, etc.

Every government relations and public affairs professional has a network of such sources, which has been cultivated and maintained over the years.

Published Sources

The firms and organizations that specialize in publishing information on government policymaking have grown into a major American industry. There is an enormous wealth of public information both on governmental and political developments as well as specific current legislative and agency issues. The researcher's problem is less in obtaining data than in winnowing it to manageable proportions for useful analysis. (See Sources and Resources at the end of the book for information on where to obtain specific information.)

Legislative reporting services. Proceedings and documents of Congress, the state legislatures, and the larger local governments are often published by government publications offices or sometimes by commercial firms. These include texts of bills, amendments and revisions; current status and legislative histories (i.e., chronology of actions taken on particular bills); hearing transcripts; committee studies, votes and reports (including minority reports); texts or abstracts of floor debates; record floor votes, etc. For the national legislature, most of this information is published in *The Congressional Record*, except for committee documents, which must be obtained from the particular Senate or House committee.

Much of this information is also available in specialized publications and from on-line computer services covering the federal government and the states. These services sometimes offer information on regulatory developments as well, indexing or abstracting *The Federal Register* (the official record of departmental and agency procedures, rules, regulations, announcements, etc.) and its state and local counterparts. The computerized services usually offer the user the ability to manipulate data; e.g., to cross-tabulate bill sponsors by political contributors.

The press. National and regional newspapers offer important coverage of issues at all stages, though rarely in vast detail. Some, like those listed in Sources and Resources, are must daily reading for certain kinds of issues. Other can be covered by subscription to a clipping service, which will provide copies of stories covering particular topics or names (both individual and organizational).

Television and radio monitoring services provide transcripts to clients on broadcast coverage of particular problems, issues, or organizations. The electronic media are sources of news and comment, but rarely of in-depth data. It is important, however, to know what the public is being told about relevant issues and developments.

Commissioned data. Market surveys, public opinion polls, and sociopolitical analyses can be commissioned from specialized firms to help ascertain the state of the public and business environment with respect to particular problems and issues. A large variety of commercial and academic resources offer services in these areas. Indeed, existing data of this kind may well be available through networking or other resources.

Government publications. Federal, state, and local departments, agencies, and commissions are generally invaluable sources of specialized studies, analyses, and compendia of information.

Trade associations and other interest groups. Virtually all organizations involved in the legislative process publish bulletins and other publications to update members on governmental/political developments affecting the industry within their geographic purviews. Many of these publications provide the most authoritative information available from any source in their subject areas.

Trade journals and newsletters. In many industries, privately published newsletters report in greater or lesser depth on governmental developments. Some are four-page monthly newsletters. Other appear daily, may run to nearly 100 pages, and include full texts of important documents.

Trade newspapers and magazines, typically published weekly or monthly, also cover legislation and regulatory developments affecting the industry— though usually in less depth than specialized newsletters or trade association publications.

Researching Federal Issues

Of the sources of information about the federal government, there is no end. New directories, almanacs, newsletters, tracking systems, and data bases appear—and sometimes disappear—with dizzying frequency. Indeed, information about the structure, personnel, and doings of Congress and the executive and regulatory agencies has become so plentiful that the user's problem is how to sort through it all.

Virtually every industry and issues group is served by specialized issue tracking services, mostly in the form of newsletters or other periodicals. Some of these are published commercially, others by trade associations and similar interest groups. There are also a number of broad-spectrum tracking and information services covering the federal policymaking structure.

Researching State and Local Issues

Obtaining sound information has always been more of a problem for those who lobby in the states (and even more so for local lobbyists) than for their Washington counterparts. Advance warning, particularly at the regulatory level, continues to be a problem in many states and localities. Resources are improving, however, thanks particularly to computerization. There is much more information available now, and on a more timely (though also more expensive) basis. But timeliness does not always mean immediacy; even some of the on-line computer services may be several days late in reporting events and developments.

Interest Group Ratings

Many interest groups compile ratings of legislative voting records, particularly members of Congress. (State legislative vote ratings are far less common.) A number of these resource groups are listed in Sources and Resources. Such voting record indexes are popular because of the positions of individual legislators on issues of concern to the interest group and its members.

These ratings should be treated very cautiously. For one thing, the issues selected are chosen more or less arbitrarily. For another, the votes selected are usually recorded floor votes, and not all votes are on the record (e.g., voice votes). Moreover, the particular vote included in the rating may or may not always be the most significant one on a particular issue; e.g., a vote on a key amendment or a vote to table a bill may be more important than the vote on final passage. It is therefore possible to make any legislator look good or bad, depending on which votes are picked for a particular issue. Some groups are also much more careful than others in using objective language to describe the issue and its relevance to the interest group. Finally, a legislator's actions in committee (not usually rated) may be more significant in some cases than floor votes.

A company or group with relatively few priority issues is likely to be more concerned with a lawmaker's actions on those bills than with how he or she scores on a broad, often ideologically selected index of issues.

It is not difficult to develop one's own analysis or index on issues. All that is required is to pick the key votes on priority issues, tally each lawmaker's vote on those issues, and run a percentage of the total. (Some groups consider an absence or other failure to vote the equivalent of a negative vote, which may be quite unfair.) If the index is to be disseminated, the description of each vote included should be set forth as objectively as possible.

ANALYZING TOMORROW'S ISSUES

Issues never arrive unannounced. They arise out of developments and potentialities that emit advance signals of their arrival. Analyzing emerging issues is something like consulting the Oracle of Delphi. The clues to the future are all there, if only they can be read; with the acuity of hindsight, they are always perfectly clear.

The dilemma lies in being able to discern which of the vast number of possible issues is likely actually to materialize and do so in ways that will materially affect the company or organization. Thus, assessing the probability of impact is a critical element.

The development and growth of the environmental movement, for example, were telegraphed long in advance by Rachel Carson and many other writers. As the literature on environmental concerns and problems expanded, long-standing conservation groups adopted environmental agendas, and activist groups began to spring up. After a time, the likelihood that the public agenda would shortly include environmental issues became predictable. But which issues? Around 1970 it might have been reasonable to conclude that air and water quality, solid and toxic waste would all be early candidates. Air and water turned out to be, of course. But toxic waste problems did not become truly major governmental issues until the 1980s—and the 1990s now seem likely to be the decade of action on solid waste disposal issues.

Forecasting which of these issues will impact on any single enterprise is more difficult, although it becomes easier the nearer one gets to the event. On the other hand, the closer one comes to the explosive "critical mass" of the issue, the more difficult and expensive it is for individual companies to cope with it—and therefore the greater their reluctance to act proactively and the fiercer their resistance to mandatory government remedies.

This is the dilemma for many business executives. Emerging issues are often too diffuse, too distant, and too hard to filter into the reality of the present to gain high corporate attention—even though they are far easier to cope with than they will be once they become current issues. Once tomorrow's issues become today's, the company knows what it is confronting, but by then its economic, social, and political costs may well be vast.

There is often a psychological obstacle to recognition of an emerging trend. Many executives treat the unpleasantness such an issue would create by dismissing it as unimportant and its advocates as troublemakers. Being able to put aside such blinders to evaluate trends and issues objectively is not as common a trait among executives as might be wished. Yet, objectivity is critical in being able to evaluate the significance of emerging issues (and, for that matter, current ones).

Business executives are by no means the only ones who find the future's signals hard to discern. For example, few union leaders realized, or would have been able to accept, that labor's political influence would decrease sharply in the 1980s as a result of the decline in the nation's "rustbelt" industries, the pressures of overseas competition, the stabilizing of both inflation and unemployment at low levels, and the conservative political trend that swept the country during the Reagan years. Even with some moderation of those trends in the 1990s, only the most optimistic labor seer would forecast today that union power is likely ever to be the economic and political force it was from the 1930s into the 1970s.

The advantage of spotting issues early is that often something can be done at that early stage to mitigate the worst effects of the issue on the company or organization, if indeed not to forestall it altogether. There are two drawbacks, however, to recognizing emerging issues.

First, out of the many trends that can always be identified at any given time, it is extraordinarily difficult to know which few will mature into major issues with great impact on the organization—not impossible, but very hard.

Second, even when this has been done and steps have been taken to alleviate the potential worst effects, it is rarely possible to state with assurance that the issue would not have died without help anyhow, as most such public trends and concerns do. This problem is complicated by fears among many government relations and public affairs professionals that their managements will mistake effective fire prevention programs to mean that the risk of fires has now died out and that the organization no longer needs to employ firefighters.

Notwithstanding these difficulties, a clear understanding of the value inherent in emerging issues identification can significantly alter the public issues agenda for many interest groups. Especially for businesses, so frequently on the defensive in issues debates, programs to identify and manage such issues can enhance opportunities to utilize the techniques of government relations and public affairs to open the public agenda for beneficial objectives.

The Evolution of Issues

The Path of Emerging Issues

CONCERNS → PROBLEMS → TRENDS → ISSUES → LAWS → REGULATIONS

Issues first originate as concerns of an interest group or some other segment of the public. If that concern increases sufficiently, it will escalate into a need for that group and pressures for change will begin to be felt. As the problem evolves, it will get a name, a very critical point in the evolution of issues for several reasons.

First, a thing does not exist psychologically until it has been named so that to label a concept is to give it life. Second, naming that concept also defines it; certain characteristics are defined in, others are implicitly defined out. Third, the name itself can empower the concept and turn it into an issue of public concern and debate. For instance, the concept that the public should have increased access to certain data in government files was at best of modest public interest, but naming it "Freedom of Information" turned it into an issue with vitality and excitement.

Isolated events may begin to develop into a pattern and then into a trend. Or a historical pattern may begin to increase in frequency or magnitude. The judgments of experts, a public crisis of some sort, an attention-getting book, or a court decision all can be crystallizing agents that begin to move an issue toward the critical mass necessary for legislative or regulatory action.

As the issue develops, the interest group that "owns" it will seek to broaden its support base. Other groups may begin to take an interest in the issue. It may become the subject of articles, first in specialized or even obscure publications, but then in the general media, electronic as well as print. Once an issue has reached this stage, it becomes possible to begin tracking it—to identify patterns and trends in its development.

It is generally around this stage that political figures become aware of the issue. Perhaps there is a constituency interest. Friendly interest groups may bring it to their attention and urge them to become involved. They may see an opportunity to "ride" the issue to more personal visibility and political influence. They may see it as a cause consistent with their personal beliefs. Any or all of these can be critical factors in building legislative support for an issue.

An issue at this point will inevitably become the subject of governmental consideration: legislative, executive, or regulatory. Most bills and issues will not survive the process of policy consideration, but some will. If the issue continues to gather momentum, it may eventually be enacted, though not necessarily in its original form. Now a law, the issue moves into the hands of the regulators where, as a government mandate or program, it will continue to evolve through regulatory and perhaps judicial case law.

When the issue, or rather the problem or concept underlying it, first began, there were a number of courses it might follow as it evolved. But at each of the phases in the issue's development, options disappeared. At some points, the issue might have been completely dissipated if certain private sector actions had, or had not, taken place. At other points, resolution of the issue might have been possible prior to governmental action. At still later points, one governmental strategy might have been substituted for another, perhaps weakening, perhaps strengthening it.

This pattern of issues evolution is essentially pyramidal. At the beginning, there are almost an infinite number of courses along which the issue might develop, but these become fewer and fewer as the issue evolves, until finally there are only a few alternatives open, and then, at the end, only one.

Issues development is pyramidal in another sense, too. The vast majority of potential issues are culled and winnowed at each progressive stage. Only a tiny fraction ever makes it from one stage to the next. And here is the dilemma of emerging issues analysis.

Clearly, the earlier the stage of an issue's development, the easier it is for an interest group other than its sponsor to influence or transform it. But how is one to know which issues will eventually become full-blown, and which will fall away? Careful tracking, research, and analysis can provide valuable clues.

Emerging Issues: Leading Indicators

By the time issues reach the stage of legislative or other policy action, they are well advanced in their evolutionary cycle. The introduction of a bill is a *lagging indicator*, a strong signal that an issue already has developed fairly extensively. Spotting the *leading indicators* of issues is what emerging issues analysis tries to do. The process of analyzing emerging issues utilizes a number of techniques that are part of a process called "issues management" (a possible misnomer since it is not the issue that is being managed as much as the organization's analysis and response to it. Issues management also includes action planning and implementation phases.) These techniques are discussed below.

Scanning and Tracking

Once someone has identified a potential problem, articles and papers about it begin to show up in periodicals. Research about scientific and technical problems is reported in professional journals, then in specialized magazines, newsletters, and reports, and often in major newspapers. Social and economic developments are similarly analyzed and reported.

Content analysis data bases and services are available that report to clients on the trends in media coverage of current and potential issues. Other data bases and services track changes in the focus and concerns of particular stakeholder and interest groups.

Futurism is a specialized field of several research and consulting organizations that forecast trends, conditions, and potential issues. Some of these develop scenarios of possible events that could lead to significant social, economic, technological, or political developments. Others use different forecasting techniques such as Delphi surveys, model building, matrices that analyze the impact of a variety of socioeconomic and technological variables on each other, and so on.

It is also worthwhile to track social developments in Scandinavia and some other European countries where important trends (like consumerism) sometimes arise before they do in the United States.

Several states are often pacesetters whose innovations others (sometimes including the federal government) tend to follow. Among the pacesetting states are California, Florida, Massachusetts, New York, Oregon, and Wisconsin. New York City was also once in this category but has been less innovative since its financial crisis in the 1970s. Some smaller local governments are becoming pacesetters, including Suffolk County, New York, and Berkeley, California.

Coverage, analysis, and public interest increase, of course, as issue indicators move from leading to lagging, or at least to immediate. *Public opinion surveys* are a principal signal of trends among major demographic groups or in the public at large. Surveys can be commissioned by individual clients on particular topics, but several survey research organizations offer subscription services to groups of clients in which they regularly report on public opinion trends and developments.

Less systematic but nonetheless potentially valuable can be "brainstorming" seminars with academic and issue experts. Dialogues with leaders of activist groups, so often the issue makers, can also point up concerns that may develop into future issues.

Screening and Evaluation

Hundreds of potential issues will surface through the tracking and scanning processes. These must now be screened and culled to produce a list that is meaningful and relevant to the company or organization. While specialized consultants can help in the winnowing and evaluation process, it is also possible to use an internal committee or task force for the same purpose.

Such a task force will be engaged in work that may well be speculative in its process and sensitive in the implications of its findings. For that reason, it should not be attempted without the strong backing and participation of the highest levels of management. In the case of membership organizations, support must also come from the board of directors where the political power usually lies.

Members of the task force should be talented and imaginative individuals with a variety of skills, training, and expertise. While some of these will be staff experts, it is important also to include line personnel from operating units. They will not only add different and valuable insights and viewpoints, but will also give the study group a credibility within the organization that will avoid the taint of "another report from the ivory tower."

In a company, the mission of such a group is to assess the possible or likely impact of each potential issue on the company's existing or planned lines of business, markets, products, or services. In trade associations and other membership groups, the impact analysis will necessarily be somewhat broader: on the industry's future development or on current or planned programs.

To the maximum extent possible, these impacts should be quantified so that they can be compared and prioritized. The probability that events will materialize should also be estimated on a time scale. The interrelationship of impacts and probability can be charted as a guide to prioritizing issues for action planning (see figure below).

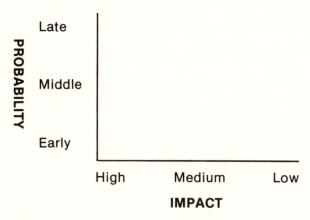

Dissemination

To be useful, the products of emerging issues analyses must be communicated to decision makers as inputs to the strategic and business planning process. This might occur through distribution of an annual or semi-annual issues inventory to corporate and operating managements, or to association boards of directors and members. As an alternative, a periodic emerging issues newsletter could be developed to disseminate research findings and analyses. Special reports are still another approach to communication. Whatever the medium, it should provide the following information:

• Name and brief description of the emerging problem, concern, or issue.

• Its background, history, and origins, sponsoring/opposing interests, causes and symptoms of its development, etc.

• Assessment of the time frame of its potential emergence and its potential *internal* impact on the organization—along with an evaluation of its possible beneficial or adverse *external* consequences. This assessment should also rate the issue's priority, based on the cross-evaluation of impact against probable emergence.

• The relationship of the issue to other existing or potential situations, problems, or information including recommended positions and strategies.

Plans and Action

Some emerging issues will be potential threats. Others will present marketing or other kinds of opportunities. Many will have mixed or unclear significance. But all should be assessed with an eye to the possibilities of influencing their course to the organization's advantage. That, after all, is the purpose of an emerging issues analysis.

Issues that cluster at the lower left corner of the graph clearly demand priority attention; their impact will be great and they are very close to being current. That is not to say, however, that other issues should be ignored. Issues are fluid creatures; those of medium and low impact should continue to be monitored to be sure that they are not reshaped by someone else in ways that could be injurious. Conversely, it may be possible to take actions that would increase their potential for beneficial impact on the organization.

The most effective time to neutralize a potentially adverse issue is before it has become politically polarized. Once positions have hardened, interest groups and lawmakers publicly committed, and emotions are starting to ride high, issues are much more difficult to resolve amicably than before they became adversarial.

Action plans are imperative for high-impact issues, although the nature of the action will depend on where the issue falls on the probability axis. Early issues, close to being current, should probably be treated as such tactically, utilizing as appropriate the various techniques of government relations. Longer range issues, however, are susceptible to broader planning.

Those plans may call for action that is external, internal, or both. An issue may warrant a publicity drive, a series of speeches or publications, advocacy advertising, an effort to reach out to thought leaders or public interest groups, or some other communications program. Or it may be that the issue could be defused if some internal actions are taken. This is not always easy unless the company or group has a mind-set that is open to potentially unpleasant information and willing to act on it. For instance, it may be difficult to accept the implications of an issue if it means scrapping or drastically modifying a line of business, withdrawing from major geographic markets or expanding into sensitive new ones, or the need to develop wholly new and expensive alternative technologies. Such situations underscore the necessity for the active support and involvement of both top management and line executives in the emerging issues process to maintain internal credibility.

An example of the value of early action on an emerging issue occurred in the early 1970s when the potential environmental dangers of atmospheric ozone depletion first came to light. A consumer marketing company assessed the situation and concluded that it could modify its aerosol packaging to eliminate the use of fluorocarbons. It coupled this internal action with external public communications, noting in both labeling and advertising that the company's products no longer contained fluorocarbons. Some other companies followed its lead. Still others, confronted with the technological and financial difficulties of early action, chose to wait more than fifteen years before phasing out the use of fluorocarbons.

Pre-emptive voluntary action may be an effective strategy for some organizations in some sets of circumstances. In other circumstances, companies sometimes actually prefer regulatory action to avoid taking steps that would raise costs and thereby give competitors a possible cost advantage. This regulatory strategy ensures that all competitors are given equal treatment in terms of economic costs, although perhaps at a sacrifice of political or public relations benefit.

Each of these strategies may have merit if it is the result of careful analysis and planning of an emerging problem area. Too frequently, though, action may be postponed because of management reluctance to accept unpleasant information and its consequences. This can prove enormously expensive in the long run.

On the other hand, it can be equally risky to act precipitously. For example, because of consumer preference, several companies have shifted their packaging from glass to plastics just as the problems of solid waste disposal begin to threaten the future of plastic packaging. Careful action planning has to assess the merits and implications of all significant inputs, not merely the comfortable ones.

This cannot be a static process. By their very nature, emerging issues are in a state of constant movement. This means that monitoring, analysis, evaluation, and review of the issue have to be continuous, and that both internal and external strategic action planning must be flexible to accommodate new developments, pressures, and insights.

3

The Internal Environment: Strategies and Plans

O! that a man might know the end of this day's business, ere it come.

Shakespeare, *Julius Caesar*

Organizations with similar needs and issues may deal with those issues in very different ways, depending on the strategic posture the company or association has adopted. Strategies affect the ways in which issues are analyzed, the evaluation of their impacts, the positions adopted, and the tactics with which those positions are implemented. It is one thing to respond to someone else's agenda and quite another to develop one's own.

Every organization that deals with government and the public environment has a strategy for doing so. But not every strategy is the result of a conscious and deliberate process.

This chapter deals with the manner in which strategies unfold or are built, the analysis of internal issue impacts and options, and decision-making systems.

THE SEVEN LOBBYING STRATEGIES

Every company and membership organization initially approaches its involvement in government relations with a reactive strategy: either seeking to defeat or ameliorate adverse legislation or regulation . . . or to use governmental power to alter some unfavorable social, economic, or political condition.

As a company confronts more and more issues, it will begin to evolve from a single-issue orientation toward an eventual realization that it can influence the development of issues and the public environment in which the orga-

nization operates. The movement from early reactive phases through legislative lobbying into problem-solving and proactive strategies is a function of
two influences: (1) the scope and intensity of its issues, and (2) cultural disposition and limitations within the organization.

Trade associations and non-business membership organizations may follow
a similar evolutionary pattern, but are likely to move into the legislative
lobbying phase faster than most companies. However, they may also be less
prone than companies to move beyond that strategy.

There are seven government relations strategies that tend to build on each
other more or less sequentially:

1. *Reactive crisis.* This is an unprogrammed, purely reactive activity. Issue
monitoring is not systematic. Information on governmental proposals and
developments is gleaned almost completely from publications and trade associations. Direct lobbying action is undertaken (either by a staff executive
substantively expert in the issue or by retained independent lobbyists) only
in crisis situations affecting vital interests and in response to the initiatives
of someone else. Trade association involvement is passive; the company may
be represented on boards and committees, but little effort is made to influence
industry positions or actions significantly.

2. *Reactive-regulatory monitoring.* This is a "no-surprises" strategy based
on systematic monitoring of key regulatory agencies, including utilization of
consultants or tracking services, and use of company or organization personnel to cultivate information sources within the agencies. Legislative monitoring is less intense unless there are bills of burning concern. There is
much greater involvement in trade association position development and
action planning, but the company's own lobbying is still reactive only to
crises.

3. *Reactive-regulatory lobbying.* Issues monitoring is now more intense
and includes systematic cultivation of personal contacts within key agencies
and among other relevant sources, e.g., other interest groups and some key
legislators and staff. Serious efforts are now made to obtain early warning of
potential regulatory action and to influence its direction by frequent, personal,
and more or less systematic lobbying of regulatory officials and staff. Monitoring of legislative issues is likely to become more systematic as a by-product
of regulatory tracking.

4. *Reactive-legislative lobbying.* By this stage, monitoring of both legislative
and regulatory issues is intensive. Major efforts are now being made to lobby
on all relevant issues, although still defensively and with the degree of activity
proportional to the potential impact of the issue. The beginnings of grass-
roots and coalition activity are found, particularly on top priority issues.

5. *Proactive-political.* Grass-roots programs to involve stakeholders or
members in personal lobbying and political efforts are now extensive, tied
in with community relations activity. A political contributions program has
been developed to aid friends and expand access. The organization lobbies
extensively on pertinent issues, although pertinence is still defined in defen-

sive terms. The organization now frequently assumes leadership roles in associations and coalitions, and on occasion is even willing to act independently if the circumstances warrant.

6. *Problem solving*. This is a mixed strategy, comprised of both reactive and proactive elements. There is extensive tracking and analysis of both current and emerging issues. Direct lobbying efforts are now being supplemented by active communications programs to help shape or alter public opinion and knowledge, and by cooperative, interactive efforts with other interest groups and government officials to help solve problems at the roots of real or potential issues. There is also a sensitivity to possible needs for voluntary internal change if external circumstances warrant. This is the "enlightened self-interest" strategy.

7. *Proactive marketing*. Issues are now being identified or developed that could lead to expansion of markets or other positive benefits on the organization's own initiative. Lobbying is no longer strictly defensive and the organization actively seeks adoption of issues on its own agenda, whether legislative or regulatory. The organization utilizes all available government relations tools and techniques proportional to the importance and value of the issue, building on the problem-solving strategy to enhance prospects for success.

Let's look at a model case to see how the seven strategies evolve.

A Model of Strategic Evolution

Armand Geddon had always limited his involvement with government largely to paying taxes. He prided himself on his total lack of political involvement. ("I never vote; it only encourages them.") His entire adult life was devoted to building his home security business.

So it was with considerable shock that Geddon learned that his company, Armageddon Industries ("You'll fight to the end to get our products!"), was being sued by the Product Regulatory Oversight Department. The complaint charged that the company had violated the law by failing to register its products with PROD.

"We've been in business for fifteen years," an angry Geddon told his lawyer, Juanita Lopez. "I've never heard of such a law. Why are they attacking us?"

"Don't take it personally, Mr. Geddon," Lopez replied. "They're just trying to enforce the law the legislature passed two years ago to regulate security products. Didn't your trade association or your government relations people tell you about it?"

"I don't belong to trade associations—waste of money," the indignant Geddon responded. "And I don't have any government relations people. Why should I? I don't have any relations with the government."

"You do now," Lopez said. "Let me talk to the people at PROD and see what can be done."

Lopez persuaded PROD officials to levy a minimum fine and took care of registering Armageddon's products to get the company in compliance. A few weeks later, she visited Geddon in his office to get his signature on the final papers.

"You really need to keep on top of what PROD is doing, Mr. Geddon, to make sure you know what's happening that could affect you in the future. Perhaps you ought to hire a specialist to monitor these things."

"I don't want to add to staff," Geddon said. "Too much overhead already. You do it for me."

So for several years thereafter, Lopez kept track of PROD's activities and sent Geddon memos whenever there was something she thought he should know. She persuaded him to join the Protective Engineering Systems Organization (PESO) so he would get news on legislation, but she suspected that he rarely read the material.

Then Lopez called Geddon. "Did you see the trade association bulletin that arrived Tuesday?" she asked.

"Getting ready for next week's sales meeting. Don't have time for anything else," he said.

"I think you may have to take time, Mr. Geddon. PROD is proposing government standards for your products. If they're adopted, you may have to redesign your products from the ground up," Lopez told him.

"Let PESO handle it," Geddon said. "Isn't that what they're supposed to do?"

PESO did handle it, and the regulations were substantially modified before they were adopted. Unfortunately, Armageddon had some features on its products that its competitors did not. Since no one from the company attended PESO's meetings on the subject, the association did little to take care of Armageddon's unique needs. The end result was new PROD standards that raised Armageddon's costs by 7 percent.

After Geddon's blood pressure went back down, he thought hard about the experiences he had been having with PROD and PESO, and decided to ask Lopez to meet him for lunch. "Well, I can't say you didn't warn me," he said to her. "We obviously have to do things differently. Do you have any suggestions?"

Lopez told him it was time to hire a government relations specialist who could devote full time to Armageddon's growing problems. "That's exactly what I've been thinking," Geddon said. "I'd like you to take the job." Lopez agreed, left the law firm, and became Armageddon's first director of government relations.

She drew up a list of federal and state agencies whose activities could affect Armageddon and developed a program to monitor them. She also subscribed to several publications that cover Congress and the state legislature, and retained lobbying firms to watch out for anything that could affect the company. She even succeeded in persuading Geddon to start getting active in PESO. And Lopez herself decided to get involved in local politics.

By the end of her third year, Lopez had built an effective government relations program. She had developed a substantial network of contacts among officials in several key agencies, and was frequently asked for information by them. Armageddon's lobbying firm had played an active role in PESO's fight against a provision in a tax bill that would have denied tax benefits for the industry's R&D expenses. And Armand Geddon was now actually chairman of a PESO committee and had given a couple of speeches to local chambers of commerce on his committee's work. Working through several legislators in whose campaigns she had been involved, Lopez had gained a public commitment at a legislative hearing from PROD's new head that the agency would consult with Armageddon and other PESO members before developing new standards and regulations affecting the industry.

By her sixth year, Lopez had two assistants who handled most of the regulatory lobbying and issues research. Armageddon was using computerized tracking services to monitor legislative and agency activities. Lopez herself did a considerable amount of legislative lobbying and was developing plans for a political action committee. She complained to her husband that she was having difficulty getting Geddon to take time from his duties on PESO's board of directors and his chairmanship of the state chamber of commerce finance committee to discuss the PAC with him.

Two years later, Armageddon was confronted with a major issue. Legislation was introduced to require that home security device companies be required to obtain a homeowner's written permission before a sales presentation could be made. Not all of Armageddon's competitors kept to the ethical standards Armand Geddon had always insisted on, and some unpleasant publicity had resulted in this proposal. Lopez persuaded companies in several other, unaffected industries that legislation like this could easily be amended in the future to cover them, and was able to put together a coalition that succeeded in defeating the bill after several months of hard lobbying. "It would have been easier," she told Geddon, "if all our PAC contributors had good personal relationships with their legislators." Geddon, just beginning his term as chairman of PESO's board of directors, promised to get the association involved in designing a plan for a grass-roots program for its members.

Lopez, now Armageddon's vice president for public affairs, decided that something had to be done about the industry's image but also about some of the underlying ethical problems. She had no problem persuading Geddon to make an ethics program a major goal for PESO. She also retained a consulting firm to develop a solid public involvement program for Armageddon. As a result, the community relations program was upgraded, a scholarship program for talented minority students was instituted, and the company took the lead in persuading the city to redevelop the blighted, high-crime waterfront area into a major hotel and office building complex.

A year later she had lunch with Armageddon's marketing vice president. "You know, if this company is going to continue growing, we'll need a new line of business," he told her. "Why don't you do something about that state law that bars home security device companies from getting into the office security business?" Lopez went back to the office with a major new lobbying project.

On her twelfth anniversary with the company, Armand Geddon and his wife took Juanita and Hector Lopez to dinner. "I'd like your advice on a matter," he said. "I've been thinking about stepping down as C.E.O. of Armageddon. The company is doing well, and the new office security business has already increased revenues by 20 percent. Benson is ready to move into my job. But the real question is this: With the waterfront project doing so well, several of the city's top business and labor leaders have asked me to think about running for mayor. What do you think?"

Lopez smiled. "We've come a long way from the time when you didn't even want to vote. Can I manage your campaign?"

Comments on the Model and the Sequential Strategies

Not all companies and organizations will move through each strategic phase to the next as Armageddon Industries did. Some will "freeze" their development at a particular stage. The perceived importance of their issues may not provide sufficient justification for the incremental resources and effort that each additional strategic level requires. The corporate culture may be disinclined toward a "high public profile" or toward political involvement. There is also the comfort factor. Many executives are personally uneasy with a broad-spectrum strategy that requires extensive interaction with the public sector and with unfamiliar interest groups. Others feels, with equal force, that publicly visible organizations cannot shun opportunities to influence the external environment in which they operate lest they abdicate the field to competitors and adversaries.

No outsider can judge the correct strategy for a company or any other organization. The "wrong" strategy is the one settled on through inertia or emotion. The "right" one is the strategy adopted deliberately and by plan, on a basis that is consistent with the organization's internal needs, culture, and concept of its future.

The importance of sound strategies is that they affect the way the organization perceives the internal impact of relevant issues, the positions it takes on those issues, and the action programs it adopts to implement its positions.

INTERNAL IMPACT ASSESSMENTS

Issues vary in their impacts. It is important to establish the inherent significance of the issue, that is, to put a *value* on the organization's stake in it. Without such a value, it is difficult to gauge the effect, both short-term and long-term, of the issue on organizational plans. The relative values of issues can also help evaluate priorities for the allocation of resources among different needs and issues.

Like the financial executive referred to in an earlier chapter, many corporate and organization leaders instantly grasp the anticipated impact of an issue— or think they do. This is hardly a sophisticated internal analysis, however, and certainly not adequate as a rationale for external consumption. Indeed, the more important the issue, the more important it is to research its impact with great care.

Sources of Impact Data

For companies. Businesses are most commonly affected by economic issues for which a quantitative value can usually be established. What is this tax costing us? How much would our costs of compliance be reduced if this regulation were amended? What is the size of the market that would be opened up to us if this law were repealed? What will it cost us if this law is enacted?

Within companies, the best judges of an issue's probable impact are those most likely to be affected by it. Tax lawyers and accountants can give the hardest assessment of a tax bill's probable consequences. Purchasing agents will usually best understand the effects of a legislated increase in raw material costs. Personnel and labor relations professionals are the best source for analysis of a proposal to increase benefits or the minimum wage. Marketers are likely to be the experts on legislation affecting consumer packaging or labeling. The general counsel's office is still another source of invaluable input and assistance on most issues. Sometimes, internal issue experts like these, with their own specialized sources, may be the first to spot a new issue while also serving as effective resources on issues identified by others.

The important point is that all relevant sources within the company that have useful expertise need to be consulted in assessing an issue's impact. (After all, they will usually be the people who have to live with the problem on a day-to-day day basis long after government relations professionals have gone on to other issues.) Other people who should be consulted are those whose involvement is valuable for internal political reasons.

Issues should be measured in comparable terms. It may be difficult to work with a list of issues if one is measured in terms of potential market, another in sales, a third in costs, and a fourth in tax impact. Wherever possible, these varying measures should be reduced to a common denominator, such as after-tax profits. In most cases, this can be readily calculated by reference to the company's effective or marginal tax rates. Help can be sought from the firm's tax lawyers or accountants if the calculation gets complex.

For membership organizations. Within trade associations and other membership groups, the process of assessing an issue's impact is not very different than the corporate process. Issues are almost always referred to the specialized committees or task forces that are a major component of almost all organizational structures. In some cases, members may be polled, formally or informally, by the staff to gain an understanding of an issue's anticipated impact. The query may go directly to known experts within the membership, or may be channeled via official representatives, depending on the association's structure and procedures.

To the extent applicable, these member inputs should be quantified for the reason set forth above. In practice, though, quantitative data is more likely to be available from large corporate members with their greater resources than it is from smaller companies or from individual members. For that reason, if the issue is sufficiently important or to maintain confidentiality among competitors, other analytic techniques may have to be considered. An accounting firm could be asked to collect data from all members or a representative sample of them. Or an economic consultant could be commissioned to undertake a macroeconomic study of the industry.

These techniques may or may not be appropriate for labor unions and other membership organizations that wish to determine the quantitative impacts of an issue on their members. Assistance from economic consultants should be sought to evaluate these other kinds of quantitative impacts. After-tax consequences are not an appropriate measure for such groups, but an effort should be made to develop some quantifiable common denominator.

Issues Difficult to Quantify

The problem is more difficult for non-economic issues but no less important. Without some means of issue valuation, it is hard to compare needs, judge resources, or rank priorities.

An environmental group, for example, may be concerned with stopping a nuclear power plant, preserving an endangered species, and cleaning up a source of toxic waste. Without some valuation of these issues, it will be difficult to establish its priorities, allocate its existing resources, or know where to apply new ones.

Clearly, of course, subjective judgments always play a role, but the less issues lend themselves to quantification, the greater the subjective element and the greater the risk the organization may make incorrect assessments.

Many issues, however, are difficult to quantify, especially those that are essentially social or political. Groups dealing with abortion rights, whether pro or con, are involved with moral questions that for them transcend any statistics. A civil rights organization trying to get a favorable nomination confirmed or an unfavorable one blocked is dealing with a political issue on which emotions can run high. Sometimes, the emotional intensity of issues can be higher than their intrinsic importance, thereby possibly jeopardizing a rational allocation of resources.

For precisely this reason, some effort to evaluate inherent significance on a quantitative scale is even more important on social and political issues than on economic ones. (This is not to say that economic issues lack emotional content, as anyone who has ever been involved in such contentious issues as right-to-work can testify.)

Issues can be evaluated on a linear scale that provides a basis by which to test resources and priorities. One way to get started is to undertake a Delphic survey. Although the process may be a bit complicated, it can be a worthwhile first step, followed by a simpler version once the issues evaluation approach is in place.

1. Select a panel of people to survey. This could be a group of managers or executives, in the case of a company. In the case of an association or union, it could be a board of directors, a government relations committee, a specially chosen representative task force, or even the entire membership. Executive judgment will determine if the panel needs to be statistically representative of the whole, or if it should be comprised of technical experts or decision makers.
2. Ask the panel to assess the organization's basic needs, using the needs analysis described in Chapter 2.
3. Based on those needs, poll the panel again to develop a comprehensive list of issues. To make the process workable, a tentative list of actual issues should be suggested, allowing each panel member to add other issues.
4. Edit the resulting issues list to be sure each is descriptive and workable. The editing process should be as objective and fair as possible; the process is defeated if obvious distortions or biases are injected.
5. Poll the group a final time, asking now that each panelist assign a value to every issue (on a scale of one to ten if the list is short, or one to 100 if it is long). Little harm is done if a panelist gives the same score to more than one issue; if enough people are polled, the values will sort themselves out in the aggregate.
6. Compute the score for each issue, and then rank the list by these total values.
7. Develop priority rankings for each issue based on these values, modified as necessary by assessments of the political factors affecting each.

Let's take the XYZ Corporation and see how it handled this process. In step 1, XYZ created a panel consisting of officers, department heads, and key managers. In step 2, a statement of company needs was developed and then, in the third step, a tentative list of issues. The issues were edited in step 4 and in the fifth step once again presented to the panel, this time for the value rating computed in step 6.

By the end of the fourth step, the company's panel had narrowed its issues to the following list:

1. Sales tax increase. The company's products may be less attractive to its customers if sales tax hikes raise their cost.
2. Widget use licensing. The widgets XYZ makes may not sell well if consumers must be licensed in order to use them.

3. Employee education tax. The company makes educational grants to its employees and does not want them to have to pay income taxes on those grants.

4. Raw material import bars. Import restrictions on raw materials the company buys from overseas would raise costs.

5. Gizmo safety regulations. New safety regulations would impede the marketing of gizmos, a product made by another firm that competes directly with widgets. Safety restrictions imposed on gizmos but not widgets would give XYZ competitive advantages.

The XYZ Company panel gave the following values to its issues, with 10 being most important and 1 least:

Sales tax increase	6
Widget use licensing	9
Employee education tax	2
Raw material import bars	8
Gizmo safety regulations	4

Comment: Because licensing requires a substantial pre-purchase effort by the consumer, the panel viewed it as a major deterrent to the marketing of XYZ's widgets, substantially more so than an increase in the sales tax even though that would increase the price consumers must pay. Almost as important are the proposed raw material import restrictions because of the increase in costs and ultimately price to consumers. While placing safety restrictions on the competitive gizmos would give XYZ an edge in the market, there are difficulties in doing so and, besides, the sword has two edges and XYZ could be the company affected next time around. Although it wishes to benefit its employees and their education, the impact of the proposed tax is spread among many companies and, in any event, is clearly of less importance to XYZ's interests than the other issues.

Political Considerations and Other Factors

The panel survey procedure brings out the relative intrinsic importance to the company of the issues. From time to time as new issues arise, the panel can be asked simply to rate these questions on the linear scale.

The opinions of these experts will be a weighty factor in determining the position the company should adopt on the issues—but they should not be decisive. Experience and expertise in engineering, marketing, or the law do not necessarily endow an executive with political judgment. Political factors, such as evaluations of the issue's legislative significance, may not bear on internal issue assessments, but they are a critical element in determining the company's tactical position.

The widget licensing proposal, for example, may be less significant as a local bill in Anchorage, Alaska, than as a federal issue. On the other hand, the Anchorage bill may become *more* important if it is clearly going to pass while the federal legislation is going nowhere. Political factors like these have to be taken into account and the panel may not have the expertise to do so. This, therefore, is a task for government relations professionals.

In addition to political considerations, other impact factors should be evaluated. These might include consistency with previous issue positions, public and consumer image, and legal matters—or implications for employee morale, stakeholder, and community relations, or some other aspect of the company's business.

The final ratings of priorities should be based on evaluations of both the intrinsic importance of the issues, and the judgments made on these political and other factors.

ESTABLISHING ISSUE POSITIONS

The issue has been researched, its potential impact evaluated, its prospects assessed—all within the parameters of the organization's needs and strategies. Now, how should all this information be pulled together to facilitate determining a position on the issue? What are the alternative choices?

Options Papers

An issue options paper can focus the available information and distill out the alternatives in a way that will facilitate decision making. Note the model options paper below. It is relatively brief, even sketchy. Supporting documents, if needed, can always be appended, but the shorter the document the more likely it is to be read and utilized.

Model Issue Options Paper

Date:

Issue name:
Senate Bill No.:   House Bill No.:
  Main sponsor(s):   Main sponsor(s):
  Date introd.   Date introd.

Key provisions:

Probable impact on our organization:
  Is impact unique to us, or shared with others? Who?
  Other factors bearing on our decision:

Likely supporters (legislators and interest groups):
Rationale and arguments pro:
Likely opponents (legislators and interest groups):
Arguments against:

Alternatives (legislative or other):

Our position options:
  Support
  Support if following changes made (or not made):
  Oppose
  Oppose if following changes made (or not made):

Other considerations

Decision: Priority:
  Fall-back positions (if needed):

Implementation by:

Comments:

The options paper pulls together in concise form the basic data relating to the issue—bill numbers, sponsors and opponents, key provisions, arguments pro and con, etc. It also requires that thought be given to several important considerations, noted below.

1. *Probable impact.* What is the likely impact on the company or organization, together with an assessment of *potential allies*, i.e., other interests likely to be similarly impacted? If the impact would be shared among others in the company's industry, then this is probably an issue for a trade association. If the impact would be shared among companies outside the industry or with non-business organizations, major tactical considerations will include utilizing a coalition. If the impact would be both high and unique to the organization, than a major lobbying campaign will have to be geared up.

   Although the impact description should be concise within the options papers, it should be backed up with the more detailed assessment described above. This information might be included as an appendix to the options paper. It will also provide crucial raw material in preparing the *position paper* described below.

2. *Likely supporters* (and their rationale). What other legislators (especially leaders and committee chairmen) can be expected to support the sponsors? What is their justification for the bill and the major arguments they are likely to use? What other interest groups might back them, and why? Which major elected officials, departments, and agencies will lend support. Similar questions for the *opposing side* also require answers.

3. *Alternatives.* Are there other bills that are preferable—or perhaps some form of executive or regulatory action? Is there a better way that could be implemented voluntarily?

4. *Decision options.* It may well be that, based on all of the foregoing questions, a decision is made to flatly oppose or support a bill. Possibly, though, that decision might be different if the bill is amended in some key respects. Perhaps flat support (or opposition) is to be the "going-in" position, but, depending on various tactical considerations, a fall-back posture (or series of fall-backs) should also be adopted so that if the other side seems likely to prevail, harm will be minimized. Fall-back positions are also important so that the organization's lobbyists will know how to negotiate or compromise if key provisions are amended.

5. *Priority or value rating*. The rating assigned the issue (as discussed earlier in this chapter under impact assessment) indicates the importance of the issue for the budgetary allocation of personnel and other resources.

6. *Responsibility for implementation*. This should be specified. In most cases, this will be the government relations staff, but if this is a state or local issue in a decentralized environment, it might be a local manager who has been assigned certain government relations responsibilities. In dispersed organization models (see Chapter 4), it will be a designated issue coordinator. In trade associations, labor unions, or other membership groups, implementation will be assigned to the appropriate staff member or department.

DECISION-MAKING SYSTEMS

Final decisions on issue positions typically are made in corporations by the chief executive officer unless he or she chooses to delegate this responsibility. Delegation might be made to another corporate officer or, in the case of decentralized companies, to the head of the operating division or unit affected by the issue. This power can also be delegated to the Government Relations Committee (see Chapter 4), but approval by the C.E.O. of the company's position at least on major issues is good management practice. Of course, this is essential where two or more units within a multi-divisional company have different views on an important issue.

Trade associations and other membership organizations generally have established processes for the adoption of issue positions. The process usually involves staff research and political inputs to a committee or task force that recommends a policy or position for ultimate decision by the executive committee or board of directors. Occasionally, policy decision on major issues may be put to a vote of the entire membership.

Informal decision making can occur on minor issues or those that are essentially variations on established issues. Where it is reasonably apparent to government relations professionals what the position of the company or organization is likely to be, an informal check with the appropriate corporate or association official is likely to be sufficient to establish a position on the matter.

Informal decision making may also be essential where time is a vital factor. This often occurs near the end of many legislative sessions when issues crowd each other and bills are rushed through for final passage or defeat. The company or association should have procedures in place so that lobbyists will know which individual to call to get a fast decision on a position. This kind of situation also illustrates the value of pre-established fall-back positions, enabling the lobbyist to make decisions on the spot when legislative circumstances require.

Position Papers

Once a decision has been made concerning the organization's position on the issue, the options paper—backed up with the basic research, particularly the detailed, quantified impact assessment—becomes a statement of the organization's position.

There is a need at this point for a document that clearly and concisely lays out this position for external use. This position paper can be used with a variety of audiences:

Legislators, legislative committees, and staffs.

Executive and regulatory agency officials.

The press.

Trade associations and potential allies.

Company stakeholders—managers, employees, retirees, shareholders, suppliers and customers, local officials in affected communities, etc.

Organization members.

Public interest groups.

A position paper should be concise, brief, and written in clear and persuasive language for a lay audience. It must be factual and accurate in content, and reasonable and moderate in tone. Firmness and conviction are always appropriate; shrillness and hysteria never are. Length should be no more than two pages, going to three or at most four only if absolutely necessary. (Readers' attention spans tend to vary inversely with length.)

The position paper also can be the basis for testimony on the issue at public hearings, speeches, press releases, employee and shareholder publications, and similar communications avenues (see Chapter 9).

Preparation of the position paper need not be difficult since it will draw heavily on the research already done for the options paper. It should contain the following elements:

• Description of the issue.

• The organization's position coupled, where appropriate, with a refutation of the other side's arguments.

If it is possible to do so, it is well to frame the argument as a question of basic fairness or other moral principles.

• Impact of the issue on the organization's operations stated, as appropriate, in terms of gain or loss in jobs, tax consequences, community effects, impacts on suppliers (especially small or minority businesses), etc.

Such points tend to have more impact than arguments relating to jeopardized sales or profits, although these will be worth making if they are dramatic enough and can be well documented.

Documentation is important. Third-party validation of the company's or organization's claims always carries more weight than self-assertions. If the validation originates with a respected and disinterested institution (e.g., university or government agency), so much the better.

• Impact on consumers or the public in general.

It is important to show citizens who probably would not perceive a common interest that they do indeed share one with the company or organization. Again, this should be documented or validated by some third party if at all possible.

"White papers" are more research-oriented versions of position papers. Intended for academics, legislative analysts, and other researchers and audiences interested in a fuller exposition of the issue, they are useful vehicles to communicate research results or other documentation of the rationale underlying the group's position.

4

Organization and Resources

Set thine house in order.

II Kings 20:1

There is nothing more difficult to take in hand, more perilous to conduct, or more uncertain in its success, than to take the lead in the introduction of a new order of things.

Machiavelli

Lobbyists often characterize government relations as akin to firefighting, describing their activities as running around dousing brush fires wherever they may flare up. But even the possibility of an occasional small blaze requires some advance preparation if only that an extinguisher be kept handy. Moreover, insurance needs to be taken out against possible losses, and affirmative fire prevention programs should be developed to minimize the likelihood and severity of problems. Nonetheless, the probability that a certain number of major conflagrations still will erupt is the reason fire departments are organized.

Government relations needs to be organized as a system for very similar reasons. Issues need to be managed. That requires planning, programming, budgeting, and implementation. It also requires evaluation and mobilization of resources within a system that either already exists in satisfactory form or needs to be reorganized or even developed from scratch.

This chapter deals with those problems, focusing on the resources and forms of organization needed for an effective "firefighting" program. (There are, of course, many kinds of resources apart from organizational ones. They include trade associations, political friendships and potential alliances, and employee or membership support. These are examined in separate chapters.)

MANAGEMENT SUPPORT

Listed in order of importance, the most essential elements in any organization's government relations program are top management support, top management support, and top management support.

Strong support from senior management is no assurance that a government relations program will succeed, but it does give it a healthy start and facilitates a favorable allocation of other necessary resources.

Without support from the top, however, no government relations program can have much hope of success. Resources available to the program will be scant. Understanding and cooperation from other segments of the organization will be given grudgingly at best. Lobbyists, assuming any are even tolerated in the organization, are likely to be viewed as practitioners of black magic whose methods are mysterious and probably unspeakable, and who certainly are not to be considered part of the management team.

Organizational Philosophies

The organization's philosophy of government relations is an important element, part of the permanent cultural value system that every organization develops and that is expressed but also often reinterpreted by current senior management. It is therefore subject to substantial modification from the top.

The following statements are stereotypes of organizational philosophies of government relations often expressed by business leaders, and (much less often) by the heads of non-business organizations as well:

- "I don't have the time or patience for a government relations program in this company," says the chief executive of Company A. "We're under extreme pressure to cut costs and there is no place here for unnecessary staff overhead. Besides, that's what we pay our trade associations to do."

- "Government relations makes an important, in fact vital, contribution to our profitability," responds his counterpart in Company B. "It has enabled us to reduce the cost burdens of government regulation. It has lowered our taxes. And it has helped us open up new markets that previously were closed to us. The benefits the government relations function has brought this company have paid for its costs many times over, and have contributed substantially to our bottom line."

- "It's all right to have a government relations person in this company," says Company C's top executive, "providing he confines himself to monitoring issues, informing management, and representing us with trade associations. But nobody in this organization is going to lobby any government officials."

What accounts for these very different philosophies, all widely found within the business community? Sometimes, differences among corporate cultures and experiences. Other times, the values and experiences of individuals. Still other explanations flow out of the different ways government relations is integrated into corporate processes of goal-setting and implementation. In most cases, the truth will lie in some combination of these factors. Each of these merits a more detailed examination.

Corporate Cultures and Business Environments

Organizations each have their own cultures, their institutional personalities. The longer the life and stability of the organization, the stronger and more distinct its culture and values are likely to be. The attitudes of the person at the top will shape the organization's cultural views and values, but the culture will also influence the boss.

The ability of an organization to affect its external environment is greatly influenced by its willingness to do so, its belief that it can do so effectively, and its acceptance of the merit of the effort. This philosophic disposition, articulated or not, will underlie everything the organization seeks to do. If the organization and its top executives question the appropriateness of trying to alter governmental policy, no comprehensive program can be organized. Government relations will be task-oriented, and results will be, at best, only marginally effective.

Different industries are likely to hold different points of view, depending on the frequency and impact of the regulatory experience.

Highly regulated government contractors, for instance, typically must conduct business under government controls that other businesses, operating exclusively in the private sector, would often find unacceptable. Government contractors are subject, by both law and regulation, to more rigid standards of performance and accountability than are private-sector marketers. Their executives frequently are highly restricted in their ability to make even routine decisions without approvals from the government agencies they service. Laws governing prevailing wage rates and other labor practices often have special applicability to companies seeking public business or financing. The effectiveness of government relations is fundamental to the ability of such companies to operate and to obtain and service contracts.

For public utilities, government regulation is the way of the world. Perhaps even more than government contractors, utilities must account to regulatory bodies and others in government for virtually every facet of their business. Utilities can also be forced by government to undo the results of decisions that regulatory bodies had previously approved—a fact of life of which the operators of nuclear power plants are painfully aware.

Retailers and other labor-intensive companies of all kinds must operate within personnel cost structures mandated in great detail by legislation and regulations, even if they are not also subject to the intricate provisions of union contracts.

Pharmaceutical companies and, to a lesser extent, food manufacturers must obtain government approvals for new products and processes, both generally extensive and expensive.

Banking, insurance, and other financial industries generally must obtain governmental approvals for many new products, business opportunities, and marketing approaches.

Some of these enterprises may conclude from their experiences that they can do little to affect the government controls that are such a substantial part of their business environment—indeed, for some, it may seem that government is the business environment in totality. Yet, others are motivated by the same kinds of experiences to initiate major efforts to alter and reshape that environment.

Personal and Corporate Values

Corporate and personal value systems are often a major factor in attitudes toward the company's ability to influence government. A top executive once told the author that he thought business was no more justified in interfering with government than government was in interfering with business. "How can we tell the politicians to keep their noses out of our business if we're down in Washington lobbying theirs?"

Personal experiences can have lasting impacts on executives' attitudes. An executive was invited to testify by a congressional committee on a financial issue about which he was considered expert. Flattered, he prepared thoroughly and presented himself at the hearing. However, during questioning by committee members, he was subjected to a merciless barrage of criticism by a legislator who had had an unfortunate experience with the company on a completely unrelated matter. Traumatized by the incident, the executive returned from Washington vowing never to become involved in government relations again.

Values toward public affairs can also be shaped by perceptions of others' experiences. A C.E.O. had spent the early part of his career in less developed countries where, he observed, companies that were publicly conspicuous seemed inevitably to become political targets, especially those that were units of U.S. multinationals. His conclusion was that the only safe strategy was to maintain the lowest possible corporate profile. He brought this philosophy back with him when he returned to the United States. For the remainder of his career, he vigorously resisted any efforts to lobby on issues affecting his company except through trade associations.

Yet, the woods are also full of executives who went to Washington or a state capital to lobby an issue on behalf of their companies, found the process successful and rewarding, and became strong advocates of government relations.

The environment in which companies operate also helps shape their willingness and ability to become involved in the business environment. Some public utilities, for example, contribute substantial executive time to socially beneficial community programs, reaping the goodwill in more favorable marketing and regulatory climates. Participation in public affairs becomes part of the corporate culture for those companies, typically transcending any adverse views held among individual executives.

Indeed, it is the nature of corporate cultures that they tend to foster the careers of executives who share the company's values and to force out individuals whose personal values are too much at odds with those of the organization. One of the best-known consumer products corporations in America "breeds" executives known for their nearly total antipathy to government regulation of consumer marketing. The story is told of two rising managers who were part of a trade association committee trying to develop an industrywide position on an important legislative issue. The two reluctantly went along with the rest of the committee in agreeing to trade off a small degree of government control in order to avoid a still larger public role. It took personal intervention by industry leaders to save the jobs of the young executives when their superiors learned what happened, but two promising careers were probably stunted.

At the other extreme are companies whose cultural values include the belief that they have an obligation to be "socially responsible" and that profitability is a secondary objective. More common are those enterprises that find it is easier to be socially responsible when they are profitable than when they are not.

Nonetheless, companies are not islands. Businesses operate in an environment comprised of many other institutions and value systems, not all of which are favorably inclined to a laissez-faire philosophy. Government relations can provide an antenna into that environment, picking up the signals of competitive and adversarial institutions seeking public policy changes. That information is not only lobbying intelligence but, if received early enough, can be valuable input for strategic and business planning.

Gaining Management Support

Whether corporate value systems tilt toward pragmatism, or in more ideological directions, the most successful government relations efforts will be those that are deeply rooted in the mainstream of corporate objectives and strategies. Most companies believe that their primary purpose is to generate a profit for the benefit of owners, to strengthen the business, and thereby to assure the economic well-being of their employees and the communities in which they operate. The government relations function must be intimately involved in serving that purpose if it is to be accepted, effective, and successful.

Wise government relations executives will therefore devote considerable energy to assuring that their efforts concentrate on those issues with the greatest impact—both short-term and long-term—on corporate profitability and other basic business objectives. If new to the organization, they will take great pains to learn its culture, absorb its folkways, and adapt their personal styles as appropriate to the circumstances. Strong programs of communications to senior and operating managements are essential to help build and maintain essential support, and to gradually reshape company values adverse to the government relations process.

Lobbying, in other words, begins at home. Some possible steps follow.

- Count noses. Who, among top corporate and operating unit executives, are supporters of the government relations process? Who are indifferent or perhaps hostile? The C.E.O.'s views can be weakened or strengthened by even the casual comments of members of the management team.

- Shore up support. Relationships with internal allies should be reinforced—and ways to win over "the sinners and the saveables" should be developed. Helping individuals in all three groups achieve their business and even personal objectives is an almost sure-fire approach. This applies not only to the top executives but also to their likely successors, those a tier or two down.

- Integrate government relations plans and programs with corporate and operating unit business objectives—both current and strategic.

- Help managers understand how the political, legislative, and lobbying processes work—how they affect the organization's goals—and how the organization can influence them. Giving them the flavor and nuances of the system is more important than a civics lesson.

- Invite lobbying participation. Even if these executives are not (yet) participating in a grass-roots lobbying program, nothing will give them a better feel for the lobbying process than a few trips to discuss issues personally with legislators.

- Organize political education seminars. An occasional management meeting at which important federal or state legislators speak is an excellent way to build greater awareness of the importance of government relations and enthusiasm for it. Invitations to a private lunch or dinner with the speaker before or after the program are an effective way to strengthen personal support and relationships.

- Communicate frequently on current issues. Bulletins, memos, or newsletters will keep the entire management team alerted to timely developments—but communicating particularly important information ahead of time and in person to affected managers is always an appreciated gesture.

Both association and company executives tend to be strongly preoccupied with current issues, and effective government relations professionals will therefore devote the bulk of their efforts to those problems that affect the organization's one-to-three-year objectives. This does not mean that issues larger than the company's immediate interests should be neglected. Tending to macro-issues is one of the reasons that trade associations and "umbrella" business groups exist.

Moreover, analyzing new and emerging issues is an important function that can alert senior management to long-term changes in the business environment. If the company wishes to play a proactive role in dealing with such issues, or to become involved in larger social and economic concerns, that is the "fire prevention" function to which government relations and public affairs should make major contributions.

But the C.E.O. and the corporate culture have to be ready to accept such activities. Many a program has stumbled and even been shut down because the public affairs department was perceived by operating personnel to be more concerned with changing the world than with protecting the bottom line.

The role of chief executives is to direct and shape government relations as their bridge to, and from, the world of public policy—supporting the function within the organization and participating appropriately in its external activities when they can make their own unique contributions.

Non-Corporate Interest Groups

The need to justify the government relations function is much less an issue today for trade associations, membership organizations, and non-business interest groups than it is for companies. For most such interest groups the battle has long since been debated and resolved.

Labor

Political and government relations involvement was perceived as a dire necessity if the organized labor movement was to survive its formative years and achieve the objectives it was unable to win in its direct dealings with management. Labor's fortunes have ebbed and flowed since its great legislative successes began in the Depression of the 1930s, but the high priority given its involvement in lobbying and the political process has not been seriously debated within the labor movement in over half a century. Individual unions, with few exceptions, have been involved in the legislative process at all levels of government, and government relations continues to be an overriding priority of labor's national federation, the AFL-CIO.

Civil Rights Organizations

Civil rights groups have been deeply involved in government relations for reasons similar to those of organized labor, namely their inability to achieve their objectives within the private sector. These organizations substantially broadened the government relations arena through extensive and largely successful use of the judiciary to alter public policy when legislative efforts stalled. Like labor, civil rights groups also successfully brought issues to Washington when they felt thwarted by state and local governments or the private sector.

Farm Groups

For American agricultural organizations, government relations has long been a high priority because of farmers' economic fragmentation and their dependence on government support to ease high susceptibility to great swings in weather and market conditions. Farm lobbying efforts have also often been fragmented, perhaps less than those of business but more so than labor's. The political power of agriculture has declined somewhat along with its relative economic importance in America, but it is still quite substantial, in large part because so many individual farmers are politically active and in frequent touch with their legislators on needs and issues. Agricultural groups are often exceptionally influential on price support policies for specific commodities, ranging from milk and peanuts to tobacco and cotton.

Consumer and Environmental Organizations

Among newer interest groups, such as those concerned with the environment and consumers' interests, the need to be involved in lobbying has rarely been in question. The few debates that have occurred have largely taken place within older organizations like the Sierra Club, which had long-standing programs that many members had feared would be lessened in importance if lobbying became a major priority. Most of the environmental and consumer groups that arose during the 1960s and thereafter were created for the express purpose of influencing governmental policies, and this continues to be an overriding objective for virtually all these groups. Indeed, the most recent controversies have centered on the question of whether these groups are *too* partisan politically.[1]

Influencing governmental policies appears to be the principal goal of most new special interest groups established in recent years. Unlike most older organizations that were originally established to defend the public- and private-sector interests of traditional economic and demographic groups, most of the newer organizations have been created to deal with very specific issues, such as abortion rights, which often transcend those traditional interests.

Symbolic, perhaps, of the modern commitment of most non-business interests to utilize government relations to achieve their objectives was the 1988 action of the American Association of Retired Persons (AARP), which discharged its executive director after less than four months on the job; the organization's board reportedly concluded that his philosophic preference for private-sector remedies to address the needs of the aging was incompatible with AARP's long-standing commitment to governmental action.

The National Rifle Association (NRA), an exceptionally effective lobby, also has undergone organizational changes in recent years, instigated by factions that felt the NRA was insufficiently militant in opposing gun controls.

Among America's major interest groups, therefore, it appears that only among business enterprises is there found such widespread reluctance to utilize the public policy process to attain important goals.

GOVERNMENT RELATIONS STAFF

No government relations or broader public affairs effort ever has enough personnel to cover all the issues assigned to their staff. Once a decision to hire a staff has been made, sophistication and awareness increase and the number of issues in which the organization takes an interest constantly grows. The perceived importance of many issues also increases within the organization. The overall effect is a staff that almost always has more on its plate than it can ever digest.

The questions management must answer are:

1. How much staff is needed to do the job?
2. What other internal resources are available to accomplish government relations objectives?
3. How should resources be organized?

The size of a government relations staff can actually be quite small and still accomplish its objectives—if it is well organized and if other organizational resources are effectively utilized. Of course, there is no optimum size. Size depends on the number, intensity, and geographic scope of the issues, overall affordability, and the manner in which the organization is structured to handle the basic functions of government relations.

Government Relations Staff Responsibilities

- Issues research and analysis and development of positions
  Staff role: Direct implementation optional; coordination mandatory.
- Direct lobbying
  Staff role: Direct implementation optional; coordination mandatory.
- Trade association liaison
  Staff role: Direct implementation optional; coordination mandatory.
- "Grass-roots" lobbying
  Staff role: Direct implementation and coordination mandatory.
- Coalitions and alliances
  Staff role: Direct implementation optional; coordination mandatory.
- Political activity
  Staff role: Direct implementation and coordination mandatory.
- Internal and external communications
  Staff role: Direct implementation optional; coordination mandatory.

Coordination of strategic planning and implementation for each of these

functions is a critical role of the government relations staff. Actual implementation by this staff is essential only for the political and grass-roots functions.

Core Functions

Research and Positions

The staff must coordinate the process of defining needs, identifying and
analyzing issues, and establishing positions. It must assure that the necessary
issues research is performed, whether within the government relations staff,
by others elsewhere in the organization, or by purchase from the outside
(see Chapters 2 and 3).

Direct Lobbying

The staff must decide, too, how direct lobbying is to be handled—whether
the ball will be carried by the company's personnel, handed off to retained
lobbyists or trade associations, or shared.

Even if the company takes responsibility for all or part of the direct lobbying, the staff may or may not do the actual personal contact work. As
discussed more fully in Chapters 5 and 6, direct lobbying is a function that
requires great skill and experience. It may be more cost-effective in some
cases to utilize outside lobbyists than to develop those skills in-house. That
is surely true when issues arise in remote locations, or require exceptional
technical or political expertise. On the other hand, inside lobbyists will tend
to have a much better understanding of the organization. Supervision and
coordination of outside lobbyists is a critical staff responsibility.

Trade Association Relations

A function often assigned to government relations personnel is liaison with
trade associations to ensure that the company's legislative positions and those
of its associations mesh. As discussed in Chapter 7, making government relations staffers the company's formal representatives is questionable. However, the *coordination* of liaison relationships is a critical staff function.

Grass-Roots Lobbying

The government relations staff plays the key role in building and coordinating the "grass-roots" network. Management of the network, communications to it, and effective utilization on appropriate issues are essential staff
functions (see Chapter 8).

Relations with Other Groups

Coalitions and alliances should be developed with other groups (both
business and non-business) that share an interest in the issues. The optimum
liaison with each group will be an ad hoc choice. If a company has a consumer

affairs director, for instance, that individual is probably the right person to maintain relationships on legislative issues with consumer groups. In some cases, outside lobbyists may be the most appropriate liaisons where good relationships pre-exist with specific groups, or where the lobbyist represents the organization in distant locations.

Although one or several people may have responsibility for maintaining these relationships on a day-to-day basis, the *coordination* of these alliances and coalitions must be the responsibility of the senior government relations staff executive. A country may have many ambassadors; it has only one foreign minister (see Chapter 7).

Communications

Public relations or employee relations personnel, or outside firms, may prepare issues information for dissemination to internal or external audiences—but it is critical that the communicators take close guidance on issues and political matters from the government relations staff. Not only facts but also nuances are critically important in such communications (see Chapter 9).

Political Action

Political activities must be closely and professionally managed, either in toto within the government relations staff or by experts who share that staff's reporting relationship. Political fund-raising and disbursement are sophisticated and highly regulated activities. Transgressions can jeopardize the entire government relations program and result in legal problems and unfavorable publicity. (Note that this should not preclude the active involvement of members or employees in both fund-raising and disbursement, but the program must be managed carefully and with political sensitivity. See Chapter 10.)

Staff Organization

There are at least three models for organization of the government relations function:

Centralized

A single staff, reporting to a common executive, and serving the entire company or organization. This is the traditional form in both business and non-business structures. Within a centralized government relations department, staff members may have functional responsibilities, or be organized by issue categories, or both.

Decentralized

In many companies, government relations is the responsibility of individual operating units. Since these units typically have broad profit-and-loss responsibility, they are assigned whatever staff functions are necessary to achieve that responsibility. (Of course, they also have the latitude to decide *not* to exercise those functions, including government relations.) Sometimes, too, government relations personnel are assigned within individual corporate staff departments, usually those that are broadly affected by government policies (e.g., labor relations, taxation, etc.). A small central government relations or public affairs staff may (or may not) exist at the corporate level in such companies, primarily for purposes of coordination but also to handle corporatewide issues.

Dispersed

A third model makes each operating unit or staff department responsible for coping with any issues that may arise to affect it. In each such unit, government relations is handled on a part-time basis by *issue coordinators*, those individuals with substantive expertise deemed most qualified to manage that issue for the company. Under the dispersed model (sometimes also called "the quarterback system"), issue coordinators have strategic responsibility for their issues. They may be responsible for undertaking or obtaining the necessary issues analysis; be deeply involved in formulating policy, positions, and strategy; play the principal implementing role through direct lobbying, trade association liaison, coalition-building, and the like. Central coordination of the issue coordinators, if it exists at all in this organizational form, is provided by an interdepartmental committee or perhaps a single individual at the corporate level who may devote all or perhaps only part of his or her time to this responsibility. (The dispersed model can also function as an adjunct to a central government relations department or to a Washington office.)

Within a single company, there may also be *hybrid* structures with one division centralizing its lobbying functions, another decentralized, a third using the dispersed model, a fourth leaving everything to its trade association, and a fifth doing nothing whatever.

Which organizational model is "correct"? There is no such thing as an ideal structure for government relations. Even within the same organization, what is ideal at one point in time may become quite imperfect at another.

The correct model is the one that will achieve the organization's objectives within the context of its culture.

For most membership organizations, the centralized form is typical; few have staffs large enough to be decentralized, let alone dispersed. The very largest, however, have sometimes taken different paths. The Chamber of Commerce of the United States, a multi-issue business organization, has long followed a form that is partly dispersed and partly centralized. Issue experts, diffused among several departments, are responsible for research, alliances, and general strategy for their issues. They share responsibility for direct lobbying and membership communications on their issues with a central legislative department, which also manages a grass-roots program. Political action is the responsibility of another, separate central department.

Within individual companies, the organization of the government relations function is likely to adhere to the firm's current overall organizational philosophy. For many multi-division companies today, this often means decentralization. Since the government relations function may not be a full-time responsibility in a decentralized structure, it is sometimes combined with other related activities such as legal, public relations, community relations, etc. In the dispersed form, government relations is always only one of multiple responsibilities.

The advantages of both the decentralized and dispersed forms are that the government relations process is never far removed from the substantive expertise on the issues. Advocates of both forms also believe costs are less; however, depending on the sophistication of internal accounting, it may well be only that costs are less visible than under a centralized system.

Two prime hazards need to be guarded against with both non-centralized forms. The first is potential lack of coordination. At its worst, this can take the form of two operating units within a company taking opposite stands on the same issue. Even short of this extreme, however, there is a need for consistency of positions and mutual support in their implementation.

The second problem is that lawmakers and other public officials are unlikely to appreciate the niceties of corporate organization and may question why they should be asked to take their time to see several people from the same company on different issues when a single individual could cover them all.

This is not to say that centralized structures are necessarily the best. Centralized government relations departments can become too concerned with governmental and political process at the expense of issue substance, and also have been known to lose touch occasionally with some of the operating realities of the business, particularly in multi-division companies.

Although numerous models exist for study by other organizations, there is no universally optimum government relations structure. What works, works.

Coordinating Systems

Regardless of whether government relations is organized along centralized, decentralized, or dispersed lines, coordinating mechanisms are essential. Such systems should take guidance from and communicate with all relevant operating unit and corporate staff executives. A permanent government relations (or public affairs) committee provides such a mechanism.

This committee should meet regularly to approve company policies, positions, and implementation plans, review the status of issues, and generally stay posted on the significance of developments and the outlook for each issue. On major matters committee recommendations should be submitted to the chief executive for final approval. (In some organizations, the C.E.O. may choose to be a member of the committee.)

In organizations where government relations is centralized, an important purpose of the committee is to help the department stay close to its constituencies. The head of the government relations department should chair the committee. Members should include his or her principal subordinates plus the heads of operating divisions or units, and those corporate staff executives deeply involved in public affairs (e.g., vice presidents or directors for law, public relations, environmental affairs, regulatory compliance, human resources, tax matters, etc.).

In organizations where government relations is decentralized or dispersed, the committee would function with a few differences. Functions would be the same. Membership would include all of the above individuals (to the extent their roles exist) plus the issue coordinators. If there is a senior government relations executive, that individual should chair the committee; if not, another appropriate corporate executive should do so, making sure that the system functions as it should on the issues.

Reporting Relationships

An important consideration is the organizational placement of the government relations staff.

If the chief executive wishes the function to be important—and to be *seen* as important—it should not be run by a manager three or four operating levels down. If the function is truly important to the organization, it should be directed by an executive reporting directly to the C.E.O. The further removed government relations is from the top, the lower the perception of its importance within the organization; in this context perception *is* reality.

The reporting relationship should be dictated by the importance of the function and the organizational needs and public issues it is concerned with, not the size of its staff or budget.

Compensation

Salaries for corporate executives in public affairs and government relations vary by geography, line of business, size of company, size of department, and other factors, according to 1987 and 1988 studies. The studies were prepared for the Foundation for Public Affairs.[2]

Salaries for the top public affairs position in 1988 ranged from a low of $32,000 to almost $255,000. Shown here are the national medians of total cash compensation (i.e., salary and bonus, if any). All data are as of July 1, 1988 except for the Washington office positions, which were separately surveyed twelve months earlier (a minor factor given the low inflation rate during that period).

Top public affairs executive	$140,500
Top federal government relations executive (headquarters-based)	96,000
Head of Washington office	128,600
Deputy head of Washington office	78,400
Top state government relations executive	91,800

Since these figures are medians (the number that 50 percent of the data fall below and 50 percent rise above), actual compensation will diverge substantially from these numbers. The FPA surveys contain considerable additional data, both for the above positions and others in corporate public affairs.

Program and Budget

If a government relations department is to operate on a cost-effective basis, it should operate by both program and budget.

There is a logical progression in the development of these management tools: Organizational needs lead to issues. Planning the management of those issues results in a program. The program, coupled with the issue priority ratings and resource allocation, produces a budget.

Both program and budget should be multi-year if they are to be useful planning guides. Three years is probably a practical limit. Both program and budget should be on a rolling basis: The old year drops off as a new third year is added. The new first and second years are amended as needs and resources dictate.

The priority or value rating system discussed in Chapter 3 provides a guide for the allocation of resources, both internal and external, including personnel.

Few issues are settled within a year or two, least of all contentious ones. In formulating the program, the best estimate possible should be made of the length of time required to resolve the issue. In the case of long-term issues—those that are very controversial or defensive issues the timing of which really rests in the hands of legislators or other interest groups—the estimate can be only approximate. It may be sufficient to note in the program that the issue is likely to still be alive at the end of the third year.

The program should contain the outline of a battle plan for each major issue, sketching out the resources to be applied. The time period during which particular resources will be needed should be indicated.

Major line items in government relations budgets may include:

- Salaries and bonuses
- Employee benefits and perquisites

- Travel and entertainment
- Consultants and independent lobbyists
- Publications, subscriptions, and tracking services
- Dues and professional training
- Rent and other costs of satellite offices (Washington and state capitals)
- Political action committee administrative costs
- Speakers' honoraria and other educational program costs

A rough rule of thumb for government relations budgets is that their total is about twice personnel costs (i.e., salaries, bonuses, and benefits).

Location of Personnel

The location of government relations personnel also affects budgeting. There are fewer incremental costs if they are based at the organization's headquarters than in Washington or state capitals, but there are other important considerations as well. The culture of the organization is one of these, as is the nature of its exposure to its issues. This question is further discussed in Chapter 6.

Utilizing External Resources

Staff and issue coordinator responsibilities and deadlines should be identified in the program to ensure accountability for performance. Other resources required to accomplish performance by deadlines should also be noted. These include *internal* resources—those within the government affairs department—as well as those *external* resources, which are elsewhere in the organization and on which the department can call as required.

This latter point is a critical element in cost-effective government relations management:

- "Grass-roots" lobbying, for example, lets the organization utilize its members—or its managers, employees, and stockholders—as a trained, enthusiastic volunteer cadre of lobbyists who can be mobilized issue by issue.
- The existing data processing system can be utilized for highly sophisticated communications to a variety of constituents and audiences.
- Coalitions and alliances can sometimes permit a sharing of costs and resources to accomplish common objectives.
- Trade association memberships can be managed to maximize the value of the dues and executive time invested.

The ability to transform such external resources can maximize the capability of the government relations staff to achieve program objectives with minimum budgetary impact. These external resources should also be detailed in the annual and three-year programs. The budget includes those current or planned expenses needed to make the most effective use of external resources and otherwise to achieve objectives.

This kind of program and budget requires strong support from top management. Without such support, inadequate funding and organizational politics will cripple the achievement of government relations goals.

Performance Evaluation

Judging both the effectiveness of the government relations function and the performance of its managers is more difficult than for other business functions that typically are appraised quantitatively. Government relations personnel can, and should, be evaluated, but fair measures of performance must reflect the nature of the function.

If 100 adverse bills died in a particular legislative session, it is probably unrealistic to give the government relations manager full credit for all the scalps. For one thing, most of the bills might have died anyhow for lack of general support. For another, credit may be deserved but should be shared with other organizations that may have worked equally hard. It may be more significant that an important favorable bill was passed, if only because enacting legislation is usually much harder than defeating it; but if it took three years to get this bill passed, does the manager get a cipher in each of the first two years and then A+ in the third? Lobbyists at best are persuaders; decision-making power lies exclusively with public officials.

The advantage of a formal annual government relations program is that it can be used to hold personnel accountable for performance: What was to be done? By whom? By when? With what resources? Was it accomplished? How well? On time? Within budget?

For this approach to work, the program must be quite specific. Each task, function, or role should be assigned to a named individual. Any computer can then print out a list of the responsibilities for which each individual can be held accountable, and who should agree in advance with the statement of his or her accountabilities.

At year's end, the manager will have a basis for evaluating individual performances: Was the grass-roots training seminar actually organized by July 24? How good a job did Smith do on the project? The PAC fund-raising drive under Jones was to raise $50,000 by September 1; what factors account for the fact that only $40,000 was raised and that only half the fund-raising budget was spent?

This approach assumes that an executive whose program is regularly meeting its objectives on schedule and on budget is probably also achieving positive results over time and in the areas where measures are softer and less direct.

XYZ Corporation
Model Government Relations Program

ISSUE: *Widget Use Licensing*

OBJECTIVE: (1.) Oppose all legislative/regulatory proposals to require licenses for widget use. (2.) Support efforts to repeal existing license requirements.

VALUE RATING: 9

PRIORITY: *High* in Ark., Pa., Utah, Seattle, & Boston—serious threats.
Medium in Ariz. and Tenn.—repeal interest growing.
Low elsewhere including Congress—little activity.

COMPLETION DATE: Open—long-term problem.

ACTIONS PLANNED: *Research*—Impact paper by Jones of Law Dept. and Smith of Marketing Dept. Legislative analyses commissioned in three *high* states & two *high* cities. Background papers underway for Ariz. and Tenn.
Direct Lobbying—G.R. resp. in Pa. (Hodges) & Seattle (Dixon). Local lobbyists hired in Boston, Ark., & Utah. Local legal counsel monitoring in Ariz. & Tenn. Trade assn. field staff helping as feasible.
Grass-Roots Lobbying—Employees in Philadelphia, Seattle, & Nashville plants being alerted to contact legislators; information booklets already distributed. Other action plans in preparation.
Coalitions—Widget user groups to be formed, using warranty records as base. Unions closely involved. Negotiations underway with ACLU and consumer groups.
Political—Good access where needed.
Communications—P.R. dept. (Harrison) developing targeted messages for stockholders, employees, public officials, and press in High and Medium locations. Outside P.R. firm providing backup, speech material, and media interviews.

RESOURCES: *G.R. dept.:* Mason mgr.; D'Elia, backup. Field reps: as noted above. Outside lobbyists as noted. *Other external*: P.R. (Harrison—1/2 time + outside firm as needed); Law (Jones—1/4 time); Marketing (Smith—1/8 time); Data Proc. (three man-days); Human res. and investor rel. personnel (as needed).

COSTS: See budget for data by year and quarters.

BENEFITS: See marketing impact paper for estimates of potential revenue preserved or regained.

NOTES

1. Douglas P. Wheeler. "A Political Handbook for the Environmental Movement." *The Washington Post National Weekly Edition*, September 19–25, 1988.

2. *1988 Compensation Survey of Public Affairs Positions*. Prepared by TPF&C, a Towers Perrin Company. Washington, D.C.: Foundation for Public Affairs, 1988. *1987 Washington Office Salary Survey*. Prepared by Peat Marwick Main & Co. Washington, D.C.: Foundation for Public Affairs, 1987.

5

Direct Lobbying

Man is by nature a political animal.

Aristotle

Direct lobbying involves two essential functions:

1. The collection of unpublished intelligence about issues and other governmental and political developments of significance to an interest group.
2. The communication of the interest group's positions on issues and other information to lawmakers or other government officials with the intention of shaping or reshaping public policy.

Direct lobbying is the oldest and best-known form of government relations; indeed, to most laymen it is probably the only form of government relations with which they are familiar. Direct lobbying commonly and typically involves personal, face-to-face communications. It is distinguished here from the other avenues of government relations that have grown up to supplement it and that are treated in other chapters of this book.

Qualities of a Good Lobbyist

- Personal integrity
- Empathy
- The ability to listen
- Strong communications and persuasive skills
- Intimate grasp of both formal legislative procedures and informal folk ways
- Political sophistication

- Intellectual strength and substantive competence
- Strategic skill

THE LOBBYIST'S CREDENTIALS

The lobbying field is rapidly changing. As government grows and becomes more complex, the credentials essential for effective and successful lobbying have also increased. Modern lobbyists must be superb communicators, yet know how to listen. They must not only be armed with knowledge of governmental and political processes, but also be able to deal with increasingly complex issues and new technologies. Lobbyists must have a strong strategic sense, be flexible and adroit, yet possess high personal integrity.

These qualities merit closer examination.

Communications Skills

Government relations is, in a sense, a specialized form of marketing. In that same sense, direct lobbying is often face-to-face selling.

The same qualities that make a successful salesperson also are needed in a successful lobbyist: cordiality and charm, persistence, understanding of the product (i.e., the position the "issue salesman" is advocating), and the persuasiveness needed to make the "purchaser" (the public policymaker) want to buy the wares.

Empathy, the ability to see situations from the viewpoint and self-interest of others, is also an invaluable trait. The lobbyist needs to understand not only the positions of the opposition but also their attitudes and even feelings, to counter and defeat them. And empathizing with the self-interest of legislators is important to winning their friendship and support.

The lobbyist needs to know how to listen. Listening is important for two reasons. First, lobbyists need to be sensitive to the reaction their message is getting, a reaction that may or may not be verbally expressed. (The ability to listen carefully to what clients or superiors have to say is equally critical, not only to success but sometimes to survival.) Second, and even more important, a major part of lobbyists' effectiveness lies in gathering information about developments and outlook, and this requires a personality that makes others want to share information with them.

Although lobbyists typically communicate "one-on-one" with policymakers, they also frequently speak before audiences and write for publication. The lobbyist must therefore be effective when speaking to larger audiences whether in the form of legislative testimony or speeches to various groups. The ability to clearly express in writing often highly complex issues, arguments, and developments is important not only to persuade other groups but also to keep clients, members, or headquarters executives fully informed about what is happening and what it means.

Personal Integrity and Political Ethics

Because the ability to communicate and persuade are such essential traits, many lobbyists of the nineteenth and early twentieth centuries sometimes offered little else. They may have had personal charm, political backgrounds, and knowledge of governmental processes, but too often gave their trade a spotty reputation through a tendency to walk near or over the line of integrity. (The law is not always consistent in its judgments of improper behavior. During the trials that resulted from the Teapot Dome scandal in the 1920s, the secretary of the interior was convicted of taking an illegal payment that the briber was acquitted of paying!)

Modern journalists and historians of lobbying have had an unfortunate preoccupation with incidents of illegal payments, improper influence, excessive campaign contributions, and the like. Today, the press continues to report cases in which former (and sometimes incumbent) public officials have traded on relationships and reputations.

Over the years, changes in public opinion have broadened and extended standards for both lobbying and official behavior. Reflecting those revised standards, Congress and many state legislatures have tightened, perhaps sanctimoniously, the regulation of lobbying and campaign finance while frequently remaining regrettably reluctant to apply the same standards to their own behavior.

Yet, it is not only the public that is injured by improper lobbying behavior. Sometimes it is the client. Stories are told of unscrupulous lobbyists like the one who connived with a friendly legislator to have an adverse bill introduced every year so that the lobbyist could later claim credit with his employer for having killed it.

The cynicism can also be subtler. One veteran Washington corporate representative privately attributed his long success to a call he would make from time to time to his company's chief executive. "I've just found out," he would say, "that Senator X is getting ready to introduce a bill that would just put us out of business." After a little while, he was usually able to report back that, thanks to his superb skills and contacts, he had succeeded once again in getting the bill killed.

Playing to executive fears may be a good ploy for personal survival and frequent pay raises in an unsophisticated company, but it can also exacerbate businessmen's anti-government reflexes and their personal suspicions about the ethics of the lobbying and legislative processes.

Much of this has changed, particularly with regard to corporate and organizational lobbyists. Most lobbyists today are men and women of probity and depth with the personal integrity required to meet higher and higher ethical and legal standards. Operating as they must in an environment in which a publicly shady reputation is the kiss of death, yet in which compromise is an integral skill of success, continuing to meet those ever-rising standards is a constant challenge for all lobbyists.

Professional Competence

The legislative process is highly complex and growing more so—technically, politically, and substantively. The effective lobbyist must be competent in all these areas.

Technical Legislative Knowledge

Among the fifty-one national and state legislatures, there are very broad similarities in the legislative process but also innumerable differences in detail. The "typical" legislative process is widely taught in elementary and high school classes. In reality, however, there are vast differences in legislative procedure. The crucial details differ greatly—not only from legislature to legislature, but to some extent even from chamber to chamber in the same state.

The "Typical" Legislative Process*

Congress and 49 of the states have two-house (bicameral) legislatures; Nebraska's is unicameral, one house. Most local lawmaking bodies are unicameral. Any member can introduce a bill, i.e., a proposal for a new law, which is then numbered: e.g., S-123 for a Senate bill; H-456 (or A-456) for a House (or Assembly) bill. A bill must be considered, possibly amended, and approved by an appropriate committee in the house in which it is introduced. It next "goes to the floor" (the full chamber) for debate, possible further amendment, and passage. A similar process occurs in the other house. Any differences between the two versions must be reconciled through a joint conference committee or other means. Only then may it go to the chief executive (president, governor, mayor, county executive, etc.) for signature. If he or she vetoes the bill, it is returned to the legislature for another vote. Passage the first time usually requires a simple majority; a vote to override a veto generally needs a higher majority.

*Note that this is a very general model description; the process never works this simply. Note, too, that a bill must pass every hurdle in the course to be enacted, which is why it is far easier to defeat a bill than to pass one and also why only a small percentage of bills ever become law.

The lobbyist must thoroughly understand these often intricate rules. In some legislatures, for example, bills may be "pre-filed" (introduced before the legislative session begins) but during the session may be introduced after a deadline only under restricted conditions; in other legislatures, including Congress, bills may be introduced at any time during the session. To take another example, every legislature requires that a bill pass both houses in identical form to be enacted, but while some provide for formal conferences between the two houses to resolve differences, others do not relying in effect on informal negotiation. Recorded roll-call votes are common in some legislative bodies, rare in others. Many use electronic tally boards for such votes, but not all.

In addition to the vast body of formal procedures, every legislature has customs and folkways that are at least as important as the formal rules. For instance, legislative hearings may be quite common in one legislature and virtually non-existent in another. Committee meetings may be open to the public or closed. Strategic decisions on controversial issues, which are generally made out of public view, may be reached in closed-door party caucuses, in a rules or policy committee, or by the majority party leadership.

A clear grasp of these technical details, both formal and informal, is absolutely essential for the lobbyist. Mastery of the process has very frequently made the difference between victory and defeat on an issue.

Political Sophistication

The lobbyist also has to understand the current political situation, which may be even more complicated. The minutiae of the legislative process, though critical, seldom change, and once they are mastered keeping up is fairly easy. The political climate, on the other hand, is very fluid, constantly shifting, and an important factor in almost every piece of legislation.

Private sector executives, particularly those in business, often have little understanding of politics but sometimes great disdain. "Politicians have no conception of the bottom line" is an oft-heard comment. Nothing could be further from the truth. Political figures have a bottom line that is every bit as critical to them as the statement of profit or loss is to people in business.

Election or re-election is the political version of the bottom line. Winning is every bit as critical to a political career as profitability is to a career in business. As dollars are the units of economics, so votes are the currency of political power.

The ebb and flow of political power pervades the legislative process. Every piece of legislation is considered, not only on its substantive merits, but also in terms of its impact on power relationships. How will it affect the individual legislator's re-election prospects? If not a likely re-election problem, could it be a problem within the lawmaker's party as a possible danger to re-nomination? How will the various interest groups important to the legislator's success regard the issue?

Even legislators from safe seats (an increasing pattern in the U.S. House of Representatives and many state legislatures) must consider the effect the issue might have on prospects for retaining, or gaining, control of the legislative house in the next election. Next to the legislator's personal re-election prospects, political control of the chamber is always the overriding consideration. Control means the leadership, committee, and subcommittee chair-manships and staffs, personal perquisites of many kinds, and power generally over the levers of legislative process and policy.

This drive for control and power also extends to the presidency, governorship, and other elected executive offices—and to regulatory and judicial offices as well where these are filled by election instead of appointment. Success in these elections for the legislator's party means enhanced influence and the opportunity to assist political friends and allies by helping to place them in key appointive positions. "Clout" is the term frequently used to describe this kind of influence and power.

Nonetheless, politics deeply involves personal and working relationships that often extend informally across the aisles that separate Republicans and Democrats in most legislative bodies. These cross-party relationships also profoundly affect legislation. Party affiliation notwithstanding, legislators of different parties may share a common point of view or an interest in a particular subject, or be in a position to engage in the favor trading, which is such an ingrained part of the political (and lobbying) process. Personal friendships and mentor relationships may also cut across party lines, influences that should not be underestimated.

Coalitions of Republicans and Democrats often form on various issues or subjects. Members of both parties will typically be found on both sides of issues ranging as widely as capital punishment, environmental control, economic development, immigration reform, and fiscal policy.

Usually, party loyalties are strongest on issues relating directly to electoral prospects or legislative control, but even here there may be occasional breaches. California Assembly Speaker Willie Brown, a power in the Democratic Party, was originally elected to his post by a coalition of Republican and Democratic legislators opposed to the then incumbent speaker; the Republicans were temporarily able to share power until the new speaker succeeded in consolidating control among the Democrats. Bipartisan coalitions in leadership contests have also been found from time to time in Connecticut, New Jersey, New York, North Carolina, and other states, but the phenomenon is still basically rare.

Lobbyists must be extraordinarily aware of all this political jockeying. Directly or indirectly, it affects the prospects for every issue in the legislatures in which they operate. Political sensitivity may be an innate trait, but it is developed to an art form only through long personal involvement and exposure.

For that reason, lobbyists typically (though not invariably) have spent a substantial part of their careers in politics or on legislative staffs. Sometimes they are former legislators themselves or have held other elected or major appointive positions in government. They are thus intimately familiar with political nuances and relationships because they frequently have been part of the process themselves, and indeed often still are.

Lobbyists, too, often have clout and use it. Although as a group lobbyists tend to stay out of intramural legislative power struggles in order to maintain goodwill with all sides, it is not at all unheard of for lobbyists to play a role in some battles for leadership or the choice for a committee chairmanship or other key post. As a generalization, labor lobbyists seem more inclined to act as power brokers of this kind than those for business.

Substantive Competence

As important to lobbyists' success as is their legislative and political savvy, they must also have the ability to grasp the substance of issues, an increasingly important quality as issues grow ever more complex.

When federal or state bills on tax policy, labor relations, environmental control, education, health, resource management, economic development, international trade, and a host of other issues commonly run now to hundreds of closely typed pages, the lobbyist must be able to become expert on the finest details. Indeed, it is frequently in the fine print that wins and losses are determined and measured. For instance, an entire specialty of tax lobbying today centers around obtaining tax changes that sometimes benefit only a single company or individual even though the language may be written in apparently general terms.

Most legislation integrates in some fashion with existing public policy, often amending current law or superceding a regulation or executive action. The lobbyist must be able to analyze these legal connections. Moreover, legislation invariably involves change—change in social or economic practice or behavior, change in governmental programs and priorities. Change that affects people's lives and livelihoods must be carefully and competently analyzed— an imperative for both lobbyists and lawmakers.

Increasingly, the intellectual ability to handle issues of great complexity is an essential quality in a lobbyist. It is quite likely that the lobbyists of the future, particularly in Washington and the capitals of at least the larger states, will be specialists in particular substantive fields rather than the legislative generalists that they traditionally have been. Lobbyists sometimes develop a "buddy system" in which one partner contributes technical expertise, the other the political contacts.

The best lobbying often requires considerable creativity in legislative problem solving. If a particular position cannot be implemented, ingenuity and expertise may produce a very different approach to accomplish the goal, or at least to reach an acceptable compromise.

(A wonderful story is told about a debate in the New Jersey Senate, which was considering a proposal to end a long deadlock with the Assembly on an issue. After several years of dispute, several lobbyists and legislators came up with a compromise that the Assembly had reluctantly agreed to accept. A cantankerous senator rose to object. "I'm not against compromise," he said, "but why should we compromise with them? Let them compromise with us.")

Lawyer or Not?

The increasing intricacy of many issues raises the question of whether a lobbyist need necessarily be an attorney, a profession centered in detail. Many lawyers do make effective lobbyists for many of the same reasons that attorneys predominate as legislators. They generally combine an orientation to substantive detail with knowledge of existing law and public policy, and often are skilled advocates—but not invariably.

A lawyer will be a good lobbyist only if he or she combines substantive ability with legislative and political skill and with that specialized form of advocacy needed to "sell" effectively in one-on-one communications.

Conversely, non-attorneys may be excellent lobbyists if they possess these traits. Clearly, though, the lobbyist who is not personally an attorney needs ready access to one for aid with analytical research and the drafting of legislative language.

Making the Presentation

Lawyers or not, lobbyists must know how to present their case to the legislator. That means understanding all sides of the issue to be able to rebut the arguments of the opposition if the need to do so arises. It means knowing how the issue affects the legislator being lobbied so that the lobbyist can play to strengths, without putting lawmakers in difficult situations in their districts or at odds with positions on previous issues. It means making a carefully prepared presentation, backed up by a position paper to be left with the legislator and staff. Finally, it means knowing how to follow up appropriately; if he or she can "close a deal" on the spot, fine and good, but if not the lobbyist must know how and when to pursue the matter to gain a favorable decision.

The Role of Legislative Staff

If Napoleon's army traveled on its stomach, legislators travel on their staffs. In both Washington and many state capitols, service in the legislature is virtually full-time and, for many, becoming a career. Members of Congress and state legislators are more dependent on competent staff personnel every year.

Lobbyists are also dependent on those staff people. Friendly staff can help lobbyists get in the door, or determinedly keep them out. Personal, cordial relations with the staff are as essential as they are with legislators themselves. Lobbyists will make a point of knowing and cultivating the staff experts on their issues, whether personal aides to the legislator or committee staff members.

Cultivating means not just personal relationships, but professional ones—providing the staff member with useful data about both the interest group and its issues, and getting important information back in return. Working with helpful legislators almost always really means working with their legislative aides to insure that every necessary or useful detail to advance the interest group's position is carefully handled.

Professional legislative staffs are of two types: (1) personal staffs to individual members; (2) committee and general legislative staffs.

Personal staff aides help their legislators with all their duties, many of which relate only marginally to legislation. Such staff functions typically include:

- Scheduling—booking appointments and filling the calendar with constituent visits, lobbyist appointments, speaking engagements, and the like, both in the district and in the capital—as well as keeping track of legislative committee meetings, floor sessions, and other scheduled official duties.

- Casework—assisting constituents with problems they may be having with government agencies. These range across the entire spectrum of governmental activity, from helping with a delayed pension or social security check, facilitating the award of a government contract, getting a pothole fixed, obtaining an official publication, and so on. (The quality of such services are significant influences in voters' decisions on election day, and are a major reason why incumbents are usually re-elected.)

- Legislation—providing research and tracking on the issues. The size of personal legislative staffs may range from one individual to dozens, depending on the legislative body and the lawmakers' interests and responsibilities. The legislator's seniority is often a factor in the size of these staffs. Staff aides usually specialize in particular subject areas, again depending on the legislator's needs and interests. Lobbyists make a particular point of knowing well the staff assistant who covers their issues. A telephone inquiry to the legislator's office is sufficient to learn which staff assistant handles which issues.

Committee and general legislative staffs handle issues for groups of legislators or all of them. Sometimes these staffs serve only the members of their political party; in other situations they perform without regard to partisanship. Committee staffs are often controlled by the committee chairman unless the staff is partisan, in which case the ranking minority legislator on the committee will control his party's staff. In some legislative bodies, staff members report to a senior staff official who serves the entire house (or all of the party's members); even in such an arrangement, staffers typically are assigned to specific committees.

These staff members specialize in particular areas. Most will be issue or subject specialists. Some specialize in bill drafting, either preparing bills for individual legislators or approving the legal form of bills drafted by others on personal or committee staffs. Still others manage the legislative calendar of the committee or full house, or provide policy, political, or parliamentary advice to the leadership.

It is no put-down of legislators to say that their legislative staffs do most of their thinking for them. These individuals not only put lawmakers' ideas in bill form, but also advise them about substance. They research the issues, receive—and commonly solicit—information and inputs from lobbyists, weigh the effects on key constituencies, negotiate with interest groups and with counterparts on other legislators' staffs, write the speeches and the press releases, and do whatever is necessary to make their boss look good.

Sometimes these staff aides (both personal and committee) are actually the intellectual founts of the issues their legislators champion. They may search out public problems and devise legislative remedies, acting in some cases as in-house lobbyists for particular causes or points of view, working closely with allied interest groups. Such activities are perfectly legitimate, so long as the staff aides act with the full knowledge and consent of the legislator they assist and represent.

The lobbyist seeking the originator of a particular issue often needs to look no further than the legislative sponsor' staff. Identifying who does what on the staff takes only a call or two. Harder, because it takes considerable time and effort, is the development of good personal working relationships with these individuals, essential for any lobbyist.

Legislative Voting Influences

One of the most critical judgments lobbyists must make is understanding the forces likely to be the most influential determinants of each legislator's voting decisions on particular issues. The variations will be substantial depending on the character of the legislative body, the time and political climate, the issue, and, of course, each lawmaker's own personality. Among the major influences are these:

- Personal ideology or political philosophy.
- Previous positions on related issues.
- Recommendations of respected peers and staff aides.
- Committee recommendations.
- Advice from outside experts.
- Positions taken on the issue by: party caucuses, leaders and activists, and platforms; respected constituents; interest groups and lobbyists; campaign contributors and supporters.
- Intensity and volume of constituency communications.
- Media coverage and editorial pressure.
- Issue advertising.

Also relevant is each legislator's personal theory of representation. One theory holds that legislators are "trustees," elected by the constituents to rely on their consciences and best judgment in deciding what is in the public interest. Much more commonly held is the "delegate" theory, which holds that the lawmaker should vote in accordance with the desires of the bulk of the constituents, reflecting and representing their views rather than his.

The delegate theory is more commonly held, by far. Legislators who have a record of voting only as they think best and not as their constituents wish tend to have brief careers.

Strategic Skill

Legislation always involves struggle. Issues benefiting one interest group will probably be at the expense of another. Even where no organized opposition exists, the forces of inertia must always be overcome. "If it ain't broke, don't fix it" remains a common legislative maxim.

The most finely honed persuasive skills are rarely enough to prevail on an issue. There must also be a belief among lawmakers that the lobbyist's positions represent the views of involved stakeholders, preferably vocal ones in large numbers—and that the public interest will be served in some way. It is hard to win on a visible issue if there is no legislative perception of larger public gain. Groups often do win on very narrow issues, but rarely if there is an inadequate defense to widespread public criticism.

The ability to strategize is therefore an essential skill among both lobbyists and legislators. Both must be able to plan and execute legislative campaigns—framing positions, martialing backers, neutralizing opponents, enlisting allies, mobilizing publicity and public support, and knowing how to use time and other resources for maximum effect.

The various techniques of government relations discussed throughout this book require strategic management and coordination if the interest group is to prevail on its issues. A well-honed strategic sense is therefore a vital quality in the lobbyist or government relations executive in charge of a legislative campaign.

SELECTING AND ORGANIZING LOBBYISTS

Companies and membership groups in need of lobbying services must deal with some basic questions:

Should lobbyists be in-house or retained?

Should in-house lobbyists on federal matters be based at corporate or organization headquarters, or in Washington?

Should state lobbyists be retained or in-house—at headquarters or the state capital?

How to choose the right person?

Scope of Exposure on the Issues

The answers to the above questions require analysis of the breadth of the issues confronting the organization or company. There are four degrees of exposure to issues, each of them requiring a different kind of lobbying service:

1. The one-time issue.
2. Clusters of recurring issues.
3. Epidemics of related issues.
4. On-going general exposure.

The One-Time Issue

This is the bill or regulation that occurs in a single legislature or agency, arising perhaps out of a local situation of some kind. Once dealt with, the issue is unlikely to recur, in this jurisdiction or elsewhere.

In such situations, the best solution is to retain a knowledgeable lobbyist experienced in that issue or that governmental body. How much back-up that individual will need is a function of how politically or technically complex the issue is, but most issues can be readily dealt with by a single competent lobbyist.

The Cluster of Recurring Issues

These are legislative or regulatory problems that continue to crop up within a single governmental jurisdiction—local, state, or national. The issues may be on related topics or different ones.

A retained lobbying firm probably is the most convenient and cost-effective answer for the short term. However, if the issue cluster gives indications of settling in for the long haul, then it may be worthwhile putting a local lobbyist on staff. This may be particularly true if the cluster requires special technical expertise or an insider's knowledge of how decisions get made in complex or exotic governmental environments—e.g., Congress, the Pentagon, the California state treasurer's office, or the legislature of Suffolk County, New York.

Retained lobbyists, consultants, and technical experts tend to be expensive; some charge by the clock and others by the issue or project, but most prefer a retainer (often sizeable) covering a legislative session or calendar year.

The question of whether to rely solely on them or to open a government relations office staffed with full-time employees is, in part, an economic cost-benefit judgment. But there may also be considerations of visibility and image. Even if a closely calculated economic analysis does not seem to justify a full-time office in Washington or the state capital, the company or organization may still consider it worthwhile "to show the flag," i.e., to become known as a permanent and involved member of the government relations community.

The Epidemic of Related Issues

These are issues arising in a number of governments around the country more or less simultaneously that treat the same problem or subject matter. Examples include seat belt laws, drinking age increases, mandatory paternity leave, and AIDS issues.

In such situations, the organization is likely to have the substantive expertise on staff (or quickly develop it), but may not know its way around the various state legislatures or agencies. The larger the number of states or localities in which the issue is active, the more likely this is to be true. Here, retained lobbyists may provide a different kind of service. Instead of handling the issue largely on their own, they may act as guides for the client's in-house experts—teaching them the governmental and political fine points of law-making in that state or community and introducing them to the right decision makers and staff.

At this point, there is likely to be a need for an additional resource: an individual to *coordinate* the lobbying activity in the different states to assure compatibility among positions, actions, and agreements. The client's substantive expert may or may not have the political sophistication or broad-gauge understanding to be able to provide such coordination. Typically, this is the role of an in-house public affairs or government relations manager.

In actual practice, the company's government relations manager tends to provide both the substantive expertise and the multi-state coordination, operating through retained local counsel in each state or locality. If the number of jurisdictions is so large that one person cannot be the traveling in-house expert while also providing policy coordination, then the functions will be split with the coordinating role residing with the headquarters-based government relations manager. In some organizations, this executive directs an in-house group of regional lobbyists, each responsible for a state or group of states.

On-Going General Exposure

Because of the nature of their operations or interests, many industries and organizations must deal on a continuing basis with a wide variety of issues across the country at the federal, state, and local levels. Large manufacturers, for instance, are constantly confronted with labor, tax, and environmental issues wherever they have facilities—and with consumer and marketing issues wherever their products are sold.

The greater the number of issues or jurisdictions facing the organization and the more complex and varied those issues are, the more likely it is that the company will move away from sole reliance on retained lobbyists and in the direction of having its own staff. The variety of issues may be broad, but each is unlikely to be unique. Staff personnel can develop familiarity with a number of issues and travel to the fires wherever they break out, either through a regional manager system or by utilizing on-site independent lob-byists as guides to the local scene, as needed.

Renting Contacts vs. Building Equity

One additional factor should be considered in deciding whether to retain an outside lobbyist or hire one onto the staff. Each prospect has his or her own set of personal skills, talents, contacts, and expertise. Retaining the out-sider means *renting* those credentials. Bringing such an individual on staff, however, enables the company to develop *equity* in its government relations program.

Independent lobbyists may represent Client A on Issue X today and Client B on Issue Y tomorrow. Actually, they may talk to a legislator about the needs of both in a single visit, thereby making maximum use of their time as well as the legislator's. But it is the lobbyist and not the client who tends to have the relationship and visibility with the lawmaker.

On the other hand, when a government relations executive of a particular company or organization goes to visit the legislator or official, the situation is reversed. The company or group now begins to develop its own visibility in the person of its full-time representative and is able to build its own network of relationships.

Relationships, though, take time to cultivate. With the independent lobbyist, the client can get instant access—but it is the lobbyist's access, not the client's. The organization gets the best of both worlds when the individual it adds to staff brings knowledge and connections with her. But even if the staff lobbyist is new to the local scene and the relationships therefore take longer to develop, once built (and maintained) they become an asset of the organi-zation. The organization *and* its representative have now become familiar to the lawmaker.

LOBBYISTS AND RELATIONSHIPS

Personal access to legislators, staff, and other public officials is essential to success in direct lobbying. Personal access flows from relationships developed over long periods of time between individuals who have come to trust and rely on each other. The legislator or official has learned that the lobbyist is discreet, loyal to friends, a source of reliable information on issues and their background, interested in the official's career, and frequently politically sup-portive. The lobbyist, in turn, has learned that this lawmaker or staffer, that public official, is a reliable source of accurate and authoritative information on a particular subject, and often inclined to be helpful to interest groups with a shared point of view.

Like any other political relationship, theirs is pervaded by discretion, a degree of trust and particularly "back-scratching"—the informal exchange of favors and mutual aid. Perhaps the lobbyist has aided the legislator with fund-raising or some other political chore, or helped a career agency official win a promotion. The legislator may have recommended the lobbyist for a job or to a client. This "favor exchange" operates on a rough barter principle. An accounting is rarely kept, but neither side can go to the well too often, or take too much of the water, before it starts to dry up. The requests made must be appropriate both to the stature of the favor-giver and to the nature and sensitivity of the relationship.

A critical ingredient is the lobbyist's knowledge that the goodwill of the relationship is more important than any one issue. The story is often told of the lobbyist who was asked by his client if he had convinced Senator X to support their bill. "I saw him," the lobbyist replied, "but I recommended that he vote no." "Why on earth did you do that?" asked the incredulous client. "Because this issue would hurt him back home. He'll help us behind the scenes if he can, but we need him back here after the election more than we need his vote on this single bill."

This is the stuff of politics. It is the stuff of lobbying as well.

THE COLLECTION OF INTELLIGENCE

Gathering unpublished information on political and issue developments and their significance is, in many ways, the most important single function direct lobbyists perform. Intelligence collection depends much more on the lobbyist's personal relationships even than does the ability to open doors and sell the organization's message. Most lobbyists spend far more time collecting and disseminating information than they do advocating positions and points of view.

Good lobbyists develop networks of contacts with whom they frequently touch base, contacts who can alert them to new legislative ideas still in gestation; the rationales and motivations of sponsors and opponents; the issue's political prospects; and the like.

The singular value of back-channel data of this kind is its timeliness. Early warning information is always the most useful because it can so often facilitate remedial action while issues are still in their most formative or vulnerable stages. As a result of private information, more bills are killed, stimulated, or reshaped before formal introduction then ever are once they have seen the light of day.

The liability of private information is that it may sometimes be speculative and subject to considerable change. Its reliability is only as good as its source, and developments that can outdate it may occur moments after the lobbyist departs the source's office. The lobbyist's ability to evaluate the validity and usefulness of private information is a talent that is hard to teach and that comes through judgment and experience.

Private information is at least as important on executive and regulatory issues as it is in the legislative process.

In the case of regulations (the agency equivalent of legislation) and other formal agency actions, proposals are typically published for a period of public comment before being finalized and officially promulgated. A published regulatory proposal, though, is often more difficult to alter by interest groups than is a bill introduced in the legislature because the proposed regulation usually represents an all-but-final agency position. Once top officials go public with a proposal, t'.ey are committed to it. But if the official and the agency can be reached before they take a position on the public record, they will be much more open to data, points of view, and other inputs. Private information on proposed regulations before they are issued for public comment is therefore particularly valuable to interest groups.

Much the same phenomenon is found among executive branch personnel during the policy development process. Whether the embryonic policy issue relates to possible legislation, agency actions, a future speech, or other public pronouncement, officials are loathe to share their thinking lest it be revealed prematurely or in a way that opponents can use to embarrass them. Indeed, the more sensitive the subject, the greater the reluctance to discuss it. Yet, this is precisely the stage at which policy is most susceptible to—and will benefit from—the information and insights that lobbyists can provide.

Individual legislators are not greatly different in this respect. Their views are likely to be most malleable before they take public positions on a particular issue.

There is much more of a difference, however, between the view of a single legislator and the final decision of the legislative body on the one hand, than between the attitude of a top official and the final decision of the agency or department on the other. A far greater share of legislative decision making occurs during publicly conspicuous processes (e.g., hearings, committee and floor debates, etc.) than does in agency decision making. The portion that is *not* visible, though, is just as critical to the outcome of the issue as it is in the departments and agencies.

The problem illustrates why personal relationships are so important in lobbying. When a relationship of confidence and trust exists, the legislator or other public official knows that he or she can tap the lobbyist's best information and advice on an off-the-record basis, comfortable in the knowledge that confidences regarding still-fluid ideas will not be revealed nor their source embarrassed. The lobbyist's reputation and access are totally on the line here; a confidence breached is a lobbyist ruined.

But there are degrees of confidentiality. The information may be for the lobbyist's ears only, not to be revealed even to the group he or she represents. Or it may be shared with the group off the record. Of course, the more people and groups the idea is shared with on this basis, the greater the risk that it will leak to opponents or the press.

Officials may also serve their own political purposes by *wanting* a leak, exposing the policy concept to debate while retaining the ability to deny its parentage if it proves unpopular; "launching a trial balloon" is the term for this kind of leakage.

In every case, the lobbyist has to understand the basis on which the private information is shared. Mistakes can be disastrous in terms of their impact on continuing relationships. If they lose their access to private information, lobbyists' sources will be reduced to press handouts.

Types of Data

Private sources are not to be wasted in the collection of standard data. Information on the status or contents of a bill, for instance, is readily obtainable from published sources. Hearing schedules or floor calendar questions are either published or are generally available to anyone by calling appropriate legislative staff. The same is true in the agencies on regulatory matters. However, their typical response to public inquiries about an issue's *prospects* is that it is "pending," even if it really has no chance, because the question is a political one.

Back-channel sources should be reserved for such sensitive questions, not readily answered elsewhere: What are the inner politics of this issue? Is the best person to talk with Senator Smith a colleague, or is there someone among his family, friends, or business contacts to whom he is particularly responsive? Why is Representative Jones dragging her feet in committee on this issue if her enthusiasm is really as great as her press releases say? Is there some kind of political connection between this bill and a seemingly unrelated issue? Pressure group X is opposed to this bill but not as opposed as they are to another bill; are the makings of a deal in the wind? Will the governor support our bill if we lobby for his budget, or will that just antagonize legislators opposing his budget?

The list of such questions is endless, but to an extent they tend to fall into three rough categories: Those that relate to political aspects of an issue—WHY questions; those that pertain to legislative outlook—WHETHER and WHEN questions; and those involving lobbying and legislative decision making—HOW questions. These categories are very approximate, however; in practice, there will be much overlapping, and some questions will fall into none of these groupings.

The essential point is that the most important information may never appear in print, or may be questioned and denied if it does. Such data is typically unpublished and private, available only through back-channels of varying degrees of sensitivity and reliability.

6

Lobbying Applications

Self-interest speaks all sorts of tongues, and plays all sorts of roles, even that of disinterestedness.

La Rochefoucauld

Direct lobbying seeks to influence public decision making in a variety of ways:

By influencing specific legislation.
By helping shape executive branch policies and programs, including budgets.
By impacting decisions on key personnel appointments.
By offering opinions on pending judicial cases.
By affecting pending regulatory matters.
By influencing decisions on government grants and contracts.

Direct lobbying is only one of the techniques utilized to accomplish these purposes, although it is the one most frequently used and, on smaller issues, probably the only one. The more important the issue is, on the other hand, the more likely that grass-roots lobbying, coalitions, communications tools, and the other techniques of government relations will be utilized.

THE PRACTICE OF DIRECT LOBBYING ON LEGISLATION

Direct lobbying on legislative issues is the best-known form of government relations. In any one campaign, the lobbyist may function as both advocate and strategist—or the strategic generalship may be in the hands of a senior corporate or organizational government relations executive. The following fictional model illustrates how direct lobbying often works, and how other techniques of government relations may be meshed with direct lobbying.

Direct Issues Lobbying: A Strategic Model[1]

The State of West Carolina is considering the imposition of an excise tax on laser pens, a new consumer device that writes on air without benefit of paper.

Laser Pen Corporation (LPC), the largest manufacturer of these writing instruments, believes that sales would be seriously impaired by such a tax—not only in West Carolina but elsewhere if other states should adopt the idea. It therefore resolves to oppose the excise tax vigorously.

Week 1. Steven Advocate, a lobbyist for LPC in West Carolina's capital, is discussing the state's new fiscal problems with a member of the governor's staff at a political fund-raising party. "We've got a serious revenue problem," the staffer admits. "Are you considering new taxes?" Advocate asks. "Possibly," replies the governor's aide. "Maybe something you'd be interested in. Why don't you come see me tomorrow."

Advocate meets with the staffer the next afternoon. She tells him that a package of excise taxes is likely to be proposed by the governor to the legislature. The list of affected products includes laser pens, but she agrees to study information from LPC on the impact of such a tax.

Advocate returns to his office and immediately calls LPC's vice president for public affairs, Bob Boss, to fill him in on the conversation. "How serious do you think they are?" Boss inquires.

"There's a large revenue shortfall. They feel they can't cut spending any more and need new money from somewhere. We're one of the candidates," Advocate answers, adding his own question: "Do you have any idea what the impact would be on laser pens?" "Not yet," Boss replies, promising to look into the matter immediately.

Week 2. LPC's Government Relations Committee meets to consider the ramifications of the excise tax issue. Advocate has flown in for the meeting at which Boss presides. In addition to public affairs staffers, standing members of the committee include the general counsel, Harvey Law; vice presidents for marketing and operations, Philip Vend and Marvin Maker; and the finance v.p., Magnus Dollar. C.E.O. John Chief is also present today.

The agenda for the meeting is essentially the framework of the options paper. Boss opens by pointing out that the issue is so early that a bill has not yet even been introduced, adding that the excise tax would likely be only a single provision in the governor's tax package. "So far, the principal proponents of the tax are the State Tax Department and Budget Office," says Boss. "The governor is seriously considering the idea but since he has not yet committed to it so far as we know, there is always the possibility that the tax could die stillborn." Boss adds that the exact tax rate is still undetermined, as are the other products that might be affected.

Boss notes that is important to identify these other products as quickly as possible. "These are potential allies and the sooner we can enlist their help, the better," he says. LPC's manager of consumer and community relations, Bertha Goodfriend, will be responsible for seeking allies on the excise tax issue, including consumer groups, as soon as Advocate can give her the list of affected products.

Advocate adds a word of caution: "So far, this is not public information. We got it because of our relationships with the governor and the legislative leadership, so let's be careful not to violate any confidences on this issue."

Magnus Dollar interrupts. "This could be very expensive to us. I think we should go all out to kill this now and not worry too much about the political pussyfooting."

Marvin Maker agrees, pointing out the impact of the issue on plans to expand laser pen manufacturing capacity. "We've got to commit soon to the plant expansion or the whole schedule will be out the window. If this tax is passed, we'll be talking about cutting production, not expanding it. The capital budget has to be nailed down in a few months and we need to know where we stand."

Boss responds that they understand the urgency and that they seek a quick kill, but that LPC's political relationships are a long-term asset. Chief sides with Boss: "We've put a lot of effort and PAC money into building good relations with these people. This is an important issue for us, but we're going to need the governor on other matters over the next few years, too."

Vend and Law express concern about what Law calls "the contagion factor." Says Law, "If West Carolina enacts this tax, other states will, too. These legislators and state officials have their own professional associations and are forever swapping new ideas. We could have an epidemic on our hands."

Vend adds that the laser pen market is price sensitive, and very competitive with other writing instruments. "If we don't want people to go back to old-fashioned pens and pencils, we'll have to lower prices to offset the tax, and that will seriously affect our profit margins," he says.

The committee considers who their opponents could be, apart from the administration and its legislative allies. Advocate says that if he were advising the governor, he would urge him to line up support among all the groups whose interests might be hurt by spending cuts. "There's new money in the budget for health and hospitals, the homeless, and higher education, as well as for economic development programs for some hard-pressed industries and regions," Advocate says. "These groups have a lot to lose if new revenue isn't found to support their programs, and they have a great many friends in the legislature."

Chief leans back and gazes out the window. "It seems to me that we have to help the governor find another way to solve his fiscal problems if we don't want the solution to come at our expense. Let me call him personally on this and see what we can come up with." He stands and the meeting adjourns.

Week 3. Chief talks to the governor and fills Boss in on the conversation. "I thanked him for giving us early warning on the excise tax, and told him that we saw serious adverse impacts on us from this tax. He said he regretted that, particularly because of the good relationship between LPC and his administration, but there was going to be a revenue shortfall and he needed to come up with new money quickly if his social and economic programs weren't to be short-changed and undercut. He told me that West Carolina has never had an excise tax on luxury products and that this was a new revenue source that would apply to a number of products besides ours. I replied that we don't consider laser pens a luxury product but a very useful new consumer product based on advanced technology. He said he was skeptical, but would certainly listen to supporting facts. Then I asked if he would consider other ways of dealing with his fiscal problem and said that I would gladly pull together a broad-based study group to advise him. He responded that he would welcome the help provided it did not jeopardize his program. He said he would have to proceed with the luxury excise tax but would be happy to look at other options whenever we came up with them. We ended it at that."

"John, that was excellent," Boss responds. "You got some very helpful new information for us. We'll work up points and arguments on the luxury goods issue, and start talking with some of the other industries that will obviously be affected. How do you want to proceed on the fiscal options study?" "Why don't you put those economic consultants of yours on this?" Chief says. "When you're ready, I'll send out invitations for an initial meeting of a study group."

Week 4. Boss has now completed the impact assessment and the options paper, having gotten further inputs from LPC's marketing and tax experts, and circulated drafts for Government Relations Committee approval. The laser pen market is considered price-sensitive and a 15 percent excise tax would decrease sales by 5–10 percent unless LPC dropped its price by the amount of the tax. Either alternative would cut LPC's profit margin on the product by at least half.

Advocate and Boss put together a position paper explaining LPC's problems with the excise tax proposal and the adverse impact it would have on sales, the plant expansion, and the new jobs the expansion would create. The paper also states that, if other states were to adopt a similar tax, the sales fall-off would result in major production costs and even layoffs.

Advocate delivers the paper to the governor's staff. He also starts using it in the conversations he begins having on the issue with legislators.

He discusses the excise tax with the chairman of the Senate and House tax committees. Both believe there is a need for new revenue although the House chairman believes more could also be done to cut spending. She also thinks excise taxes on products like laser pens are anti-consumer. The Senate chairman thinks further spending cuts would be unfair and he is inclined to support the governor in whatever revenue additions the administration develops. Both stress that their views are subject to change with further data.

Week 8. There have been a number of developments on the excise tax issue. LPC has adopted a three-pronged strategy. First, it has organized a coalition to oppose an excise tax on luxury goods. Second, it has asked the research department of its national trade association to prepare a paper refuting the argument that laser pens are a luxury product. Third, it is mobilizing the economic study of fiscal alternatives to the tax.

Boss and Advocate have had meetings with consumer groups and with luxury product manufacturers, retailers, and their trade associations to get them involved in opposition to the tax. Although LPC organized this coalition, it prefers not to lead it; Harry Furrgold, a retailer politically active in the capital region, is selected as coalition chairman. The head of one of the state's consumer organizations enlisted by Bertha Goodfriend is vice chairman. Labor union representatives are also involved because of the tax's potential impact on jobs at LPC.

LPC's purchasing department has also enlisted a number of its principal suppliers in the state by pointing out to them their stake in the issue should laser pen sales and production fall off. These suppliers are now part of the coalition.

Also part of the coalition is the Laser Pen Institute. As a national trade association, the Institute has had almost no state issues up to now and none of its other members have operations in West Carolina. However, both the Institute and a couple of other laser pen manufacturers are lending lobbying personnel to assist Advocate.

LPC's economic consultants are developing a plan that would preserve the governor's program with no tax hikes, although their revenue projections are somewhat different than those of the administration. The plan is being discussed by a study group of business, labor, and social welfare executives, which John Chief has organized and is chairing.

Boss is coordinating the fiscal study project for Chief. He and Advocate stay in close touch on legislative developments.

Advocate is working with Furrgold to coordinate the activities of the coalition, while also maintaining liaison with the governor's staff and discussing the issue with members of the Senate and House tax committees whenever he can corner them.

Although the governor's tax proposals have not yet been formally announced, they are now common knowledge, and in fact the governor's staff has discussed several bill drafts with the Senate and House leadership and the two tax committee chairmen, Senator Howard Kindhart and Representative Barbara Thrift. For political reasons, both will undoubtedly sponsor the governor's bill, the Senator perhaps more enthusiastically than his House counterpart.

Week 10. The Governor's bills have now been introduced with over half the Senators cosponsoring S-123, but only about a quarter of the Representatives adding their names to H-456 (which, except for the number, is identical to the Senate version). The bill provides for a 15% tax on a long list of enumerated products defined as luxury goods. Laser pens are on the list.

Advocate learns that hearings soon will be announced, probably to be held next month. Coalition members are informed so they can sign up to testify. The Laser Pen Institute in Washington is also alerted.

Week 12. The Chief Commission, as it is being called, is mired down in controversy. The labor and other non-business members are suspicious that the group is only a device to kill the governor's tax bill, and even some of the business members are a bit skeptical. The State Budget Office is questioning the projections of the economic consultants.

Boss and Chief start making calls to commission members to convince them of the stake they all have in avoiding new consumer taxes and in a sound fiscal program that does not lead taxpayers into questioning the cost of the governor's program. The consulting firm is brought in to persuade the Budget Office that the consultants' figures have more validity than the Tax Department's.

Week 14. Hearings are held by the House Tax Committee on the excise tax bill. Administration witnesses present their revenue projections, and argue that the governor's program will be in jeopardy if new funding is not provided. They maintain that the 15 percent tax on luxuries is the "fairest" method.

Chief makes a brief statement, describing the work of his commission. He points out that he is appearing at the hearing only in behalf of the commission and not LPC, and declines to take a public position on the bill. He promises to keep the legislature posted on developments.

Witnesses for a variety of groups whose constituencies and members will benefit from the governor's program appear in support of H-456, many of them also saying that it is "only fair" to tax luxuries in order to fund programs for the needy and to put depressed regions and industries back on their feet.

Advocate has been working closely with the staffs of Chairman Thrift and some other committee members, and has developed a list of questions that are asked of the administration witnesses and their supporters. The questions are intended to expose weaknesses in proponents' presentations. They focus on the accuracy of the Tax Department's revenue estimates and also inquire why the spending program is so sacrosanct that nothing can be trimmed even if the estimates are indeed correct. Thrift wants to know what is so "fair" about asking overburdened consumers to pay for these projects, especially when she wonders if all the products in the bill are really luxuries. Television news coverage that night plays up her grilling of the excise tax proponents and their awkward responses.

Furrgold and other coalition members, including consumer witnesses, testify against the bill, arguing that luxuries are already highly taxed at the federal level, that the excise tax is basically anti-consumer, and that many of the products listed in the bill are necessities, not luxuries. The union also testifies against the bill, arguing that it would jeopardize current jobs at LPC and its suppliers, and discourage creation of new ones. The coalition witnesses also are peppered with questions from committee members—some friendly, some not.

Boss, Advocate, and the Government Relations Committee made the decision that LPC would not testify as a company (apart from Chief's presentation for the study commission). Instead, they are represented by the president of the Laser Pen Institute, Barry Beame. Beame argues that laser pens are not a luxury and should be removed from the list. He maintains that they are a technological advance, just as ballpoint pens were in their day. He says that if they are a luxury, then so are compact discs and CD players, microwave ovens, VCRs, high-resolution television, and many other new products. He says that the excise tax is nothing more than a penalty on technological innovation. In any event, Beame notes, luxury is in the eye of the beholder; one person's luxury is another's necessity. Asked why a product that costs over $100, as some laser pen models do, should not be classed as a luxury, Beame responds that many basic necessities such as cars and home appliances cost far more than $100 but are not considered luxuries. He adds that gold and silver pencils, ballpoints, and fountain pens cost that much or more but are not in the bill.

At the conclusion of the hearing, Chairman Thrift announces that the committee will vote on the bill in two weeks. Advocate's nose-count of the House committee tells him that there is a fighting chance the bill will be voted down. He has persuaded Thrift that the committee vote should be taken before members can be swayed by the Senate hearings three weeks hence, which Advocate fears will be much more favorable to the governor's position.

Thrift's staff counsel accepts Advocate's offer to help in drafting sections of the committee report.

The next day, Furrgold's coalition meets to organize a grass-roots campaign among all their members to try to barrage House members generally, and particularly those on the Tax Committee, to defeat H-456.

Joining the grass-roots effort are members of LPC's Political Action Club, managers and employees who are involved in public affairs in their communities. They talk with their own legislators about the bill, and a number of them convince their local town officials to do the same.

Week 16. The House Tax Committee meets to vote on H-456 after several weeks of intense lobbying by both sides. Mail and telephone calls from constituents have been very high, partly in response to organized grass-roots efforts but also because of the issue's visibility. The governor's aides and their allies have scoured the committee. So have Advocate, Furrgold, and coalition members. An hour before the committee meeting, Advocate is dismayed to learn that he has lost two votes he had counted on after administration lobbyists promised to support a pet bill of one member and build a long-wanted highway interchange in the district of another. The two votes are crucial. A series of amendments is voted down, and the bill is approved 26–24.

Two days later, the bill is narrowly approved by the full House without change and sent to the Senate.

Week 17. The Senate hearings are held. As expected, proponents of the excise tax dominate the proceedings with many senators trumpeting their support for the bill. Jubilant over the House action, Senator Kindhart schedules a Senate Tax Committee vote the following week.

Once again, Furrgold and the coalition, along with the LPC Political Action Club, go back to work for another barrage of constituency communications.

Week 18. The week opens with a pair of bombshells. The Sunday editions of the two largest daily papers in the state, both generally liberal in their bent and supportive of the governor, run lead editorials on the excise tax. The *Bigtown Gazette* opposes the bill outright as anti-consumer and of questionable real need. The *Capital City Monitor* tepidly endorses the bill, but urges that several non-luxury products, including laser pens, be dropped from the bill. Several editorials Monday and Tuesday evenings on local television channels contain messages similar to the *Monitor's*.

Credit for the coup belongs to Bob Boss, Barry Beame, and LPC's public relations director, Jerry Flacke, who have spent several weeks, armed with the LPC position paper and Beame's arguments, meeting with newspaper and television editorial boards and directors.

When the Senate Tax Committee meets on Wednesday, S-123 is approved as expected—but not before amendments drafted and orchestrated by Advocate delete laser pens from the list. The editorials have clearly made an impact.

Week 20. Meanwhile, the Chief Commission has made significant progress. The Budget Office has started to waffle in its support of the Tax Department's numbers, and the commission members have come to the conclusion that the revenue projections of the economic consultants are more valid than the department's. This undercuts the very rationale for the excise tax. Moreover, the group is successfully developing areas where spending cuts can be made without harming the governor's projects and programs.

Chief calls the governor personally to report these developments and to arrange a time when the commission might meet with him to present its findings. "Great timing, John," the governor says wryly, realizing that he is now in an untenable position. Chief smiles but says only, "Thank you." "When are you going to release this report?" the governor asks. Chief replies,"Governor, the intent of this project was never to embarrass you but to provide you with different, hopefully better, inputs than your tax people were giving you. If I can presume to offer a suggestion, why don't you release the report yourself? You can then ask the legislature to defer further consideration of the excise tax for a year or two until the study commission's findings and recommendations are implemented." "Excellent suggestion, John. Bring your commission over to the Executive Office next Monday and we'll have a press conference on the spot."

Week 21. The governor has asked the Senate leadership not to call up the excise tax bill for a floor vote, but to put the issue on hold for at least a year. Two days after the press conference, Advocate has a drink with his friend on the governor's staff who alerted him to the excise tax proposal in the first place. "Jane," he says, "I really need to thank you for that. I hope nobody ever considered it off-base." She smiles. "It was never a problem. You had a right to know, especially because your people have been helpful to the governor before, and really just as you were this week." "Well, you and I are going to be around this town for a while," says Advocate, "and both the governor and LPC will be here long after the tax bill is forgotten."

"Oh, we haven't forgotten about it. We've just put it off a year until experience shows up your economists' ding-a-ling numbers. In fact, we've already come up with a new bill to be introduced next year. Here's a copy to read some evening when you've nothing else to do."

Advocate takes the bill home and reads it that night. It is no longer an excise tax bill. Instead, it proposes new taxes on manufacturing equipment and corporate stock transfers.

Advocate wonders what Marvin Maker and Magnus Dollar will have to say about that.

Comments on the Model

1. The object of LPC's lobbying was to preserve its market without jeopardizing sales and profits. In other circumstances, companies might actually take the initiative to open up markets, perhaps through elimination of regulatory restrictions. Non-business interest groups also pursue legislative agendas to preserve beneficial arrangements or alter adverse ones.

2. Despite the importance of the issue to LPC, it made every effort to conduct itself so as to maintain the good relationships it had built up with the governor and legislators through its political support for them. Those relationships brought it early information and helped result in an ultimate success.

3. A key role was played by the C.E.O. He was a strong supporter of LPC's government relations programs and a personally active participant himself. When circumstances required personal discussions with the governor, the C.E.O. was able to initiate them himself. Yet, he was not a domineering force who hogged the limelight.

4. The role of the vice president for public affairs was also important. He coordinated the entire campaign, devised the three-pronged strategy, and was instrumental in executing it without hampering the day-to-day work of his lobbyist in the capital. At the early stages, he acted to be sure that the necessary research (impact assessment and options paper) was done and also helped prepare the position paper that was used in direct and grass-roots lobbying and in press communications. A

subordinate organized the coalition that the lobbyist used to help achieve company objectives. He also enlisted the trade association in the campaign and worked closely with it to obtain maximum benefits from the company's membership. He also used the Government Relations Committee to insure that inputs were obtained from all relevant interests within the company and, with the C.E.O.'s support, developed a consensus strategy that met all needs.

5. The company's direct lobbying was a prime factor in its success. The lobbyist obtained and utilized early, private information at several important stages, drawing on his personal relationships with key figures in both the legislative and executive branches to achieve objectives. He prepared for the hearings, organizing witnesses and planting questions that would advance his side's cause. He helped draft the committee report and amendments and arranged their best use. He had the resiliency to overcome an unexpected defeat in one house, and to capitalize on the asset of surprise press support in the other chamber.

6. LPC utilized its allies and developed an effective coalition that included consumer and union support along with involvement from other business interests. These included its suppliers who shared a stake in LPC's business success.

7. LPC organized its alliances along two fronts. Through the legislative coalition, members and employees were utilized in grass-roots lobbying, not only contacting their own legislators but also getting local government officials to make similar communications. The fiscal study group amounted to a second coalition and was also instrumental in the legislative success.

8. LPC's press contacts resulted in invaluable support for the direct lobbying campaign.

9. It is unusual, of course, for a legislative campaign to mobilize all these components effectively, and even rarer for all to work as smoothly and successfully as this one did. The purpose of the model, of course, is not to disseminate fairy tales about government relations but rather to show what can be accomplished when all the pieces work as they can and should.

OTHER ARENAS OF DIRECT LOBBYING

Apart from legislation, direct lobbying is utilized to affect policy in other branches and agencies. It is also often used to procure government contracts and grants.

Executive Departments

The elected chief executives of federal, state, and local governments, the individuals who head the principal departments and agencies, and the top staff personnel of both are all deeply involved in the public policy process in ways that both rival and interact with the legislative branch. As in the foregoing model, policies that may or may not require legislative approval are frequently developed in the executive branch. There will be substantial interaction, too, during the give-and-take of the legislative process, and executive branch officials frequently play essentially a lobbying role to get a final product as close to their initial proposal as possible. Following enactment, executive officials will have to enforce or otherwise carry out the law, often with considerable latitude as to how to do so.

Had Advocate, in the legislative model, learned what was being developed at an even earlier stage, he undoubtedly would have devoted substantial effort to influencing, first, the Tax Department's interpretation of its data; second, the Budget Office's analysis of the situation; and third, the policy assessments and conclusions drawn by the governor and his policy staff.

He would have utilized at least some of the same techniques he applied to the legislative process:

- He would have obtained and communicated research data to influence the thinking of the various executive officials and staff.

- As soon as he felt at liberty to do so without violating confidences or jeopardizing relationships, he and Boss would have organized much the same kinds of coalitions to bring the pressures of other interest groups to bear on the situation, very likely including both the study group and the legislative coalition, while stimulating a variety of grass-roots communications on the subject.

- He would have sought to mobilize the press early on as a potential ally.

If he had failed in all this and in the legislature, too, he would have been back to the executive branch once the bill had been enacted. At this stage, the Tax Department would have been developing rules, regulations, and procedures concerning the enforcement of the new excise tax law. Advocate would have wanted to be involved in this process. Later, as particular compliance problems arose, he would be in frequent contact with the Tax Department to assure at least even-handedness if not the most favorable possible enforcement policies. He undoubtedly would seek help from friends in the legislature to bring about such a situation.

Lobbyists also get involved in a variety of other types of executive actions. They may try to shape the budget, to the extent that it affects government programs in which they are interested; for the same reason, they may also follow through with the legislature's authorization and appropriations processes.

Lobbying on Personnel Appointments

Lobbyists may also try to influence key departmental, agency and judicial appointments to assure that friendly people are named, or at least that hostile ones are not. Any or all of the tools in the lobbyist's kit may be utilized as appropriate to the circumstances. Such campaigns are usually conducted behind the scenes to minimize embarrassment to the personalities involved, but highly controversial appointments or nominations from time to time have become major public issues.

For instance, several nominations to the Supreme Court by Presidents John-son, Nixon, and Reagan became the subjects of major lobbying campaigns to deny Senate confirmation of the nominees, and direct lobbying was only one of the means used for the purpose. The battle in 1988 over President Reagan's nomination of Robert Bork to be an associate justice illustrates the intense use of various tools of government relations by both supporters and opponents:

Intensive research into Judge Bork's background, writings, and past decisions.

Direct lobbying of vast scope, not only targeted at members of the Judiciary Committee but at all senators.

Extensive coalitions among interest groups, organized largely along ideological lines.

Grass-roots lobbying on the part of many of these groups to muster massive communications from their members to senators.

Political finance, at least to the extent of pointed reminders to senators of the strong interest, both pro and con, of past contributors and support groups.

Communications utilizing advocacy advertising, promotion of major press editorials, and the placement in news stories of research results, among other means.

Major campaigns like the one on the Bork nomination, or that of John Tower to be secretary of defense in 1989, are relatively uncommon, but in some respects are easier to organize than battles over legislation. Personality issues are easily painted black and white, and therefore are more readily communicated. There are few gray areas or questions of complex amend-ments to confuse the public. Compromises and trade-offs often may be ar-ranged for nominations to lesser offices, but the more controversial the individuals involved, the harder it is for the normal legislative and lobbying processes of compromise to come into play. In many ways, highly contro-versial battles over nominations resemble the politics of elections more than they do the normal legislative processes.

Indeed, the 1986 campaign to remove several California Supreme Court justices was an election in reverse, with the voters of the state using their power to disapprove the judges' continuance in office.

Lobbying the Judiciary

Important court decisions can also be the focus of lobbying. Direct lobbying in such situations is quite formal, taking the form of "friend-of-the-court" briefs and oral arguments before the judges by interested groups who may coalesce for the purpose. Political pressures and grass-roots lobbying are largely inapplicable in such situations because of judicial ethics, and may in fact be self-defeating. However, public communications tools may be utilized on highly visible issues. News stories and editorials, for example, have been heavily used in a number of Supreme Court cases including those on school desegregation, abortion rights, capital punishment, congressional budget controls, and the legitimacy of special prosecutors.

Regulatory Agency Lobbying

At every level of government, agencies exist that exercise authority over some aspect of the economy or society. Such agencies are most commonly involved in fields directly or indirectly affecting public and consumer health and safety, but they also regulate many aspects of business and the economy. Civil rights and education are the most common examples of government involvement in social fields.

These agencies generally have broad authority granted by the legislature to both write and enforce rules, regulations, standards, etc. Thus, the Securities and Exchange Commission issues regulations controlling, let us say, some aspect of stock market transactions. The same agency will investigate possible transgressions of these regulations, prosecute violators in a trial-like proceeding, and, if it finds them guilty, impose penalties. The SEC's operations are not different in principle from those of some local agency supervising restaurant sanitation.

Lobbyists seek to influence the actions of these agencies in many of the same ways that they use to affect executive and legislative decision making. Lobbying can occur at two stages of regulatory action: rule making and compliance.

In the rule-making stage, the agency is developing rules or regulations over a particular problem area. The rule-making process is essentially a legislative one. A problem will be identified and a possible solution conceived, formulated, and publicly proposed. Except in emergency situations, the proposal is offered for public comment, either at hearings or by mail. Following the comment period, the proposal may or may not be modified before final adoption. The agency's final action may be appealed to the courts in some cases.

At each step in this process, the lobbyist can provide information and analysis to influence the proposal. Early information is particularly important because there are fewer stages in regulatory rule making than in the legislative process, and because lobbying is sometimes virtually prohibited in some later stages if it involves private communications with an agency official. Psychologically, politically, and procedurally, the earlier lobbyists can begin influencing the thinking of agency officials, the more successful they are likely to be.

Within the bounds governing each agency's rule-making procedure, the lobbyist can use all the available tools. The research function is essential. Direct lobbying and the use of coalitions are always appropriate, subject to some restrictions. The intervention of influential legislators can be enlisted. Communications can be helpful and sometimes a necessity. Grass-roots lobbying and political action may or may not be effective; some state and local regulatory officials are elected but others are appointed, sometimes for fixed terms to insulate them from political pressures. (At the federal level, all such officials are appointed.)

Lobbyists are likely to play a much more informal role in the compliance stage. Because no agency ever has enough funds, employees, or other resources to saturate the field it is regulating, agencies depend on voluntary compliance often supplemented by informal, even off-the-record warnings. Lobbyists who are well acquainted within the agency may be quietly told that such-and-such an action or practice by the lobbyist's client, company, or members could well result in an enforcement proceeding if it is not changed. More often than not, the entire matter is satisfactorily worked out. Many activists consider such informal communications improper and perhaps sometimes technically illegal, but the practice is necessary to insure that regulatory objectives are met with minimum economic, social, and political strain.

Iron Triangles

Another kind of political influence pervades many regulatory situations. Regulated economic sectors begin to develop strong common interests with career officials in the regulatory agency, as both groups do with certain legislators (and staff) who have a strong constituency or committee interest in the regulated field. These relations are called "iron triangles" and they tend to be strongly self-protective of all concerned.

Examples of iron triangles abound. Veterans' organizations like the Veterans of Foreign Wars and the American Legion, the Department of Veterans Affairs (formerly the Veterans Administration), and senior members of Congress interested in matters affecting veterans; farmers producing particular commodities, the legislators who represent them in Congress, and the Agriculture Department bureaucrats regulating those commodities; teachers and their unions, federal, state, and local educational agencies, and friendly legislators; truckers and the Teamsters Union, legislative allies, and regulatory agency officials.

Activist and "public interest" groups have their own iron triangles: for example, environmentalists and their legislative and agency friends, or consumer groups, consumer protection agencies, and supportive legislators.

Iron triangles are perhaps the ultimate form of coalition politics and involve every form of government relations activity. The regulated group is usually highly organized, vocal, and communicative from the grass roots, and politically active in behalf of friendly legislators and other elected officials. The legislators ensure that the regulatory agency gets the funding and resources it needs and often give career boosts to cooperative bureaucrats. The legislators also use their oversight and appropriations authority to hold the agency in line, if need be, to make sure that constituents' interests are protected. Agency officials provide useful research and other assistance to the legislators.

Lobbyists play a significant role in iron triangles, acting not only as representatives of the regulated group but frequently as liaisons among all three partners in the relationship to make the system work.

Procurement Lobbying

A specialized field of lobbying influences legislative, executive, and sometimes regulatory decision making to obtain government contracts or funding for companies or organizations. The spectrum of this kind of lobbying is enormous:

- Defense contractors not only solicit Pentagon business to build a new weapons system but also often help to lobby Congress and the White House to get the system authorized and funded in the first place.

- Universities seeking federal or state funds for particular projects utilize independent or on-staff specialists who are expert in the complex processes of obtaining government grants.

- Associations of state or local officials lobby Congress to authorize new education programs, and then lobby the Department of Education for some of the new subsidies.

- Local agricultural organizations lobby state legislatures and agencies for funds to promote sales of their particular commodities—and national farm-related groups seek federal money so that their members can go abroad to explore and promote export opportunities.

The list literally grows daily and is virtually endless. The practitioners of this specialized field can avail themselves of the same set of government relations techniques used by other lobbyists to achieve their objectives.

Procurement lobbying is also frequently characterized by iron triangle relationships, in this case the close and on-going ties that develop among the seekers of grants and contracts, and legislators and bureaucrats friendly to them.

LOBBYING THE FEDERAL GOVERNMENT

Monitoring and influencing the policies and programs of the federal government is, for most companies and organizations, the dominant government relations activity. The number of individuals concerned with federal government relations is well into five digits, if the size of some of the published directories is any measure. These individuals work either for membership organizations or companies. Thousands of other men and women pursue federal government relations as independent practitioners with law firms, consulting and advocacy organizations, and the like.

The membership groups, including thousands of trade associations as well as non-business groups, are largely, and increasingly, based in Washington (although there are still considerable numbers headquartered in Chicago, New York, and other cities).

Corporate federal government relations personnel are usually based either at company headquarters or in Washington. The trend toward maintaining full-time Washington offices, which began in the 1950s and 1960s, has continued into the 1980s, although it has abated somewhat in recent years. A survey of 300 companies by The Conference Board[2] found that 157 of them had opened Washington offices to handle federal government relations: 40 percent had been opened prior to 1970, another 40 percent during the 1970s, and 20 percent since 1981. Less than 13 percent (20 companies) subsequently closed the Washington office, although, interestingly, 14 of the 20 had not opened the office until after 1980.

The current pattern seems quite mixed. Within the banking industry alone, two major institutions (Chase Manhattan Bank and Chemical Bank) closed their Washington offices, while their larger competitor, Citicorp, decided to open one—with a staff of twenty headed by the company's executive vice president.

Some companies seemed to conclude that, with the advent of the Reagan administration, the likelihood of federal regulation had virtually disappeared. Although regulation substantially diminished during the 1980s, any belief that the federal government would shrivel was as much a fantasy even under Ronald Reagan as it undoubtedly will be under George Bush. A Washington corporate representative explains why:

The effect of the federal government on all phases of national life is pervasive. It's a taxer. It's a granter. It regulates the workplace and the marketplace. Any organization—be it a trade union or company or association—is taking a chance if it didn't have a presence on the Washington scene and an ability to have an input and to have its interests represented.[3]

Many of the companies without a Washington office are headquartered within easy traveling distance of the capital. The pattern, however, is to open an office in Washington once the number of government relations personnel reaches two or three.

The pros and cons of having a Washington office have been debated for many years. The arguments in favor relate to the personal relationships and information sources that are developed with much greater ease by a resident—akin to the reasons nations place ambassadors in each other's capitals. An on-site representative becomes part of the local scene with far greater opportunities to develop contacts than a visitor from out of town. Apart from cost, the principal argument against a resident representative is the added emphasis some people believe a matter may be given because an executive traveled from corporate headquarters for an appointment with an official especially to discuss it.

This is a rationalization, not a real argument. Those who have tried it both ways, including the author, generally conclude that over the long run, federal government relations are more successfully conducted from a resident office if the organization has on-going issues in Washington. For example, effective participation in coalitions, a technique utilized more and more in government relations, is much harder for the traveler than the resident.

Lobbying is a prime function for many Washington-based government relations offices, but not necessarily the most important. For companies particularly, a major Washington staff role is tracking and analyzing federal policy developments and proposals affecting their organizations, and communicating that information back home.

Often, the initial justification for a Washington office—indeed, sometimes the federal government relations function itself—is the need to focus on regulatory issues, primarily to keep posted on governmental requirements the company or industry will have to comply with. Involvement with the process tends, sooner or later in most organizations, to evolve into a desire to influence regulatory decisions before they are made—and later still to attempt to shape the legislative decisions on which regulatory programs are based. Ultimately, the organization may seek to broaden its influence both at the grass roots and politically.

Thus the pattern is likely to look something like this:

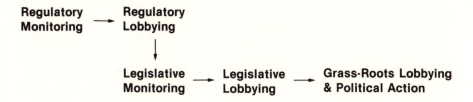

It should be noted, though, that some organizations, particularly companies, deliberately choose to freeze the pattern at a specific point: refraining from legislative activity, for instance, or choosing not to go beyond lobbying into the political arena.

According to the Conference Board study, government relations personnel spend about one-third of their time on issues monitoring. Those that devote "considerable" time to government relations are more likely to focus on legislative issues, whereas those who devote only "moderate" time or less are likelier to stress regulatory or executive branch topics.

Another one-third of their time is spent on advocacy, directly or indirectly, with much the same pattern.

The remaining time is divided among state/local government relations, coalitions, marketing support, and legislative and business planning and reporting.

Not included per se in the Conference Board study are activities that most government relations personnel devote vast time and attention to: providing policymakers with information, and networking—cultivating and developing contacts and relationships among people in Congress, the agencies, political groups, the media, associations, and allies (including others in the same industry), and anyone else who is a real or potential source of information and support.

Procurement lobbying occupies a large amount of time for Washington representatives representing defense contractors and other companies for whom the federal government is a major customer.

Choosing a Washington Representative

Selecting a Washington representative for a company or organization based elsewhere involves much the same criteria as those in selecting a lobbyist. An important additional consideration, however, is political sophistication to a higher degree than is found, perhaps, in the state capitals of all but the largest states.

Notwithstanding Washington's rapid growth as a city, the nation's capital is in many ways a village. Political/governmental Washington has its own culture, its own ways of doing business, and a certain disdain toward people who do not appear to grasp the nuances of politics and government "inside the Beltway"—for example, the importance and prevalence of iron triangles. Successful veterans in the village understand the culture and how to make it work for them, and generally have a strong network of contacts and relationships. But many a newcomer succeeds who exhibits that grasp of the nuances and who therefore can quickly gain both acceptance and a networking base.

Organizations, especially companies, preparing to open a Washington office frequently consider whether it is better to transfer an experienced corporate executive to Washington or to hire someone with political sophistication and, perhaps, an existing contact network. The issue is sometimes put this way: Is it better to get someone who knows Washington and teach him (or her) the company, or transfer someone who knows the corporate culture and teach him Washington?

As critical as understanding of the company's culture and problems is to success in government relations, they are easier to learn and absorb than are the culture and process of Washington.

Of course, an individual who is experienced in federal government relations and who also has grown up in the company fits in with both cultures and is therefore in an ideal position to hit the ground running.

Federal Regulation of Lobbying[4]

The Federal Regulation of Lobbying Act was passed in 1946. In 1954 the U.S. Supreme Court (*U.S. v. Harriss*) struck down many of its provisions as violations of the First Amendment. What remains is widely considered toothless, unenforced, and indeed largely unenforceable. It is, in fact, entirely possible to conduct major campaigns to influence federal legislation without being more than nominally subject to the law, or even coming under its jurisdiction at all.

Its major provisions are these: Lobbyists, if paid, are required to register with officials of Congress and to file financial reports; unpaid lobbyists and groups that spend their own money are not. Organizations are subject to the law only if lobbying is their "principal purpose." Thus interest groups that can claim their activities are principally educational or informational are not covered.

Only direct contacts with members of Congress are considered lobbying, not contacts with congressional staff, testimony at hearings, or grass-roots contacts—nor contacts with executive and regulatory officials. Contacts with one's own senators and representatives are also exempt, and this is probably true as well of an organization contacting the lawmakers representing headquarters and other facilities.

Because the law is so general and unenforceable, Congress has occasionally considered revising or replacing it but has never actually done so, in large part because of concerns about constitutionality.

A 1976 tax law tried to limit the lobbying expenses of nonprofit groups. As of early 1989, the Internal Revenue Service was still attempting to frame implementing regulations that would withstand constitutional challenge, especially regarding restrictions on grass-roots lobbying and efforts to treat small groups differently than larger ones.

Other categories of lobbyists are treated in widely varying degrees by the law.

- Executive branch personnel are supposedly barred from lobbying Congress. In practice, this prohibition is totally disregarded by both branches.
- Former high-ranking executive branch officials are also restricted in their ability to lobby Congress and their former agencies in behalf of foreign or private-sector clients for one year, and in certain matters for life. (The celebrated trials of former White House aides Michael Deaver and Lyn Nofziger flowed from this ban.) Congress passed legislation in 1988 to bar former top officials from lobbying any other high officials for a year, not just those in their former agencies, but the bill died on President Reagan's desk. New ethics legislation is likely early in the Bush presidency.
- In the 1988 legislation, Congress also sought to apply the same one-year cooling-off period to lobbying of members of Congress by former senators and represen-

tatives. Senior congressional staff personnel were to be restricted only from lobbying staff members in their old offices or committees, but not otherwise.

The Internal Revenue Service considers some kinds of lobbying activities tax deductible, others non-deductible. Costs of direct lobbying are deductible by companies. Expenses for "indirect lobbying," including grass-roots communications and advocacy advertising, are not. Trade associations can deduct expenses of exhorting their members to lobby legislators—but not if they ask them to urge employees or others to do so.

Lobbying Expenditures

How much do lobbies spend? Because of the vagueness and virtual unenforceability of federal lobbying requirements, the real total is unknowable. Filings with congressional officials[5] indicate that $63.6 million was spent in 1987 just to lobby senators and representatives, up from $60.9 million in 1986 and $49 million in 1985.

These amounts are undoubtedly narrowly defined and also exclusive of sums spent on federal executive and regulatory lobbying, grass-roots activities, and other exempt categories. It does not seem too far-fetched to guess that an actual total is probably in excess of $1 billion annually for federal lobbying. Adding in estimates for state and local lobbying expenditures brings the probable national grand total into the $3–5 billion range.

LOBBYING STATE AND LOCAL GOVERNMENTS

There is an interesting dynamic that has long existed between federal and state governments and the private-sector interest groups that lobby them. Until the middle 1960s, business organizations opposing certain legislative proposals in Congress often used the argument that the subject of the legislation was inappropriate for federal action and was best left to the states. In part, this was a sincere argument, but it was also useful because those advocates knew that the states in general had little interest in legislating on those topics. Conversely, labor unions, civil rights groups, and others interested in engineering social and economic changes urged Congress to act— partly to achieve national uniformity and partly because they were making little progress on their agendas in the state capitals.

Then, beginning in the middle and late 1960s, a revitalization of state government and policy innovation began, facilitated by the development of revenue sharing (a device to provide some of the federal government's tax collections to the states, initiated for philosophic reasons by one conservative president, Richard Nixon, and terminated for fiscal reasons by another, Ronald Reagan).

As the states became increasingly active in areas of consumer, environmental, workplace, and other social issues, many business lobbyists reversed course, urging Congress to enact national legislation that would pre-empt state action in order to protect interstate and national markets from fragmented regulation. Businesses have also often been reluctant to trade federal deregulation for new and possibly incompatible state and local regulation, especially if they believe they are less influential in the states than in Washington.

Liberal interest groups supported federal pre-emption, though with a twist, often arguing that federal legislation should pre-empt conflicting state laws that were less stringent than federal requirements, while leaving the states free to enact tighter standards if they wished.

Many state and local governments have taken a third road, asking that Congress not pre-empt them at all so that they are free to act as they desire.

This philosophic conflict is likely to continue well into the next century as state and local governments continue to experiment with widely varying legislative and regulatory interests and approaches. This is particularly true for those states and communities that tend to be regulatory innovators and pacesetters (or, as one disgruntled business lobbyist put it, those "on the cutting edge of trouble"). These are states like California, New York, Massachusetts, Oregon, and Wisconsin, and local governments like Berkeley, California, and Suffolk County, New York.

Liberal interest groups whose agenda includes much social and economic innovation are generally happy with a variety of federal and state experiments on their issues, believing that diversity tends to produce public policy more to their liking. Conservative interests, whose economic agendas tend to oppose *any* governmental activism, maintain such a constitutional aversion to Washington's involvement that the frequent effect is the promotion of state activism, whether they wish it or not.

The interests of business are often caught in the middle. Many businessmen and women may be philosophically conservative, but they are operationally pragmatic. It is costly to be compelled to do business under fifty different sets of rules and standards, and ultimately both the consumer and economic productivity suffer.

It is not only activism that has led to the rapid growth of state government relations. Other factors include:

• The enlargement in size and power of legislative staffs, many of whom have become power brokers in their own right, often with their own personal ideological agendas for public policy initiatives.

• Increased careerism among legislators, a growing number of whom hold safe seats and who today often consider their legislative pursuits as full-time vocations.

• The fragmentation of power in many states and its shift away from legislative leaders toward individual lawmakers. Once leadership-dominated power centers, many state legislatures have become, like Congress, bazaars of entrepreneurial activists. There are still some exceptions like New York that are notable and important, but even there changes are tending away from strong power centers.

- The growth of legislative calendars. Almost all state legislatures now meet for at least a quarter of the year, and the legislatures of the larger states are, like Congress, virtually in year-round session.

- Federal fiscal restraints that have the effect of shifting the program initiatives of interest groups away from Washington and toward the state capitals.

State government relations is of varying importance to companies, depending on the nature of their business and their exposure to regulation. Public utilities, banks, and insurance companies operate predominantly under state regulation, and a potent state lobbying capability is critical to them. Retailers, some manufacturers, and other companies that market goods and services to consumers are sensitive to state and local regulation of marketing, merchandising, health, and safety; these are often the same firms most concerned about diversity in state regulation. Manufacturers are also susceptible to a broad variety of state and local involvement where their plants are located.

Depending on the nature and scope of the exposure, state government relations can be carried out in one or more ways:

- By full-time government relations professionals with responsibility for a single state or perhaps several states in a region.

- Through independent lobbyists retained in each of the state capitals (or localities) in which there is significant exposure.

- Through state trade associations, themselves growing in size and importance.

- Through the use of plant and facility managers and other grass-roots executives whose responsibilities include some degree of state and local government relations.

Modes may differ by industry, by individual company, and even within companies and divisions, depending on needs and resources. Whatever the approach, the principles discussed in other pertinent chapters of this book apply.

Regulation of Lobbying

There are fifty different patterns of state requirements governing lobbying registration and filings—and more, if local requirements are counted. Some are as vague and loose as the federal lobbying law; others, very stiff, rigid, and bureaucratic.

Lobbying regulation laws typically have two kinds of requirements: registration and reporting.

Registration

All fifty states require paid lobbyists to register with a state official if they will be contacting legislators on issues. Thirty states also require registration if the lobbyist will be in contact with executive and regulatory agencies. Typical registration information includes name and address, identification of employer or clients, description of the issues, and sometimes even the names of legislators or officials the lobbyist expects to contact. Many states require an employer or client authorization statement; some require a registration fee which, in the case of Texas, can be as much as $100; some, like California, Illinois, and Massachusetts, require a photograph of the lobbyist to be published in a directory of lobbyists or used on a badge that the lobbyist must wear. Badges are fairly common. In Connecticut, for instance, the badge must state the client's name, with a separate badge for each client; multi-client lobbyists are often seen festooned like Christmas trees.

Reporting

Most states require lobbyists and/or clients or employers to file periodic financial and activity reports with the state, although Arkansas, Georgia, Louisiana, Utah, and Wyoming do not. Some reporting forms are simple, like those of South Carolina and Ohio; others are very complex, such as Maryland, Massachusetts, and Rhode Island. Some reports are carefully checked for accuracy, others merely filed. Some reports must be filed monthly, others quarterly or semi-annually, a few annually.

Information to be filed also varies widely. Lobbyists may be asked for statements of compensation and expenses; who they have contacted and on what issues; and for specific entertainment details (who was entertained, where, when, how much, etc.).

Even though most state lobbying laws are more restrictive than the federal law, there has not been a court test of their constitutionality before the U.S. Supreme Court since its 1954 decision in *U.S. v. Harriss*. As recently as October 1988, the Court declined an opportunity to hear an appeal of a case[6] upholding a Minnesota law requiring disclosure of expenditures over $250 a year for both direct and grass-roots lobbying. Other state laws are considerably more restrictive than Minnesota's, and some might be viewed as infringements on First Amendment rights. It would seem appropriate that, sooner or later, the nation's highest court should reconcile its decision in the *Harriss* case with what the states are doing today.

Each state publishes information on its own lobbying requirements and forms. Sources of this information for each state are indicated in the *State Legislative Sourcebook*. A frequently up-dated compendium of lobbying requirements is *State Lobbying Laws*, published by State and Federal Associates. A biannually published reference work is the *Blue Book* of the Council on

Governmental Ethics Laws. (For citations to these publications, see *Almanacs and Directories* in the section on Sources and Resources at the back of the book.)

REFERENDA AND INITIATIVES

About half the states extend the legislative process to the polling place by permitting voters to decide the fate of individual issues. "Direct democracy," as some call it, takes two forms, the initiative and the popular referendum. Both are important to government relations professionals in these states because they provide the public with means either to override an act of the legislature or to circumvent it altogether.[7]

Initiatives

In twenty-three states, the District of Columbia, and many localities, citizens may petition for placement on the ballot of proposed new laws or constitutional amendments. In states with the "direct initiative," the proposal goes directly on the ballot (assuming it gets the required number of petition signatures) and, if approved by the voters, is adopted. Some states have a variation, "the indirect initiative," which requires that the proposal first be submitted to the legislature, which is given a chance to act on it before it goes to the voters.

Referenda

The term "referendum" is commonly used to describe any ballot question that the voters are asked to approve—constitutional amendments, bond issues, and the like. Most of these are more accurately described as "referred measures" since they do not involve citizen petitions but are referred by some governmental body or are required by the state constitution.

"Popular referenda," in contrast, give the voters a chance to approve or disapprove legislation already passed by the state's lawmakers. Like initiatives, popular referenda require that a minimum number of voters sign petitions to have the issue placed on the ballot. The popular referendum exists in twenty-five states and many localities.

Both initiatives and popular referenda can result in significant legislation. A 1982 Massachusetts referendum resulted in approval of the state's "bottle law," for instance. The initiative in California was the instrument of the famous "tax revolt," which limited property tax rates, spreading to other states during the 1970s and early 1980s and even resulting in the recall of two Michigan state senators. Stringent environmental measures have also been adopted through use of initiatives.

The initiative process can have its peculiarities. In 1988 California voters were faced with two different and inconsistent campaign reform proposals, and approved both!

Recalls

Fifteen states permit the voters to remove elected officials from office, and others require periodic votes on certain officials' continuation in office. These are seldom used but powerful devices. Arizona voters filed enough signatures to force a recall election on their governor in 1988, had the legislature not first removed him from office. In 1986 Californians refused to reconfirm the chief justice and two associate justices of the state's supreme court, ejecting them from office. Both events were front-page news across the country.

The laws governing initiatives, popular referenda, and recalls vary widely. Petition signature requirements for initiatives and popular referenda, for example, range from 2% to 15% of the most recent statewide voter turnout. Signature requirements for recalls are generally higher.

NOTES

1. With thanks and apologies to the Public Affairs Council for the concept of the *dramatis personae*.

2. Seymour Lusterman, *Managing Federal Government Relations* (New York: The Conference Board, 1988).

3. Ricardo R. Alvarado of Allied-Signal Inc., quoted in: Kirk Victor, "Being Here," *National Journal*, August 6, 1988.

4. The history and provisions of federal regulation of lobbying are well summarized in *The Washington Lobby*, 5th edition (Washington: Congressional Quarterly, Inc., 1987).

5. Compiled by the Associated Press and reported in *The New York Times*, August 23, 1988.

6. *Minnesota Ethical Practices Board v. National Rifle Association*. NRA appealed a decision of the U.S. Court of Appeals, 8th Circuit. Certiorari was denied by the Supreme Court, October 11, 1988.

7. A useful explanation and analysis of referenda and initiatives is in: Patrick B. McGuigan, *The Politics of Direct Democracy in the 1980s: Case Studies in Popular Decision Making* (Washington: Institute for Government and Politics of the Free Congress Research and Education Foundation, 1985). McGuigan also edits a monthly newsletter on the subject (see section on state information sources in Sources and Resources). For a scholarly history and analysis, see: David B. Magleby, *Direct Legislation: Voting on Ballot Propositions in the United States* (Baltimore: Johns Hopkins University Press, 1984).

7

Alliances: Trade Associations and Coalitions

Friendship needs a certain parallelism of life, a community of thought, a rivalry of aim.

Henry Brooks Adams

Leveraging government relations capabilities to a higher level of influence through alliances creates a synergy that can exceed the effectiveness of its components. Multiplying influence through membership in trade associations and other membership organizations is one way to do this. Joining with other organizations in an ad hoc issues coalition is another. Each is an important instrument of government relations success.

The dictionary defines "alliance" as "a bond or connection between families, states, parties, or individuals; an association to further the common interests of the members." "Coalition" is defined in turn as "a temporary alliance." One might talk about an alliance of companies or an alliance of environmental groups—but a business-labor-consumer coalition since the latter is more likely to be temporary and oriented toward a particular problem or issue. Trade associations are really permanent alliances.

TRADE ASSOCIATIONS

Trade and business associations serve a wide variety of purposes for their members' companies, but representing the interests of their industries with governments at all levels is increasingly the most important. For many firms, trade associations are their principal lobbies, sometimes their only ones.

These groups range from the national giants—so-called "umbrella" associations like the Chamber of Commerce of the United States, National Association of Manufacturers, and the Business Roundtable—to local chambers of commerce in communities across the nation. They also include the vital national, state, and local associations that represent industries and professions with lawmakers and government officials in behalf of the members who pay their dues. These members are sometimes individuals, but more often companies. (In general, professional associations or societies are comprised of individuals; trade associations are usually made up of companies.)

There are thousands of such groups at the national level, and at least as many again at state and local levels. An individual company may belong to several, or to several dozen. Indeed, the largest companies may belong to hundreds.

Trade associations are a principal means through which American corporations relate to each other, to governments, and to the public. In the area of government relations particularly, trade association participation can be a highly cost-effective means of achieving a company's public policy objectives. Indeed, trade associations are probably the first lines of both defense and offense for most companies.

A point not often recognized is the distinction between an association's *opponents* and its *competitors*. Groups with potentially overlapping memberships compete with each other for dues dollars, and therefore for prestige points, even though they are often (but not always) allied in their legislative aims. For instance, the AFL-CIO opposes the National Association of Manufacturers (NAM) and the U.S. Chamber on many legislative issues, but it does not compete with them economically because there is no common constituency. The Chamber and the NAM are rivals for dues precisely because there is a substantial commonality of membership.

Competing associations are usually allies but sometimes opponents. When competitors share positions on issues, they vie for leadership and effectiveness. When their positions are opposed, they fight to protect the interests of a distinctive membership element but also for organizational self-interest.

Merger pressures are common in industries or movements with multiple associations. Food retailers and wholesalers for instance, are represented by a number of associations, and efforts to merge some of them are a constant in the industry—sometimes successfully, often not. The question for the individual member is how it can best be represented, but there is rarely a unanimous view among members. Associations themselves, both elected leaders and staff, have a broad sense of organizational identity and deep streaks of self-protectiveness.

Some companies are wary of trade association participation because of antitrust concerns. A few companies decline to attend certain meetings or even to join at all. Actually, a well-run association has little problem complying with the law, particularly if an attorney is present at key meetings. The law is both clear-cut and well established with respect to trade association activities. Such groups have wide latitude in the government relations area particularly.[1]

Associations are one of the most valuable and efficient resources available to companies. They can also be a great way to waste money. Both dues and even more costly executive time are wasted if the company does not take steps to assure that the goals, priorities, and performance of its trade associations meet the company's established needs.

Coupled with their potential for effectiveness is their generally modest cost—often less than the cost of adding a professional to staff. However, companies tend to look mainly at dues, neglecting the real expense of membership, which at the very least includes executive time.

It is important to calculate both the true costs and also the true value to the company of its association memberships. The latter is measured by the extent to which each association fulfills the individual company's goals and priorities for that group. The point is not whether the association is doing a good job for its industry, but how well it is performing for the individual member-company, not at all the same thing.

From the company's point of view, the critical concept is *value*, and value should be evaluated as a cost-benefit relationship.

Analyzing the Real Costs

Many businesses take their trade associations for granted. They tend to leave policy development to the staff or to a committee of association experts on which the company may or may not be effectively represented. While often acutely conscious of the dues they pay, companies seldom calculate the real costs of membership, which go well beyond mere dues. Firms that have not established written goals and purposes for their memberships have no way to evaluate whether they are getting true value.

Dues may be only a small percentage of a company's real cost of association membership. This is especially true of associations whose individual annual dues may be only a few thousand dollars or less. Dues are only the visible part of the iceberg; the submerged portion, less visible but substantially larger than dues, is executive time.

What does it cost a company each time an executive spends a day on association activity? That day may be spent attending a meeting, traveling to the meeting, or doing anything else that's directly related to his or her involvement with the association.

These expenses can be measured. The measurement formula should include personnel costs, office overhead, and travel expense. Based on input from various companies, here is what it costs, on the average, to send an executive to an overnight meeting.

Executive's Salary	Real Cost of Single Overnight Meeting
$50,000	$900
100,000	1,300
150,000	1,600
200,000	2,000

Source: Author's estimates.

Those are the costs of sending one person to a single meeting. However, if that individual is moderately active, he or she is going to board and committee meetings several times annually, and also attending seminars, the annual convention, etc. As a conservative estimate, the executive probably incurs the equivalent of six overnight trips a year in connection with association business and events.

On top of that, considerable time is generally spent on telephone, correspondence, and reading on association-related matters. Add all that in, and the costs to a member company (in 1988 dollars) become substantial:

Executive's Salary	Minimum Annual Real Cost of Association Participation
$50,000	$7,800
100,000	12,000
150,000	15,600
200,000	18,500

Source: Author's estimates

Since even a moderately active company will have several executives involved in the association, attending meetings of its board and committees, conferences and conventions, and so on, a subtotal of real costs may well be in the annual range of $50,000 to $60,000—to which must then be added dues, special assessments, and fees, etc.

For associations with low (under $10,000) dues levels, this is a very high cost multiple. But even those companies that pay their associations large annual dues—$50,000–100,000, or even more—may find that their total real membership costs may well be at least twice what they believe.

The critical issue for the member-company at this point is "What are we getting for all that money?"

Evaluating Benefits and Value

Corporate executives often assess their trade group with the comment that "the association does a good job for the industry." This may be true, but it obscures a critical issue. The question should not only be whether the association is doing a good job for its industry, but how well it is doing for the individual member-company actually paying the bills.

Many managers regard their associations as they would some charitable organization pleading for the donation of some executive time. "Look," said one in a typical remark, "we pay our dues, we have a seat on the board of directors, and we go to the annual convention. What more do you want? We can't spare the man-hours to put people on every committee."

The point this executive overlooks is that his company belongs to each association for important business objectives. If his company is to stay in the association, it must be sure that those goals are being met. If the group is not meeting the company's goals, then steps should be taken either to cure that condition or to reassess the value of membership in the trade association in the first place.

What is generally not appreciated is the extent to which an individual company can shape the goals, policies, and even performance of its associations. Moreover, an individual company can exercise influence far beyond what might be expected from its size and share of market—typical measures of association influence.

To maximize the benefits of its association memberships, the member-company should formulate a set of goals for each trade association to which it belongs. Then it should become deeply involved in the association's affairs, striving to achieve and maintain positions of leadership and influence over objectives, policies, and priorities. Finally, the association's performance must be evaluated—not only against the group's own goals but also those of the company.

How to Evaluate an Association

The process should begin with a close review of each trade association to which the company belongs. This review should take place at least annually and consist of two parts:

1. Evaluating goals and performance of the trade association.
2. Evaluating the role and effectiveness of the company within the association.

Company Goals for the Association

Individuals and companies join associations for a variety of reasons, of which government relations support may be only one. Others could include education, trade relations, group insurance programs and other economic benefits, industrywide public relations programs, contact opportunities, and just good fellowship with peers and colleagues.

Step 1: Analyze the respective roles of the association and the member-company and understand the relationship. What business is the association in? "I don't consider myself to be in the association business," a trade group executive told an industry publication. "I'm in the business of helping [the members] move forward to meet the challenges the industry faces."

Actually, he has to be in both businesses. The head of a drug industry association is neither a pharmaceutical manufacturer nor a druggist. It is his or her job to look after the needs of the membership, but he also has an association to run. Revenues must be raised, programs planned and conducted, and a budget maintained. The association must serve the industry it represents, but it also has its own needs and objectives of survival and prosperity quite apart from those of its membership. As an economic institution, it must do both—just as any business must take care of its customers while also managing its own affairs.

For the members, the critical issue is whether the association is meeting their needs while also meeting is own, or whether it is pursuing an independent agenda devoted to its own aggrandizement. Says a former staff member of a large, well-known national business group, "I left when I realized that the association's only real purpose was the betterment of the executives on the top floor."

Much of the blame for this kind of situation has to be placed at the doorstep of the members who not only failed to cure the condition but unquestioningly went on paying dues year after year to support it.

Step 2: Calculate the real costs of company membership in the association. First, list the direct outlays: dues, special assessments, contributions to the association's foundation or political action committee, etc.

Next, list the executives active in the association, and estimate their daily cost to the company, including salary, benefits, secretarial and other staff support, and office overhead.

Third, ask them to approximate the number of days each spent during the past year on association activities, including not only committee and board meetings, educational conferences, conventions, and the like, but also telephone, correspondence, and meeting preparation time. Add in meeting registration fees, travel costs (including travel time), and entertainment.

Multiply the daily cost by the number of days—by individual for a reasonably precise number; by average cost and number of days for a rougher approximation. (Given the fact that both daily costs and time are at best estimates, the total almost certainly will be on the low side, whichever method is used.) This is the indirect cost.

The total of both direct and indirect expense is the *real cost* of membership in that association.

Step 3: Prepare a list of the company's basic objectives in belonging to the association. Why does the company belong? For government relations information and services? News of developments within or affecting the industry? Executive education? Statistical and economic surveys and services? Industry standards setting? Trade relations with suppliers, customers, and competitors? Industrywide promotion and marketing? Group insurance and similar benefits? Other specific benefits from attendance at conventions, conferences, and committee meetings?

Within such major categories, list the priority goals that the company wishes the association to meet within a finite and reasonable time, perhaps a year: passage, defeat or amendment of specific legislation or regulations; expansion of a particular educational tool or economic service; development of a new insurance or group discount benefit, etc.

Both the major categories and the priority goals should be understood as being of considerable significance to the member-company in terms of its basic strategies for the industry the association represents. If that industry's needs are important to the individual company's, then so is the trade association representing the industry. That priority should be reflected in the intensity of the company's participation within the association. (The converse is also true; if the association is not all that important to the company, then perhaps it is not worth belonging at all.)

In the case of government relations objectives, the company's goals for the association should be extracted from the firm's overall lobbying aims as determined in the needs analysis (see Chapters 2 and 3). After all, trade associations are a vehicle for achieving lobbying objectives and the whole purpose of analyzing and monitoring association performance, at least in the area of government relations, is to make sure the vehicle is traveling the right road toward the member-company's desired destination.

The list of major purposes should not need to be altered frequently, although it should be reviewed at least annually. The list of goals under each major purpose should also be updated as often. Of course, the matters on both lists should be realistic and within the association's purview.

The company should maintain close relationships with association leadership and staff to ensure that it is represented on every association policy body bearing on the company's priorities, working within those bodies to make sure that company objectives are reflected in association policies and programs. The member-company's representatives to these bodies should understand that they are accountable as part of their job performance reviews for effective lobbying of the association so that the company's objectives become an integral part of association policies and programs.

Note that even if the association's goals are those of most of its members, it is still important to be sure that the individual member-company's priorities are fully reflected. If the company's needs are primarily legislative while most of the association's other members are more concerned with education and training, then there clearly is not the best fit.

These priorities should be finely tuned. If Issue X is the member-company's top priority concern but is only number three for the association as a whole, then the member's needs are not likely to be fully met.

Step 4: Evaluate the association's performance. Is the association delivering for the member-company on top priority matters? If so, thank it and reward it, perhaps with a voluntary increase in that year's dues. But if the association is not performing, consider why and what can be done about the situation.

A few companies assess trade association performance from time to time. Even fewer do it regularly and systematically. One way to undertake such an analysis is to retain a consultant who is knowledgeable about both association management and corporate public affairs to undertake an audit of the association's effectiveness from the member-company's point of view. Another approach is to survey from time to time the company's executives who receive services from the association or who are active in it.

Some companies have queried a panel of such managers about goals and performance for each association to which the firm belongs. The advantage of this approach is that these executives usually know what the associations are doing and what benefits they are deriving. The disadvantage is that they often have a loyalty to, and an emotional vested interest in, the association that can cloud objectivity. Because some firms have found that these attitudes can hamper an objective analysis, they have chosen to take the consultant approach, sometimes in lieu of the panel survey and sometimes in tandem with it.

The kinds of questions a survey or audit should pose include the following:

- Is the staff competent in all the dimensions of government relations and public affairs? Do staff lobbyists have authority to negotiate deals on the spot if circumstances require? Are the legislative positions and strategies politically and substantively sound? How well are non-public affairs objectives being met?

- Is the association staff-led or member-led? Neither is inherently good or bad, but a staff-led association in which the members provide only lip service rather than strong backing for the staff is in trouble. Should such an association encounter serious difficulties—e.g., financial problems or a loss on a major issue—there are likely to be few leaders who will champion its cause in the face of membership anger. A staff-led association to which members feel little emotional attachment will have problems with membership involvement in areas like a grass-roots lobbying program.

- Does the staff have the resources to do what the members demand of it or is it left to cope as best it can? Is the staff backed up with formal objectives, programs, budgets, timetables, and the like? How is it held accountable? For that matter, how are the elected leaders held accountable? (Hardly any are; as volunteer leaders, the benefits are largely psychological and the sanctions virtually non-existent—unless accountability is required by the companies that pay them and whom they represent.)

- Is there a dissident faction within the association that must be mollified? What about competitive trade groups? Competition strengthens companies, but it frequently weakens associations and dilutes their effectiveness. In government relations particularly, public officials expect an industry to speak with a single voice on pertinent issues. When there are multiple voices—and particularly when they convey conflicting messages—then the industry's ability to achieve its goals is severely reduced.

• Does the association take an ideological or a pragmatic approach to its mission? Every organization needs to have a point of view, but highly ideological groups tend to be partisan and muscle-bound, and have difficulty negotiating. They can also attract needless hostility from those with whom they have to deal. Some major organizations have been criticized for preferring to retain a highly polarizing position instead of being willing to compromise and thereby help shape the legislative nuances. Despite their size, such groups must take their wins in the relatively small number of black-or-white issues; their influence is little felt in the gray areas where most legislation is shaped.

• Is the association flexible and able to move quickly as the legislative situation changes? Sometimes the association has to be agile, able to modify its stands and negotiate positions and amendments on the spot. As a general rule, associations with large numbers of members find it more difficult to resolve competing interests than more narrowly based ones. A position often represents a general consensus, which can fall apart when a decision has to be made on a crucial amendment.

Evaluating the Company as Member. Once the survey or audit results are in hand, they can be validated by an informal check with a few other members of the association to see if their experiences and observations are parallel. (If not, the study methodology should be re-examined.)

The next step is to interpret the conclusions in the light of the member-company's role in the association. This is another area in which an expert consultant can be helpful, particularly in the development of the remedial action plan that should logically flow out of the Step 5 analysis.

In a sense, trade associations are only as good as their staffs and elected leadership. But in a deeper sense, they are really only as good as their membership wants them to be. A vital aspect of this is the question of how active and involved the members are.

Step 5: Evaluate the effectiveness of the company as a member of the association. Assuring that the association's goals and priorities closely parallel the member-company's is an important strategy for the achievement of company objectives. It will not happen simply by writing a letter, even from one chief executive to another, and leaving it at that. The strategy works only if the company takes pains to involve its people deeply on all the relevant committees and the board, making an intense, on-going effort to influence, if not actually dominate, association decisions.

Contrary to what many businesspeople believe, this is not a power limited to the largest companies in the association. Any company can do it if it knows how to go about it and where to invest the executive time. There is a great myth about trade association participation and governance:

The *myth* is that the largest members run the association, indeed that their very size in the industry entitles them to dominate the association almost by divine right. The *truth* is that regardless of size, involvement and achievement in associations lead to influence—and influence is power.

There is an unfortunate converse to this situation—the tendency of many association members to take free rides on the coattails of the largest members. It is not only that the smaller company believes it must concede association leadership to the larger, but that in many cases the "smalls" are actually happy to do so. Their reasoning is that the "bigs" have more resources to work with and that, after all, the interests of both are identical: another myth.

From issue to issue, companies may well have common interests; else, why belong to trade associations? But they do not have common interests as competing members of the industry. The "bigs" have larger market share and wish to maintain it; the "smalls" want to take it from them. And even companies of similar size have different business needs, plans, and objectives.

Companies that content themselves with the role of free riders in their trade associations concede to their competitors a powerful instrument to achieve individual goals and priorities.

Here are criteria that can be used to evaluate the effectiveness of the member-company's trade association participation:

- Is the company achieving the benefits it wants, as determined in Step 3 above? Do these benefits equal or exceed in value the real cost of membership, as calculated in Step 2? If the answer is negative to either question, and yet the Step 4 analysis indicates a strong and healthy association, then there is a prima facie case that there are deficiencies in the company's involvement.
- Is the company represented on the board of directors? Is it on the committees and other key policy bodies whose actions bear on the company's aims for the association?

Equally important, what is the *quality* of the company's representation on these groups? "Quality" representation means:

- Being prepared for the meeting, not only in terms of the association's agenda but also armed with goals advancing the company's aims with respect to that committee—indeed, diplomatically communicating with the staff and committee chairman to help shape the agenda.
- Effectively participating in the meeting—contributing meaningfully to the discussion in behalf of both the association's and the company's agendas.
- Staying in close touch with the staff after the meeting to insure that decisions on matters important to the company are followed through—where appropriate, volunteering to aid in implementation.

Effective committee participation involves contributing to the achievement of the association's aims as well as the company's. The extremes of committee behavior need to be avoided. Dominating the discussion produces only hostility, but sitting silently throughout produces nothing.

Equally critical to the effectiveness of the company's participation in the association is the identity of its principal representative on the association's board of directors. In many companies, it is the chief executive officer of the operating company if not the parent corporation. In others, it is the senior public affairs executive.

Usually, it should be neither, but rather a top manager in the area most closely affected by the association's programs and activities. All too often, though, this responsibility is inappropriately delegated—sometimes down, sometimes up.

In the case of downward delegation, a lower level manager or staff assistant is sent to the association's meetings. "Don't make any decisions," he or she is instructed. "Just take notes and brief us on what takes place." What sometimes happens, however, is that an important discussion occurs on a key policy issue. A decision is then made without the company's input and sometimes to its dismay.

Upward delegation may be almost as bad. Many associations insist that the seats on the board be held only by the chief executives of member-companies. This assures a certain amount of prestige for the association. Since C.E.O.'s don't always have the time to be intimately involved in trade association affairs, the practice tends to result in a staff-dominated association. Moreover, while the C.E.O. comes to the board meeting briefed by his operating people, he often possesses very little understanding of the underlying issues. Should the staff, or an unusually informed peer, bring up a deep issue for a policy determination, the decision may be made without really meaningful company participation.

The optimum "ambassador" from the company to the association should be the highest ranking executive whose operations will be directly affected by association actions.

Dues for this association should be in his budget, not some corporate catch-all line item. Liaison with the association should be a responsibility included in this executive's job description, and part of his personal annual performance review should include accountability to top management for the performance of the association on both association and company objectives.

This will, of course, require intense involvement on this executive's part in association affairs, time and effort he may be reluctant to invest unless true accountability to superiors is present. But if the trade association is not important enough to invest the money and managerial time required to assure that the association performs for the company, then the association is probably not worth belonging to in the first place.

Member-companies should regard their trade association memberships as on-going investments made to achieve specific company objectives. Like any other investment, performance must be constantly monitored to assure adequate payoff.

Maximizing the value derived from a trade association does not require the company to sacrifice its right to take independent action on issues when, despite its best efforts, the association's position is not in the company's interest. Acting independently of the association on certain matters has its risks, but it can also have benefits. The member may be embarrassed within the industry if it loses after going its own way, but even such a situation can be played politically to enhance the firm's long-term position within the association. Win or lose, it is always an embarrassment to an association to be seen publicly as having a divided membership. The association may be willing to take steps to placate an aggressive member that it otherwise might have disdained. The association may be even more willing to do so should the member-company's minority position prevail in the public arena.

The Trade Association's Stake

The trade association and its staff executives have an interest at least as great as those of its members in assuring that its goals and performance meet both collective and individual member needs. In a very real sense, the association's members are its clients and must be treated as such if the association is to continue receiving their "business."

For that reason, if the member-company is unhappy with what it is getting from its association, the association executive should be, too. Either the association is not giving the company what it needs—or the company has not made a substantial effort to influence the work of the association—or, most likely, both.

If either party believes it is not winning full value from the relationship, then both are losing. The development of a "win-win" strategy requires a mutual assessment and understanding of the other's needs. It is in the trade association's interest to pursue a marketing strategy intended to satisfy the needs of each of its "clients" as fully as possible.

COALITIONS

Within "families" of like-minded groups, coalitions are quite common. Environmental, consumer, civil rights, labor, and agricultural organizations and many other categories of interest groups come together with relative ease on issues of mutual concern. So do business groups on many issues. Indeed, coalitions of companies and associations are an increasingly common mechanism to manage broad issues in Washington and in many state capitals as well.

Less common are coalitions that cross "family" lines. Clearly, however, when interest groups that do not normally find themselves on the same side of the fence can come together on an issue in a mutually supportive relationship, the credibility of the position they advocate is multiplied substantially. A business group may disagree with the League of Women Voters on public financing of elections but be able to ally with it to promote international trade. A company or trade association interested in protecting domestic industries threatened by imports from other countries could broaden its effectiveness through an alliance with the AFL-CIO.

The fact that the groups have opposed each other on other issues sometimes makes it difficult for them to leap emotional boundaries. Coalitions of this type must be organized and managed with extraordinary care and tenderness. It is easier if the parties involved keep in mind that they are not getting married but only dating, and for only as long as everyone benefits. The more diverse the coalition, the harder it is to put, and keep, together—but the greater is its public credibility.

There are two types of coalitions:

Consultative coalitions: groups with a common position on an issue that consult with each other on legislative tactics and strategy, perhaps dividing the burdens of research, intelligence collection, and direct lobbying, while coordinating with each other on utilization of their separate grass-roots systems.

Managed joint coalitions: a coalition with its own management and staff that not only utilizes the capabilities of its members but may develop its own as well. Trade associations are really coalitions of this type but on a permanent rather than ad hoc basis. (In fact, such a group is more an alliance, in the dictionary sense, than a coalition, which is why some associations began life as coalitions of this kind.)

The first step on the part of a company seeking to create and mobilize a coalition (of either kind) is to identify potential members. A good technique is one suggested by Edward A. Grefe.[2] Instead of the usual classification of groups as either friends or foes, Grefe suggests refining the first category:

Family: These are employees, shareholders, retirees, spouses. Utilization of these groups is discussed in Chapter 8, Grass-Roots Lobbying.

Friends: Customers and suppliers, and others with an economic relationship to the company (also covered in Chapter 8).

Strangers: These are groups that might be interested in the issues if they know of the measure and understand its impact. Grefe includes in this category business organizations, academicians, the press, and communities in which the company has operations (see Chapter 9, Communications).

"The family should share an emotional interest," says Grefe, "the friends an economic interest, the strangers an intellectual interest. At least that should be the beginning point of approaching one or more of these groups to become involved in the coalitions being formed."

Potential allies should be identified from among those the issue would affect: Who gains? Who loses? Who might have an interest that they might not be aware of? (For example, in the latter category might be local officials and merchants if an issue would have a significant impact in the community in which a facility is located. So might interest groups whose economic interest might not be directly involved but where there is an underlying principle that bridges to another issue that does impact on those groups.)

Thinking as broadly as possible, even group brainstorming, may be useful to develop as large a list as possible of potential allies.

The second step is recruitment of those potential allies. This is still another of those points in the government relations process where C.E.O. support is so important. C.E.O.-to-C.E.O. communications (oral or written, depending on the relationship) are much likelier to gain both attention and a successful recruit than solicitations further down the table of organization.

Whoever makes the contact, however, it is important to explain the issue in terms of its effect on the potential ally and framed from his or her point of view. "Strangers" and perhaps even some "friends" may view the solicitation with suspicion unless it is extended from an empathetic basis.

If the group being solicited to join the coalition should decline the honor, it is worthwhile to try to get a commitment of neutrality, thereby at least denying the other side a recruit.

The third step is to call an initial meeting of the group to discuss the stake of the participants in the issue, its importance for each, and the position the coalition will take. This latter point is ticklish. If the issue is clear-cut, the logical position should be obvious to everyone. But many issues are complex. The impact of the measure on Group X may be ambiguous to it for one reason or another. Group Y may be concerned with only part of the bill. Group Z may like one section of the bill and dislike another. The priority of the issue also may differ from group to group.

These matters must be discussed and resolved in a completely amicable and understanding manner or there is likely to be no coalition at all. If one member tries to push its position down the throats of the others, it may end up sitting at the conference table alone.

The fourth step concerns the nature of the coalition. Will it be a consultative coalition or a jointly managed one? Even if the former, someone is needed to provide coordinating functions—calling meetings, taking minutes, assuring that assigned responsibilities are carried out, maintaining communications among the members between meetings, etc.

If the issue is complex and important enough, then coordination and staff needs may require bringing in a manager. This could well be an executive from one of the coalition's members. But it might be preferable to retain someone independent, perhaps a consultant specializing in coalition management.[3]

The allocation of costs is another potentially touchy point. On the one hand, non-business members of the coalition may not have access to the economic resources of the corporate members. On the other, many of the non-business groups may be sensitive to appearances of being "bought." Careful and sensitive handling of this question is important.

Step five relates to tasks and functions. Once the structure and positions of the coalition have been determined, it needs to develop and carry out a government relations plan as any single organization or company would—particularly the research and analysis, direct lobbying, and grass-roots phases. The difference is that these functions will probably be divided up and apportioned among coalition members. It is important for the coalition's leadership and/or staff to identify who can be depended on to perform and who may be shaky, and to handle the division of labor thoroughly but also sensitively.[4]

Step six covers the critical elements of negotiation and compromise, important in any lobbying campaign and particularly hazardous points for coalitions. Some members will be willing to yield on points that others will not. The very timing of negotiation and compromise may become highly controversial within the coalition.

One business coalition opposing an environmental measure successfully held off enactment for ten years. As proponents began to succeed in building momentum, it became clear to some coalition members that a credible alternative was needed. The nature of the alternative became hotly controversial within the coalition, and a weak choice, at the level of the lowest common denominator, ultimately was made to keep the coalition from disintegrating. Despite vigorous pursuit of the alternative, it never achieved sufficient credibility and the coalition was ultimately defeated by its adversaries, environmentalists operating through their own coalition.

Preserving the business coalition was important, for reasons that went well beyond the legislation, but the price ultimately paid to do so—defeat on what turned out to be a very expensive issue—was higher than the coalition's value to a major segment of its members.

Sensitivity to the needs of coalition members is important, but so is leadership. Vigorous leadership willing to risk consensus to achieve the larger goal is essential to coalition success.

Step seven involves time. Some legislative issues are resolved within a short time frame. Others drag on for years. Between crises, the coalition has to be maintained, the members stroked and kept motivated and informed. This is not easy during periods when attention is distracted by more immediate concerns, but unless it is done carefully and systematically, the coalition will not be there when its existence and effective operation are most needed. Personal and organizational relationships, the awareness of the individual and shared stake, and motivation must be maintained. Unless there is a permanent staff, in all likelihood the company or group that initiated the coalition's founding will also need to accept responsibility for its continued care and feeding during the quiet periods that are typical of long-term issues.

NOTES

1. See, for example, George D. Webster, *The Law of Associations* (New York: Matthew Bender), 1986.

2. Edward A. Grefe, "Creating Winning Coalitions," *Public Affairs Challenge*, Fall 1983.

3. For an analysis of the potential pitfalls in selecting such consultants, see: Mary Ann Pires, "Initiating and Renewing Advocacy Group Contacts," *Impact*, December 1987.

4. Ten principles of coalition management are discussed in: Anne Wexler, "Coalition-Building: How to Make It Work for You Now and in the Future," *Public Affairs Review*, 1982.

8

Grass-Roots Lobbying

Glendower: "I can call spirits from the vasty deep."

Hotspur: "Why, so can I, or so can any man; but will they come when you do call for them?"

Shakespeare, *Henry IV*

With all the skills the most talented lobbyists can bring to bear, there is one thing they cannot do for most of the legislators they cultivate, and that is vote for them. Like everyone else, the lobbyist votes where he or she lives. To almost every legislator, therefore, the lobbyist is someone else's constituent.

In each legislator's eyes, the wants and needs of one's own constituents are paramount. Satisfying them is key to the legislator's "bottom line": re-election. Legislators are elected to represent their constituencies' best interests as they see them, but in practice that generally means responding to the opinions of the electorate and particularly to the views of vocal, well-organized, and active local groups.

Such groups tend to be more influential than the average citizen because, on the issues that concern them, they care more deeply than most other people do. The public at large may or may not share the views of the National Rifle Association, for instance, but it will not be a tenth as expressive about gun control as are local gun owners. "You just have a ton of grief in your district if you don't vote with them," said an Illinois congressman after a 1988 House vote on a gun issue. "They really turn up the heat locally. You just don't want to spend every district appearance talking about that one vote."[1]

In consequence, lubricating the frictions and stress points of local interest groups becomes the almost-daily task of every elected official. As the late

Senator Everett McKinley Dirksen used to say, "the oil can is mightier than the sword."

It is that principle that underpins grass-roots lobbying. By mobilizing informed local members of the organization—or the employees, retirees, and shareholders of the company—the lobbyists extend, multiply, and reinforce their efforts in every legislative district into which they can reach. Provided some understanding of the issues is reflected, 100 calls, visits, or letters from back home provide substantial and impressive support for the position the direct lobbyist is urging a legislator to adopt. Communications from 500 constituents are overwhelming, even for a member of Congress representing half a million people.

This is true whether the lawmaker is a United States senator or representative, or a state or local legislator. "All politics is local," former House Speaker Thomas P. O'Neill liked to say. So is the most effective government relations.

Certain basic principles underlie effective grass-roots organization:

- Individuals must be motivated and recruited to participate.

- They must be mobilized and trained in techniques of legislative communication.

- Issues communications to participants should be frequent, factual, and objective.

- Grass-roots messages to legislators must reflect some understanding of the issues to be credible.

- Appeals to action must be specific and clear as to issue messages, action needed, and action targets.

- Grass-roots, political action, and community relations programs should be closely coordinated.

- Participants need frequent feedback to assure them of the value and effectiveness of their efforts.

- Participants should also be encouraged to provide feedback to program managers on responses from legislators. This can be both a source of legislative intelligence and a means to assure that participants are actually in touch with their legislators.

Grass-roots programs can operate through members (or employees and other stakeholders) either as a network of individuals, or in teams. *Individuals* in a grass-roots network can be encouraged to write or call legislators on key issues. *Teams* can be used to make visits to legislators and engage in other group activities on major issues while communicating as individuals on others.

The advantage of the individual network is that it involves less training and can potentially get more people involved since less effort is required of any one of them than if they are part of an active team. Computerization also makes this approach quite easy to manage. A disadvantage is that it is often difficult to learn if requested legislative communications have actually been made.

The advantages of the group approach are that a team spirit can be engendered and that personal visits will generally make much more of an impact on the legislator. The disadvantage is that more training, organization, and other staff preparations are required, as are fairly substantial time commitments on the part of team members.

"As a rule, the larger the company, the larger the grass-roots budget is likely to be—and the more sophisticated the resulting program," comments one consultant.[2]

Most grass-roots programs utilize the individual network approach, largely for reasons of administrative ease and cost, especially in organizations with very large numbers of employees or members.

Actually, though, organizations can use both methods through a two-tiered system.

ESTABLISHING A GRASS-ROOTS CONTACT NETWORK

This is a network of individuals whose function is to communicate, primarily by mail or telephone, with legislators and other elected officials on current issues. In identifying the individuals to be invited to participate, it is important to note that different types of organizations have different solicitation and recruitment problems.

Individual Membership Organizations

Groups comprised of individual members may solicit participation by either the entire membership or perhaps only some portion of it. Selection criteria should include a record of local political connections or involvement, participation in the association's political action committee, or other indications of political awareness. Recruitment should also take political geography into account. For example, if it is not possible to get participation within all legislative districts, priority could be given to those districts represented by legislators who sit on committees important to the organization.

Trade Associations and Federations

Groups whose members are companies or other organizations have more complex problems. They not only have to determine which members to solicit but also which individuals within those member-organizations. Associations typically have a prime contact in each member-company, but that individual may not necessarily be the right person to recruit for a grass-roots network. However, the prime contact can be asked to recommend politically sensitive or well-connected colleagues who *could* be solicited. On the other hand, if sheer quantity of participants is considered preferable to qualitative criteria, the alternative is to solicit all employees or all managers or everyone else within readily identifiable categories.

Keep in mind, however, that *any* employee, not just executives, may be politically involved or at least know key legislators or officials: A blue-collar worker may be mayor of his town. A secretary may be a legislator. A clerk may have a family or neighborhood relationship with a key official.

When reaching into member-organizations, it is critical to start with a strong endorsement of support from the member's top executive.

Company Networks

Businesses have a number of stakeholders they can consider recruiting. These include:

Managers and executives.

Other employees.

Retired employees.

Shareholders.

Executives of major customers or suppliers—including such suppliers of services as advertising and public relations agencies, consultants, and law firms.

Spouses and other adult family members of the above.

As in associations, decisions must be made as to whether to solicit the participation of everyone within each category, or to segment recruitment on some political or other basis.

Motivation and Recruitment

Recruitment of volunteers for a grass-root network has to be predicated on an understanding of motivations. Here is what one corporate grass-roots program manager has to say:

What makes volunteers volunteer? Unless you understand that, your program will fail to achieve its potential.

Most volunteers simply say it feels good to volunteer. For some, it's an honor. They feel lucky in their own lives and feel that the company has been good to them. It's their way of giving something back. Some are stimulated by being at the "cutting edge" of the company, making a difference, helping to create new programs that help the company solve legislative challenges. Others may be prompted to volunteer for less lofty goals, such as fellowship, a feeling of belonging.[3]

Unfortunately, it is not always that easy. Constituencies are often hard to arouse in non-crisis situations and hard to keep aroused once the crisis has apparently passed. Arousal is easier if there is a fear of loss than when there is a promise of gain. Fear of lost income (jobs, government payments, etc.)

is a more powerful personal motivator, for example, than the anticipation of improved benefits (e.g., lower taxes or higher pay). Motivation in grass-roots programs is an element that needs constant tending at a very personal level. Members need to be reminded of their personal stakes in the issue, and why they need to act and to continue acting.

Various studies of corporate grass-roots participation have found that the higher individuals rank in the company, or the more shares stockholders own, the more likely they are to participate.[4]

Individual business owners, on the other hand, are more likely to respond if they perceive an economic stake in an issue, regardless of the size of their firms. Small business owners were highly instrumental in defeating or modifying a large number of union-backed federal issues in 1988, for example, through grass-roots legislative communications organized by business associations. Speaking of one such issue, an AFL-CIO lobbyist said: "The small-business community—they're the ones that did that bill in. [The associations] were able to effectively scare the hell out of every small businessman in the country.... Senators who told me they were sympathetic to the bill did an about-face."[5]

Once a target list of volunteers has been compiled, the individuals have to be requested to serve as members of the network. The essential word here is *requested*. Even within a company, individuals cannot realistically be commanded to engage in a program of this sort. The principle that "when you have them by the throat, their hearts and minds will follow" may possibly produce results in the short term but after a while will breed only resentment and foot-dragging. (Compulsion is not remotely possible, of course, in voluntary membership organizations.)

The exception to this principle is the case of certain business executives (e.g., plant managers) who have been assigned political and community relations responsibilities as part of their jobs. To be effective, such responsibilities must be explicitly part of both their job descriptions and salary-related performance evaluations.

The most effective beginning is a solicitation letter from a senior executive who is well known and highly regarded—preferably, the C.E.O. in a company, the chief staff or elected officer in a membership organization. The letter should invite participation in an important cause: utilizing the power of citizen communications to persuade elected officials to adopt sound and sensible public policies (however the group or company wishes to define such policies). The letter should make clear whether the network will seek to influence legislation at the federal, state, or local levels, or some combination of them.

The letter should also explain that the cause is important, the effort requested not burdensome, and that clear information on the issues will be provided often so that participants in the network will be able to communicate intelligently with their legislators. The network should be given a special name, e.g., "XYZ Corporation's Grass-Roots Democracy Council." A special letterhead can be designed for use in newsletters and action appeals to help promote personal identification with the network.

Although it is useful to describe the kinds of issues grass-roots network participants will be asked to write their legislators about, it is best not to ask for action in the initial recruitment letter. But do ask for the pledge: a form (with a postage-paid envelope, of course), which the individual signs, agreeing to be a participant—perhaps for a limited time period (such as two years, the length of most legislative terms) so that the participant does not feel that he or she is volunteering for a life sentence. (Invitations to re-enlist can always be extended later.)

A letter by itself will not draw an enormous response rate. That rate can be significantly increased, though, by follow-up telephone calls from a peer to reduce the hesitation and uncertainty many people will feel about participating in a program that may involve unfamiliar activity. The follow-up call is an opportunity to provide answers to questions, encouragement, and a general increase in comfort level.

This requires the establishment of a solicitation committee, broadly representative of all those being solicited. Ideal members of such a committee are individuals well known and highly regarded among their peers.

Wherever possible, it is valuable to supplement the written invitation and follow-up calls with a meeting at which the cordial but low-key invitation to join is reiterated, explanations of what is involved are given, and opportunities provided for questions and discussions.

The list of individuals agreeing to participate should be computerized, including name and address; local, state, and federal legislative district numbers; political contacts and activity; particular issue interests and sensitivities, and other useful data. All this information can be requested on the return-mail form; note that legislative district identification may need to be researched by staff since many people do not know the districts in which they live. It is important to think through ahead of time what other kinds of helpful data could be requested without arousing concerns about invasion of privacy.

Training and Orientation

Unless they have considerable familiarity with politics and government, most members of the grass-roots network will need information about the legislative process, striking a balance between what the individual has to know and how much all but the most committed are likely actually to read. A booklet could be specially written for network members, but it may be possible (and certainly cheaper) to obtain quantities of educational publications prepared for this purpose by Congress and most state legislatures. Groups such as the League of Women Voters are also good sources.

This material could also be included in a training manual or handbook that gives pointers on how to communicate with legislators, how to develop relationships with them and their staffs, and basic information about the company or industry (sales, employment, etc.). If this material is published in looseleaf format, it can easily be updated and sections reserved for federal, state, and local government directories, issue fact sheets, action appeals, etc.

In some cases, orientation seminars should be considered for network members if their locations make that feasible. In the case of employees and other company stakeholders, such a seminar could be held in a company facility during the lunch hour or immediately after office hours.

The seminar should be led by the senior government relations or public affairs executive of the sponsoring company or organization, assisted perhaps by lobbyists or others on the staff. Including the local member of Congress or state legislator as a guest speaker will increase the appeal of the seminar and boost attendance. Having a legislator provide the briefing on how laws are made and influenced not only lends authority to the seminar, but also provides the legislator with a welcome opportunity to speak to a group of constituents; an honorarium to the legislator may be politically useful but probably not essential.

A seminar of this kind should supplement the written material that participants will need for later reference.

To avoid overloading participants with more information than most are likely to be able to absorb at one time, detailed issue briefings are not a good addition to the orientation seminar, although thumbnail descriptions of a small number of issues may be useful. A packet of position papers can be provided for later reading.

The orientation seminar should be renewed at least annually—not only for new network participants but also as a refresher for veterans.

Communicating to the Network

The time to begin communication with network participants on the issues is *not* when an issue has heated up to the point that an urgent action appeal is needed. Participants need advance information on what the issue is all about and how it affects them. They also need time to absorb the information. Good communications increase interest and cooperation, and build a sense of civic legitimacy about communicating with lawmakers.

Communications can be in the form of a newsletter or a personalized letter, preferably from the C.E.O. Even when people can recognize computer-generated letters, a letter addressed personally to them—especially when first names are used in the salutation—is probably the most effective medium. The organization's issue position papers should be updated and provided to network participants from time to time.

The mails are not the only means available for communicating with the network. FAX equipment is becoming widespread in many business offices and provides the benefit of immediate receipt. So do electronic mail and similar computerized communications systems if personnel within the company or organization network have access to the necessary equipment.

Companies and other groups that find it feasible to hold orientation seminars might supplement these sessions with periodic meetings at which legislators or other officials are invited to speak on issues. During election campaigns, opposing candidates might also be invited, either to debate or at separate meetings. Such events are always popular and well attended.

Whatever communications media are used, there are several criteria for presentation of legislative information:

1. *Communications should be consistent and frequent.* If a newsletter is started, it should not be dropped after an issue or two. Recipients should be kept informed and up-to-date as often as needed, but if six months go by without receiving anything they may well assume the network is defunct or that they are no longer part of it. Some communications should go out at least bi-monthly to maintain interest and involvement, more often when there is much news. Old information is as stale in a newsletter as in a newspaper.

2. *Information about the issues must always be factual and objective.* There is nothing wrong with presenting the organization's point of view, but respect for those in the grass-roots network requires that the position of the other side also be fairly presented. One way to do this is in the form of rebuttal arguments:
   a. "Our bill would achieve the following...
   b. "Opponents argue that the bill is not needed because...
   c. "However, they fail to realize that..."

3. *Two-way communications help make network participants feel more involved.* They should be encouraged to reply to network communications with their own views. Of course, a letter from a participant should always receive a prompt and considerate response.

Even more effective might be an annual poll of network members, asking for their views on important issues and perhaps even inviting them to propose issues for inclusion. For example, employees who are working mothers might express interest in child care legislation; retirees might want to know about health issues; shareholders might be concerned about a new tax bill. Even if such issues are not ones in which the company is involved, it would be no great effort to include information on them in the newsletter from time to time, thereby further contributing to a sense of personal involvement.

Action Appeals

The payoff for its investment in developing and maintaining the network comes when the sponsoring company or organization needs grass-roots support on its issues. Not every issue lends itself to grass-roots appeals. An issue with emotional aspects will produce a better response than a very technical one.

The time for an action appeal may be when a bill is at a crucial stage of consideration by a legislative committee, or is coming up for floor debate and voting, or at other critical points. The appeal for action can take either of two forms:

The General Alert

"Now that the bill is scheduled for legislative action, you may wish to inform your legislator what you think." The network participant, having been well briefed in past communications, is encouraged in low-key fashion to express his or her own views. Not all who write will necessarily endorse the position of the grass-roots network's sponsor, but the vast majority will—and the few who do not underscore the fairness of the information provided by the sponsoring company or organization.

The Specific Appeal

This is the more common approach. It requests network participants to get in touch with their legislators and convey as their own personal views those of the organization: "Tell Senator X why you think he should vote for S. 1234. Here are some arguments you can use your own language to express . . . ."

Note the essential elements of the specific appeal:

1. Who to write or call and how to reach them.
2. The name of the issue and bill number.
3. The position to be expressed on the issue.
4. Talking points to be used, in the writer's (or caller's) own words—backed up where possible with personal experiences that can lend substantial credibility to the message.

All this information can be communicated in computerized personal letters to network participants. Software programs readily available permit coding of legislative or congressional districts and name and address of legislators, so that the personalized letter can also tell the recipient specifically who he or she needs to contact and how to reach them. Such programs also allow the sender to contact selected portions of the network by manipulating almost any number of variables.

Let's suppose that a company wishes to generate mail from its grass-roots network to members of a particular legislative committee before it votes on a particular bill. Assuming the variable data have been correctly programmed and coded, a number of different, highly personalized versions of the letter to the network are possible:

1. The name and address of the particular legislator representing that particular recipient.

2. Different versions of the letter, depending on whether the legislator's position on the bill is pro, con, or unknown.

3. Still different versions to employees, managers, retirees, and shareholders—and to any desired subgroups among them—suggesting, perhaps, different motivating arguments.

4. Different versions yet, depending on whether or not the constituent is known to have a relationship with the legislator.

5. Exclusion from the mailing of grass-roots network participants whose legislators are not on the committee—or another version of the letter suggesting that lawmakers be asked to lobby their colleagues who are on the committee.

6. Different signatures on different letter versions, depending on whose name will have the most impact.

This is not to say that every mailing should be this complex, but only that computers can provide this kind of flexibility, and more. (Chapter 11 discusses in more detail new technologies available for direct mail communications.)

Tips on Computerized Communications

To maximize response rates, seek a personalized appearance to letters. Use letter-quality printers such as laser or ink-jet printers. Dot-matrix and many daisy-wheel printers are dead giveaways that a computer was used.

Addresses should be printed directly on envelopes. Avoid labels. Omit computer codes.

Personalize the salutation. "Dear Mr. Jones," *not* "Dear Friend," "Colleague," etc. "Dear Tom" is, of course, better yet—but only if the signer knows the recipient. Many people are irritated by being "first-named" by someone they don't know.

The body of the letter should also appear as much as possible as a personal, and personally typed, letter. Content should also be personalized, but do it naturally. Shun language like "you and your neighbors on White Street in Hometown"; you are not selling magazine subscriptions. For the same reason, avoid headline- and flash-type effects.

If letters cannot be hand-signed (although secretaries and others can help), utilize personalized automatic signing equipment—not the kind used to sign checks. Some laser printers can also "sign" letters.

Some organizations enclose a postage-paid postcard to be returned when the letter is sent, or ask for blind copies of correspondence, so that they will know which legislators are being written (and, of course, see who in the network is actually working). Keep a record of which legislators have heard from which constituents, a useful aid for the direct lobbyist.

Follow-Up and Feedback

Most legislators will respond with a note of acknowledgement. This letter may say only that the legislator will take the writer's views into account in deciding how to vote—or it may say that the legislator is already inclined to a particular position. If network participants get information of this latter type, encourage them to pass it along; the organization's direct lobbyists may find it helpful intelligence.

A note of thanks should always be sent to each network participant whom the organization knows has gotten in touch with his or her legislator. Either in this thank you note or in the newsletter, the network should be told as promptly as possible what the outcome was on the legislative decision.

Expressions of thanks to legislators if their votes were favorable should be strongly encouraged.

Feedback is important to maintain interest and morale. Recognition from a manager or a peer will encourage the network participant to be even more effective in the future.

To be credible, grass-roots communications have to demonstrate an understanding of what the issue is about and how it would affect the constituent. This is where the value of keeping network participants well informed as issues develop pays off in *quality* messages. Legislators don't expect constituents to be issue experts, but an uninformed or canned message will obviously not have a fraction of the impact of a call or letter from individuals who know what the issue is about and how they will be affected.

Negative Techniques

Devices all too commonly used in promoting legislative mail by some organizations are the pre-printed letter, canned postcard, or signed petition— *all to be avoided like the plague.* The purpose of a grass-roots program is to engender individual involvement and numerous personal messages to legislators, not to demonstrate how many identical pellets can be fired out of the organization's legislative shotgun. Most legislators are turned off by this technique and some even have been known to use it against the organization.

Petitions may have some value with local officials on strictly local issues, e.g., a town zoning matter. They should be shunned for other uses. Legislators realize that most people will sign any worthwhile-appearing petition. That, after all, is how most legislative candidates get on the ballot!

ESTABLISHING A LEGISLATIVE ACTION TEAM

A second tier of a grass-roots system is the *Legislative Action Team* (LAT): individuals working at the grass roots to help influence public policy through *personal* visits with targeted legislators.

Recruitment and Training

Recruitment of team members is made in much the same way as the individual grass-roots network. However, because team members will be communicating with legislators in person rather than by mail, their selection must be made with some care. Team members need outgoing, persuasive personalities and a keen sensitivity to the political and legislative process. Remember that these are people who will be representing the sponsoring organization when they meet with legislators.

Selection should begin by identifying those legislators whose views and actions are critical to the sponsoring company or association: legislative leaders and the chairmen and members of key committees.

LAT members should then be sought in those congressional or state or local legislative districts represented by the targeted legislators. (While it may be desirable to have LAT members in every district, in practice only the largest and most broadly based membership organizations are likely to be able to achieve this goal.)

Invitations to participate should be quite personal: an initial telephone call from a respected figure in the organization or company—followed by a letter of explanation and invitation—probably followed by a second telephone call. Because team members are being asked to devote much more time than participants in the individual network, they need that much more personal attention at all phases.

Training needs to be thorough—a seminar is important, backed up if possible by a manual of legislative information and issue fact sheets or position papers. Team members need to understand not just the broad outline of legislative procedure, but also the fine details and political background. They also need to know a great deal about the issues because they will be questioned about them during their meetings with legislators and staffs.

Organization and Communications

The team will require staff support and coordination from the sponsoring group or company. Working as part of the organization's government relations staff, coordinators will be responsible for:

1. Organizing the team and assuring adequate membership on an on-going basis.
2. Keeping team members well informed about the status of the issues on which they are focusing as well as pertinent political developments.
3. Mobilizing them for action as required by legislative needs.
4. Assisting in planning and implementing major meetings and functions of the teams or, if necessary, carrying out the organization of such events directly.

Personal recognition is important. Ideally, each statewide organization should be provided its own letterhead with the names of state and regional chairmen. This letterhead should be used for internal communications to and among the teams' structure. (Communications to legislators and government officials should always be on each member's own personal or business stationery.)

An awards program for distinguished achievement should be considered, perhaps at recognition dinners, using plaques, pins, and other recognition devices.

Communications to legislative action teams must provide several different kinds of news:

- Issue briefings and legislative news, similar to that provided the members of the individual network but probably on a more frequent basis—as often as weekly during heated legislative periods—and by telephone, FAX, or electronic mail when crises arise.
- Information about relevant political matters, e.g., shifts in legislative committee chairmanships or memberships.
- News of forthcoming team events.
- Recognition of achievements of individual team members.

Team Events

A major purpose of the legislative action team is to show strength, concern, and involvement on major issues on the part of the sponsoring organization and its members, or the sponsoring company and its stakeholders. The team should concentrate on a fairly small number of top priority issues, perhaps even only one if its importance is overriding.

The most effective use of team members will be visits to legislators in their offices at the capital, to make the case for their company's or organization's position on the issues. Properly briefed (and sometimes accompanied) by the group's lobbyists, team members "from back home" can make an impressive and occasionally even overwhelming impact on the legislators they visit, particularly if the lawmakers know that the team members are going to continue to be involved and are watching carefully what happens on the issue and what each legislator is doing about it.

These visits can be of two kinds. One is almost a mass rally (if the organization's membership is large enough to produce such an event) in which hundreds and perhaps even thousands of people, often adorned with slogans on political-style buttons or wearing distinctive clothing, descend on the capital for an annual visit to press their case on their vital issues. The second kind is a series of frequent, quieter visits by small groups to lobby their legislators.

These visits, of whichever kind, must be organized in the closest consultation with the organization's lobbyists on the scene. The whole objective is to back up their efforts on the issues with demonstrations of grass-roots concern and strength, not to shunt the lobbyists aside.

Variations on these visits at the capital can also take place back in the districts. Congress and the legislatures of the larger states are now in virtually year-round sessions, but members are usually home a day or two a week at even the busiest times, and more during recesses. Members of other legislative bodies may be even more accessible. Almost all are available for conferences in their offices, or meetings over breakfast or lunch to hear constituents' views.

Not all meetings need to be "one-on-one." Sometimes it is useful to arrange meetings of team members in groups with individual legislators or with small groups of lawmakers. Depending on the purpose and context of the meeting, a delegation of team members can demonstrate strength and commitment. Another advantage is that members provide each other with mutual support and reinforcement.

Supplementing team visits are other useful events or functions:

- *Annual legislative dinners or receptions* to which lawmakers (and often their staffs) from particular states or regions are invited to break bread or bend elbows with team members. Team members can help promote attendance among legislators by follow-up notes or calls after the formal invitations from the sponsoring organization.

  The value of these events, particularly receptions, is the opportunity they provide for extensive socializing and, of course, lobbying. Speeches and receptions tend not to mix well so that if a few brief talks are needed—as perhaps at an awards event to which legislators are invited—a sit-down dinner is the better medium. Socializing is difficult at dinners, though, but can be preceded by a reception, thus providing the best of both worlds.

  Such events must be scheduled long in advance because they are increasingly popular among interest groups and legislators' social calendars are generally overflowing.

- *Plant, store, or facility visits by legislators.* These can be quite useful especially when used to demonstrate the effect a particular bill would have on operations. Legislators also welcome the chance to meet employees, whether or not they give a talk. If a talk is to be given, a few well-planted questions and comments can help underscore the position the organization wishes the lawmaker to adopt.

  Such visits need not be limited to legislators. Other elected officials and regulators may find it helpful to visit an operation in order to observe the effects a proposed law or regulation would have.

- *Annual legislative conferences for team members.* This provides another opportunity for issue briefings and meetings with legislators, and can be coordinated with a dinner or reception. The conference agenda can include a mix of staff reports on issues, panels of legislators and regulators, speeches by top elected officials, etc.

  Team members should make every effort to get as close to their legislators as possible: socializing with them, contributing and participating in their campaigns, and doing whatever is legitimately possible to build not just constituent relationships but personal friendships.

  That includes expressions of thanks whenever the legislator votes as the constituent recommended. When they do not, a very low-key note of reproach may also be appropriate to let them know they are being watched—but threats or other angry (and therefore antagonistic) statements should always be avoided.

A Grass-Roots Lobby at Work

An illustration of the power of a grass-root lobby occurred in 1988 when independent insurance agents descended on Washington to oppose, successfully, federal legislation that would allow banks to diversify into insurance lines. "In a two-day period, 720 agents representing every Congressional district camped on Capitol Hill, " *The New York Times* reported.[6] The drive was organized by the Independent Insurance Agents of American, which has a membership of 126,000.

(Even a small response rate can be impressive: With less than one percent of its members attending the association's conference, *The Times* could still say that "a phone call can bring the insurance hordes into Washington.")

Briefed ahead of time by friendly congressional speakers and association staff, the agents used lunches, receptions, and dinners to meet with state delegations of congressmen as well as private meetings with individual legislators, urging them to keep banks out of the insurance business.

The agents' effectiveness is a tribute to their salesmanship, even though their PAC contributions were only about two-thirds those of the bankers, *The Times* said. Conceded a banking lobbyist: "The agents are salespeople, individual entrepreneurs and they react in numbers. Their style is to be very aggressive. You don't negotiate with them."

COORDINATION WITH POLITICAL AND COMMUNITY PROGRAMS

Both types of grass-roots efforts should be meshed with other programs that promote political involvement or participation in community affairs where these exist.

If employees or members are actively involved in a variety of civic organizations and causes, the contacts they develop through community participation can be a strong asset in their grass-roots lobbying efforts. For example, if a bill would have a substantial impact on a company's local investments and employment, local officials could well be enlisted to aid in lobbying appropriate lawmakers on the issue.

Similarly, if a program to promote employee political activity exists, its participants already know top political and elected personalities. Their ability to constitute an effective lobbying force is already in place.

Conversely, if such a program does not exist, the grass-roots program provides both ample evidence of why one is desirable as well as the potential base to start up a political participation program.

A similar meshing can exist with respect to a PAC or other political fund-raising program.

SINGLE-ISSUE TELEMARKETING

Still another approach to grass-roots lobbying involves solicitation by specialized consulting firms retained by a company or other interest group to promote mass communications—typically mailgrams—to legislators from their constituents on a particular issue.

Using such sources as organizational membership lists or industrial or community directories, calls are made to names within targeted legislative districts to discuss the issue. The consultant explains the pending legislation and how the individual would be affected by it. The consultant then seeks permission to send a mailgram in the individual's name to his or her legislator, at the same time also soliciting pertinent personal or business details that can be used to individualize the communication.

Positive citizen response rates are reported quite high by practitioners of this technique, which can generate large amounts of legislative mail in a short time on specific issues. Of course, the approach must be both genuine and memorable enough that the citizen will confirm his or her interest in the issue if the legislator should inquire about it.

The technique is expensive, possibly risky, and should therefore be utilized only in major legislative emergencies. This is single-issue solicitation telemarketing that can produce a large volume of one-time legislative mail on a crisis issue. Note that this approach builds no "equity" in an on-going program of grass-roots citizen participation, so that the next time a crisis erupts, the same effort must be carried out all over again. Consideration should therefore be given to limiting its use to areas in which the organization has no significant membership or involvement.

MODEL GRASS-ROOTS COMMUNICATIONS

Following are three models: a model invitation, a general action appeal, and a specific action appeal.

1. Model Invitation

XYZ CORPORATION
Bigtown, New Ohio
Office of the Chairman

Mr. Thomas H. Jensen
515 Cedar Street
North Bigtown, New Ohio

Dear Tom:

This is a cordial invitation to you to join in an important new civic endeavor that XYZ is sponsoring. We're calling it the Grass-Roots Democracy Council, and it's a program to enlist active members of the XYZ community in an effort to communicate with our federal and state legislators more effectively than we ever have before.

There are many issues before Congress and the New Ohio legislature that affect us in a variety of ways: as businesspeople, as investors and shareholders, and as taxpayers and citizens. Too often, we have failed to let our legislators know what we think about those issues while they're still making up their own minds. They have an obligation to represent us, true, but we also have an obligation to share our views and experiences with them.

Because I know how active you and some of our other retirees have always been in the community, I'm inviting you to be a part of this new civic campaign. What we're asking you to do is express your willingness to write or call five lawmakers to tell them your thoughts on particular issues when circumstances warrant.

These five are New Ohio's two United States senators, the representative from North Bigtown's congressional district, and your state senator and assemblyman.

To help keep you, and the other participating retirees, employees, and shareholders completely informed on the issues, we're beginning a special newsletter, *The Insider's Report*, which will be prepared from material provided by our state and federal lobbyists and trade associations and sent only to members of the Grass-Roots Democracy Council. It will not only discuss the issues that we think are important, but also cover issues that you and other council members have a special interest in; just let us know.

Then, from time to time, we'll be in touch to let you know when you might write or call these legislators to have the greatest impact on important issues.

Please sign and return the enclosed card to let me know if you're willing to be part of this exciting new program. Incidentally, there's space on the form for you to indicate, if you care to, how well you know these and other legislators. That would be very helpful information to us in managing this program effectively.

I do hope you'll join us in this important effort, Tom. My best to Dorothy—who might also enjoy being a part of this!

Sincerely,

Harvey Howard
Chairman & C.E.O.

P.S. We're having a meeting on Thursday, the 14th, at 5:30 in the employee cafeteria to explain this program and answer any questions you and the other invitees may have. Senator Seymour Solon will also be there to discuss how our laws are made. Can you and Dorothy join us?

2. Model Action Appeal—General Alert

XYZ CORPORATION
Bigtown, New Ohio
Office of the Vice President—Public Affairs

Mr. Thomas H. Jensen
515 Cedar Street
North Bigtown, New Ohio

Dear Tom:

For the past several months, *The Insider's Report* has been telling you about H.R. 1234, the bill to increase import duties on a number of raw materials imported from Europe. This would increase the cost we pay for one of our essential raw materials, black wicker chips, which we can obtain only from European sources.

The sponsors of this bill believe that the United States has to take steps to force the Europeans to open up more of their markets to American products, and that the only effective way to negotiate is to make it harder for Common Market exports to sell in this country. The bill raises trade barriers on about twenty commodities to do this.

Opponents of H.R. 1234 believe trade barriers of this kind are a bad way to negotiate—that raising barriers is no way to remove them. Of course, you're familiar from the newsletter with the other arguments opponents have used, including XYZ's own concern about what this bill would do to our production costs and the resulting impact on our domestic markets.

The House Commerce Committee is scheduled to consider H.R. 1234 on February 24. As you know, Congressman Warren Wisdom from your district is an influential member of this committee.

Whatever your personal views may be on this bill, now would be the best time to share them with Congressman Wisdom. (If you'd care to send me a copy, I'd enjoy seeing whatever you may say to Representative Wisdom—and also his reply to you.)

My thanks and best wishes.

Sincerely,

Marvin Miller
Vice President

3. Model Specific Action Appeal

NATIONAL MANGLERS ASSOCIATION
Washington, D.C.

TO: Mr. Harris Fellowes
        Clench Mangler Industries, Inc.
        Windward, Minneconsin
FROM: Wendell Philpotte, Executive Vice President

This is an urgent appeal for your help with Congressman Stephen Statute in connection with H.R. 1234, the raw material import tax. The House Commerce Committee has scheduled a vote on this bill for February 24, and Rep. Statute remains uncommitted.

Please make these points to him, putting the following in your own words:

1. Recognize that the sponsors of this bill are well intentioned in their desire to take constructive action against the trade barriers erected by the Europeans.

2. However, the import restrictions that H.R. 1234 would impose in terms of higher duties on raw materials are not a workable negotiating tactic with the Europeans.

3. American companies like Clinch Manglers will be hurt because of the cost increases H.R. 1234 will impose. (If you can document this damage with numbers, so much the better.)

4. These increased costs will eventually be passed on to consumers, raising prices and adding to domestic inflation.

5. Thus, it is ultimately the American consumer, not the Europeans, who will be penalized by this bill.

6. A better approach would be to allow U.S. trade negotiators to work out an effective arrangement in their discussions with their European counterparts.

The sooner you can write—or call—Congressman Statute, the better. Please be sure to let us have a copy of your letter and whatever reply you may receive.

Many thanks for your help on this. If this bill should be approved by the Commerce Committee, we will probably ask you and other members of NMA's legislative action teams to visit the Congressman and his colleagues to lobby them in person on this issue.

NOTES

1. Quoted in *The New York Times*, September 22, 1988.
2. Mary Ann Pires, "Fertile Fields," *Public Relations Journal*, November 1986.
3. June Ebner, "Grassroots Key to Success: Finding (and Keeping) Volunteers," *Impact*, May 1988 (published by the Public Affairs Council).
4. Pires, op. cit.
5. *The Wall Street Journal*, October 3, 1988.
6. *The New York Times*, March 29, 1988.

9

Communications

Good government obtains when those who are near are made happy, and those who are far off are attracted.

Confucius

Not every truth is the better for showing its face undisguised; and often silence is the wisest thing for a man to heed.

Pindar

Government relations is a communications process. Other chapters in this book cover the techniques of communicating issue positions to those who write and enforce laws and regulations, and the use of other techniques and leverage to amplify the impact and effectiveness of the message.

Government relations is also a political process. Politics is a system of complex relationships, formal and informal, dependent on a vast array of communications for their establishment and maintenance.

Politics is the pursuit and use of power.

Lobbying is the use of relationships and influence to affect public policy.

Communications is the means through which both politics and lobbying achieve their goals.

This chapter seeks to bring together in a cohesive framework the different communications modes and target audiences discussed in various parts of this book.

The essence of education was once described as a teacher sitting at one end of a log with the pupil at the other. In the same sense, it is the politician and the voter who sit at opposite ends of the political log.

But lobbying communications is more complex. The process may start out with the lobbyist and the lawmaker straddling the two ends of the log, but soon the lobbyist gets up. He may yield his place to a constituent of the legislator, then to one of her campaign contributors, later perhaps to an ally and, afterward, to another government official influential with the legislator. While they are talking, the lobbyist moves around discussing the issue with legislative staff aides and journalists. He may engage in political activity, either to reinforce the legislative relationship or possibly with the thought of re-placing the lawmaker on the log with someone friendlier and more sym-pathetic. Finally he comes back to the log and negotiates the best deal he can with the official sitting at the other end.

All the time, the lobbyist has been communicating with those who make the decisions and those who can help shape the forms the decision can take. Let's look first at those with whom he has been talking, and then examine the media he uses to talk with them.

TARGET AUDIENCES

The most important government relations audiences are those who make and then administer the laws:

- Legislators
- Executive branch officials
- Regulators
- Key staff aides

Then, there are the intermidiaries—constituents and others who can help carry the message between the lobbyist's interest group and the officials who make and execute public policy.

'Family':

- Members (in the case of associations)
- Shareholders
- Executives and managers
- Employees
- Retirees
- Spouses

'Friends':

- Trade associations and similar groups
- Suppliers

- Attorneys, banks, advertising agents, public relations firms, consultants, etc.
- Customers and dealers

Other allies, actual or potential:

- Groups sharing whatever the natural community of interest may be—other business organizations, other labor unions, other environmental or consumer groups, etc.
- Groups outside the natural community of interest who still may be enlisted as allies on particular issues.
- The press—general and trade—print and electronic.
- Local community officials and opinion leaders.
- Intellectuals—academics and "think tanks."
- The general public—perhaps most important of all.

COMMUNICATIONS MEDIA AND TECHNIQUES

A vast array of communications and public relations approaches can be used with these different audiences, as appropriate to each. Development of a communications strategy is a critical first step.

Strategies can be developed for each issue on an ad hoc basis, but the organization's communications will be far more effective if it has a comprehensive outreach strategy tied into its overall business plan and objectives. Such a strategy will ensure that all the organization's messages mesh in content and tone, regardless of the issue and the audience to whom they are addressed. A communications strategy for a company or any other organization should deal with such questions as these:

- What its communications goals are—what essential corporate or organizational interests it needs to advance.
- What public image it desires, and how that image should be fine-tuned among different target audiences. How to ensure that its actions and programs will receive understanding and approval among these audiences.
- When to speak out, to whom, and on what topics. Some companies, for example, may prefer to take a low public profile, speaking publicly on just one or two issues of the highest priority. Or a union may have a policy of avoiding public comment on issues that put it at odds with another union, in the name of labor solidarity.
- How to coordinate its public voice, a particular problem for muti-divisional companies.

Audience research, including market and opinion surveys, is a valuable prelude to communications strategy development to determine how different audiences perceive the organization initially. Associations will find it helpful to know how the members perceive the group. Companies can obtain data about how managers, employees, and other internal constituencies view the firm, its policies, and its issue positions—important input before launching a PAC or grass-roots program. Both kinds of organizations may want to probe the attitudes of opinion leaders and government officials before constructing a communications program to reach them.

As in every other aspect of government relations and public affairs, the support and involvement of the C.E.O. and others in top management are critical in devising and executing communications strategies and programs. Not only is the chief executive's enthusiastic blessing essential to success in external (and indeed internal) communications, but increasingly C.E.O.s are becoming their organizations' principal spokespeople and advocates on public issues.

Within the framework of the strategy and as appropriate to the issue and the audience, following are some basic communications devices:

Newsletters:

Informative publications distributed at fairly frequent intervals to grass-roots program members, PAC contributors, selected allies. Because computerization facilitates fine-tuning of newsletter distribution, it is both possible and useful to vary the content and style of the newsletter to different audiences. Different issues could be discussed with different recipients, according to their interests. Political topics, for example, can be discussed in depth with more sophisticated groups (e.g., executives, PAC supporters) or with retirees who have more leisure time.

Newsletters usually are intended to motivate as much as to inform. While accuracy is vital, a dry recitation of dates and data is deadly. Like the content, the style and tone of a newsletter should reflect the interests of the audience. The same issue information may need to be interpreted differently to retirees then to active employees; franchisees and other small business owners tend to be more responsive to an emotional tone, even on economic issues, then corporate executives do. The purpose of the message is not only to convey facts but also to stimulate a sense of personal involvement in the issue on which action sooner or later will be requested.

Personalized Communications:

A carefully executed personalized letter is a very potent medium. After all, everyone likes to get personal mail, especially from the person at the top. Personalized letters are useful in connection with grass-roots programs, messages to allies and thought leaders, certain PAC communications, community relations, and civic messages, etc. Readily available computer software facilitates a high degree of personalization so that personalized letters, like newsletters, can be finely tuned to the interests of the recipients.

To be credible, however, the letter should look and read like a letter and not the fancy product of a well-trained computer. Form and content should be guided by purpose. A letter appealing for legislative action needs to be constructed quite differently than one appealing for funds. Direct mail consultants can advise about such matters, although it is important to be sure that the communications they produce reflect, in both tone and content, a message with which the signer of the letter is comfortable (see Chapter 11 for more on this topic).

Position Papers:

Moderately detailed analyses of the issue, its pros and cons, and the rationale underlying the organization's position can have multiple uses, by media spokespeople, lobbyists, and internal or membership communicators. *White papers* are a more comprehensive, research-oriented version of the position papers, perhaps suitable for academics, legislative researchers, and other analysts and opinion leaders. *Fact sheets* are a terser, more simplified version for use with the press and for grass-roots communications. (See Chapter 3 for more information on position papers and white papers.)

Brochures:

Position papers or white papers can be printed as brochures to present the organization's case in a visually attractive form, perhaps with graphics or other illustrations. Uses include mailings to legislators, other public officials, allies, and opinion leaders—distribution to participants in grass-roots and PAC programs—and inclusion in press kits.

News Releases:

Announcements should be made to the press of organizational developments, issue positions, issue-oriented research findings, and other news. Publication of a white paper would merit a news release, for instance, if it contains new information such as results of an opinion survey or research project.

Apart from the subject of the announcement itself, the value of news releases is their promotion of media coverage, which can not only make the organization better known to the public but can also help influence its 'image,' the way people think of the company or group. For this reason, there is enormous competition for good media coverage. No one can be sure that the press will report the news the way the organization wishes, but two things help—relationships and newsworthiness.

Good relationships with reporters and editors, in both the electronic and the print media should be cultivated. Public relations professionals develop relationships and reputations as helpful sources of accurate and reliable information, just as lobbyists do. Those relationships, built over time, can increase the likelihood of press coverage and fair reporting.

The newsworthiness of the announcement and professionalism of the press release are equally important, as is correct emphasis of the information presented in the release. Some people write the way they tell a joke, holding the punch line until the very end. But reporters (and readers) sometimes never get past the first paragraph or two. For that reason, releases or other announcements should always lead off with the most important points, followed by identification of the announcer and then with appropriate amplification and documentation. Here is what such a press release might look like:

RELEASE DATE:	For release: March 8
PRESS CONTACT:	Contact: Jerry Flacke (123-4567)
HEAD:	*PUBLIC OPPOSES LASER PEN TAX*
LEAD:	West Carolinians oppose a tax on laser pens by a two-to-one margin, a new poll has found. The same survey also found the public against new excise taxes on any consumer products, by a large majority.
ANNOUNCER:	Results of the survey were released by John Chief, chairman of the Laser Pen Corporation, and Harry Furrgold, president of Furrgold Stores and chairman of a coalition of consumer, labor, and business groups that sponsored the survey.
AMPLIFICATION:	Of those interviewed, 67% said they opposed bills being considered by the state legislature to place an excise tax on laser pens and other consumer products. Of those polled, 55% disagree with legislators that "luxury" products should be taxed.
DOCUMENTATION:	The survey was taken by Trot & Canter, Inc., an opinion research company. Trot & Canter interviewed 750 people, chosen at random to represent a cross section of the state's population. [Editors: Survey report is attached.]

There is, of course, much more to an effective press release than this sketchy model indicates, but it does set forth basic elements and style.

Press kits might include a news release, issue brochures or fact sheets, background information on the organization, etc.

Press Conferences:

These are meetings with reporters—national, regional, local, or trade, as appropriate—for important announcements. Press kits should be distributed. Press conferences need to be prepared with extra care since reporters will usually pose the most difficult questions they can, often in an aggressive manner intended to build a good story—good for the media, not necessarily for the organization.

Television and Radio Interviews:

Interviews are excellent but also potentially dangerous opportunities to explain the organization's issue positions. They are valuable because the spokesperson for the company or association can explain the group's position to a wide public audience without the problems of press interpretation. The hazard lies in the risk of a misstatement or poor answer to a tough question. *Debates* with issue opponents can be just as valuable and at least as hazardous. (Those who doubt the risks may recall the damage inflicted on the presidential candidacies of Richard Nixon in 1960, Gerald Ford in 1976, Jimmy Carter in 1980, and Michael Dukakis in 1988 as a result of debates with their opponents.) *Actualities*, taped or telephoned issue statements provided to radio stations for use in newscasts, are useful and much safer, though less exciting.

Editorial Briefings:

Meetings with media editorial writers help to explain the organization's views on the issue, usually preceded or accompanied by substantial supporting data. A supportive editorial can often be very influential with legislators and officials.

Third-Party Columns:

A supportive column, a guest editorial, or an op-ed page article by a well-known expert or celebrity with no official connection with the organization can be pure gold. Almost as good is a similar piece under the by-line of a company or association officer. *Letters to the editor* may also generate attention.

Issue Advertising:

This is the single most effective way of stating the position of the company or organization unfiltered by the press. Also called advocacy advertising, the technique was perfected by Mobil Oil. Many other companies have also used this medium effectively as a vehicle either to enunciate issue positions or to build a corporate image. It has also been used by labor unions, trade associations, and many other interest groups to express their opinions directly to the public. The legitimacy of such ads has been upheld by the U.S. Supreme Court.[1] Although many legislators say they are not influenced by issue advertisements, these communications can have an indirect legislative effect by promoting interest on the part of constituents who may be motivated to get in touch with lawmakers themselves. Ads can also reinforce enthusiasm among allies and grass-roots participants.

To be effective, an ad must be well written, readable, and interesting, with a clearly understandable message. The full-page ads of closely spaced small type often found in major newspapers, calling for the liberation of the Nairobi Nine or the overthrow of the dictator of Tyrannistan, are usually a waste of money; few people will bother to plow through all that dense prose, let alone act on its message. An issue ad should appeal to readers' self-interest, sense of fairness or justice, or in some other way reach their emotions.

GUIDELINES AND PRINCIPLES

As organizations have sought to reach out to a widening circle of constituencies and allies in their search for support on public policy issues, the arts and expertise of public relations, advertising, and communications have become increasingly interrelated with those of government relations. Indeed, in a substantial number of companies the public relations and government relations functions both report to a senior executive for public affairs. (This was the case in about three-fifths of the 300 companies surveyed by The Conference Board in a 1987 study,[2] with some variations by industry.)

The skills of these communicators should be employed in developing government relations materials for the various target audiences. In some cases, it may be appropriate to utilize outside consultants, public relations firms, or advertising agencies, either to prepare materials or at least to provide an independent and objective evaluation for advertising, publications, or the press. Such an evaluation should include an appraisal of both text and the appropriateness of the intended medium, depending on the objective of the planned communication.

On the other hand, if materials are prepared on the outside they should be carefully checked to assure that the message has not strayed from plan. It is important not only to verify facts, but also to be sure that the *tone* is right and consistent; if the point is to convey the organization's concern and caring about a public problem, for instance, tough and aggressive language is probably inappropriate.

Truthfulness is an imperative since confidentiality can never be guaranteed. As the old public relations adage puts it, "If you don't want to see it in *The New York Times* or on the evening TV news, don't say it at all."Since credibility is absolutely essential, the following checklist of generally accepted principles can help assure that the client is getting sound, high-quality public communications materials.

Public involvement. Issues should be framed to show how the public benefits from your side of the argument. Don't go public with a narrow, self-serving issue. If a morale principle is at stake (e.g., discrimination or injustice), lead with it; citizens understand that if it can happen to you, it could happen to them.

Audience targeting. Identify the target audience before choosing the medium. That way, content can be specifically addressed to the particular group the organization wishes to reach, and costs are held down.

Accuracy and fairness. If facts, data, and quotations are inaccurate or misleading, everything else the organization says will also be open to challenge. It may or may not be appropriate to include the other side's views (to arm friends and advocates and provide rebuttal arguments), but they should be reported fairly or not at all. Candor in stating how the issue will benefit your side may take the wind out of attacks by the opposition if the information is likely to come out anyhow.

Moderation and balance. Extreme statements, improbable predictions, and heavy-handed language also endanger credibility. Statements likely to be met with skeptical reactions should be documented. Threats are usually unwise since they generate anger and risk retaliation; a threat should not be expressed unless there is a clear determination to carry it out (e.g., closing a plant or facility if a certain bill passes). Political threats are always a mistake.

Simplicity and clarity. Language should be clear, arguments and statements simple. Jargon should always be avoided. If technical terms must be used, explain them. Don't overinform; excessive details produce glazed eyes and tuned-out minds.

NOTES

1. *First National City Bank of Boston v. Bellotti, 1978.*
2. Seymour Lusterman, *The Organization and Staffing of Corporate Public Affairs.* (New York: The Conference Board, 1987).

10

Political Action

Money is the mother's milk of politics.

Jesse Unruh

Jesse Unruh understood the role of money in the political and public policy process as well as any politician in America. State treasurer of California at the time of his death in 1987, he mobilized his counterparts in other states to wield great power with Wall Street merchants of public bonds. But it was in an earlier role, as speaker of the California Assembly, that Unruh organized political fund-raising to a high art. By centralizing in his office both fund-raising and disbursements, he bolstered Democratic majorities in the Assembly, and made both lobbyists and his fellow lawmakers extraordinarily dependent on his leadership. In his day he was arguably the most powerful state legislator in America.

With the huge amounts of money Unruh raised from lobbyists, interest groups, and other contributors, he poured record sums into winning key legislative districts, often spending more on Assembly contests than were being expended at the time on some congressional races.

Political campaigns in the United States depend almost totally on funds raised from the private sector. (Although public financing seems to be a slowly growing trend, the vast majority of campaigns are still privately funded from voluntary contributions.) Much of this money comes from friendly individuals, but a great deal of it has always been raised, one way or another, from interest groups keenly concerned about both pending public policy issues and the candidates running for the offices empowered to decide them.

Campaigns have become an expensive business. As recently as the early 1970s, $100,000 or less would finance almost any race for the U.S. House of Representatives. But spending soared in the 1980s. By 1988 each party was spending $500–800,000 for each contested House seat, and several House campaigns cost $1.5 million. In the 1990s, any seriously contested House seat will cost each of the major parties over $1 million, and at least one has already reached the $2 million mark.

(There may be less here than meets the eye, however, since few House incumbents are defeated anymore—only about 2 percent in both 1986 and 1988. With occasional exceptions, a "seriously contested" House race today is for an open seat, i.e, where there is no incumbent.)

Campaign spending for U.S. Senate seats is already well into the millions. Even in the smaller states, non-incumbents must raise several million dollars to be competitive. In California, battle costs for a Senate race now approach $20 million in total spending by the two major party candidates.

State legislative campaigns frequently cost $100,000 and up in urbanized states, actually reaching seven digits in a few California contests.

The total for both parties, national and state, in the 1988 elections is likely to be between $1.0 and $1.5 billion by the time all the bills are tallied. Most of this money comes from private sources even though the presidential campaigns were publicly funded after the national conventions (and partially funded with matching public funds prior to the conventions).

The political appetite for funds seems insatiable. A New York Democratic activist spoke for both parties when he said, "Candidates look at money the way Mark Twain regarded bourbon. Too much is never enough."

How all that money is used is another, oft-told story. This chapter discusses political finance from the donor's point of view:

- *Why* interest groups give to political candidates and organizations.
- *How* they give.
- *What else* they can do to influence the political process.

WHY GROUPS GIVE

It needs to be said at the outset what political contributions *do not* buy: legislative votes. Paying a public official for a favorable vote or decision is completely illegal everywhere. Hardly any lobbyists attempt bribery or other illegal payments, and the vast majority of officials not only would be mortally offended by the attempt but are likely to report the matter immediately to the nearest prosecutor. On those rare occasions when political influence and decisions are bought and paid for, the resulting prosecutions and trials are front-page news stories for months. Neither lawmakers nor lobbyists enjoy having their careers terminated by a jail sentence.

There are, however, legal—and ethically legitimate—reasons for political giving:

1. To help elect officials favorable to the group's issue positions—and oppose candidates who are not.
2. To gain and enhance access to elected officials.
3. To express appreciation for their favorable positions and actions.

In the historical course of events, acting successfully for the first reason has automatically achieved the second. Legislators and other officials look more fondly on those who have helped elect them than on those who didn't. Access has always flowed particularly to those who were there from the beginning and to those who helped along the way.

With the growth of legislative careerism, these two motivations have tended to drift a bit apart. Lobbyists can hardly be personally active in the district campaigns of all the legislators with whom they deal and wish to thank, but they can assist by contributing funds—and, since campaigns have gotten so expensive, the funds are increasingly needed and solicited, and their donors made welcome. (It is not easy to separate cause from effect. Part of the reason campaigns have gotten so expensive is that so much more money is readily available to fund them.)

There are differing views among government relations practitioners about whom to support, and why. One school of thought tends to be ideological:

We need lawmakers who share our basic philosophy. More important than access is their basic commitment to our point of view. Senator Omega may be an important leader, but he is not in tune with us on the issues. We should support his election opponent who is and who would vote with us more than 10 or 20 percent of the time. We have to take the long view and work to elect legislators who share our views even if that means antagonizing some incumbents until we can defeat them at the polls.

Another view is heavily pragmatic, tilting more to the importance of contributing to gain access and appreciation. This group tends, more often than not, to be comprised of day-in, day-out lobbyists. Their argument goes something like this:

Everybody wants to see Senator Alpha on the issues, but he and his legislative staff have only so much time. Preference is going to go to important supporters, political and financial. Gaining timely access and a sympathetic ear is not only legitimate, it's essential; we can't present our views if we can't get in the door. Moreover, if he's been helpful to us on the issues that are important to us, we have to be helpful to him when he needs it, and that means financially supporting his re-election campaign. We also have to contribute to his colleague, Senator Beta. He is more neutral than supportive on our issues, but he is the chairman of the most important committee to us and we have to have his goodwill and access to the committee staff that he controls. We can't risk antagonizing him by supporting his opponent.

A variation on this theme was expressed by a local businessman who expressed his fears of *not* giving before the New York State Commission on Government Integrity:

To characterize why I would respond to a solicitation for a contribution, I would say it's more trying to avoid a negative impact than trying to incur a positive result.[1]

Politicians respond somewhat piously when asked about the quid pro quo of campaign contributions. New York City Mayor Edward I. Koch, speaking of contributors at the New York commission hearings: "I'll take their calls. They won't get anything from me, but they get access."[2] And Andrew Cuomo, former aide to (and son of) Governor Mario Cuomo: "If they didn't give, it wouldn't make any difference, but they don't know that."[3]

Most lobbyists view such statements skeptically; politicians want and need the money too much. A prominent state legislative leader sardonically asked a business group not long ago, "Why buy a legislator when you can rent one?" The audience roared with appreciative laughter.

An association executive was involved in a series of small fund-raising meetings with another well-known elected official. At each session, the executive reported, the official asked what the industry's problems were in the agencies reporting to him. As each matter was outlined, he would dispense his decisions: "Yes, you can have that." "No, I've got problems with what you ask." "Let me look into that one and see what we can do." As each group left, its contribution would be discreetly handed to a staff aide. Not all elected officials are quite as open about the quid pro quo as this one.

Some legislators do admit that contributions occasionally affect their votes. About a fifth did so in a survey of members of Congress taken in 1987 by the Center for Responsive Politics, a group that favors tough restrictions on political finance; half said contributions do not affect their votes, and the rest were unsure. Many legislators think they have to spend too much time raising money and some even have chosen not to run again because of it.

Which philosophy is correct? In practice, motivations for contributing must be mixed. Only an interest group more interested in ideological purity than in winning can ignore the need for access and goodwill. But groups willing to totally sacrifice long-range interests for today's issues are not so much pragmatic as cynical.

Some organizations have written criteria stating what their mix is. One company's confidential guidelines actually state that 75 percent of their political action committee funds will go to candidates "who have demonstrated a clear business orientation in their public positions," with no more than 25 percent allocated to those with a pragmatic relationship.

Regardless of its concerns, needs, and issues, each politically active interest group must strike its own balance of comfort between these two poles, making the decision as a matter of policy and not mere inertia.

Each group has its own agenda that looks beyond today's immediate concerns. That agenda may be specific—to ban, compel, or permit some social or environmental practice, for instance—or philosophical—the election of more lawmakers dedicated, perhaps, to the advancement of the rights of workers and consumers, the extension of free enterprise and free trade, or the preservation of the family farm. To confine the use of political money, however given, merely to access-building undercuts the organization's ability to achieve its own long-range agenda through the election of a more supportive Congress or state or local legislature.

Many lobbyists and executives will counter with the words of John Maynard Keynes, "in the long run we are all dead"—that long-range thinking is all very well, but meanwhile there is S.1234 that must be defeated this year. Recent contribution trends, especially among political action committees, have been strongly favoring incumbents to the detriment of their challengers. Close to 85 percent of PAC contributions for the U.S. House of Representatives in the 1988 elections went to incumbents. Such extreme bias is an unfortunate development.

A support policy balanced between the needs of today and those of tomorrow is likely to prove the most pragmatically effective, and probably the most justifiable to members or corporate constituency groups as well.

HOW GROUPS GIVE

There are at least nine devices currently used by interest groups to provide economic support to favored political candidates and parties:

1. Individual contributions
2. Bundling
3. Corporate and union contributions
4. Political action committees
5. Conduits
6. In-kind contributions
7. Independent expenditures
8. Soft money
9. Honoraria

Individual Contributions

Despite the rise in political action committees and public financing, contributions from individuals remain the backbone of political funding. Most contributions are made in presidential campaign years. Projections from previous years put the number of individuals contributing to political parties and their candidates in 1988 at about 20 million people. If those who contribute to their interest groups are included, this number is more likely 25 million—exclusive of the "25 to 30 percent of federal income taxpayers [who] consistently show a willingness to earmark $1 of their income tax liability for the presidential campaign fund through the checkoff procedure."[4]

Historically, individual giving was dominated by large contributors, "fat cats" in political parlance. As late as 1972 when federal campaign finance limits were tightened, some individual contributions to both the McGovern and Nixon campaigns reached the upper six-digit range, and a few exceeded $1 million.[5]

This pattern changed as a result of two developments in the 1960s and 1970s: stricter regulation of campaign finance, and the rise of direct mail solicitations.

Political Reforms

Federal election statutes were substantially rewritten between 1971 and 1979 by a series of laws and court decisions. The changes were these:

- Limits were established on individual political contributions in federal elections (allowing spouses to give equal amounts):

   $1,000 per candidate per election (with primaries, runoffs, and general elections each considered separately).

   $5,000 annually to a PAC or state or local party committee supporting federal candidates.

   $20,000 annually to a national party committee.

   $25,000 annually in total contributions to any or all of the above.

- Contributions were disallowed in cash over $100, and political candidates and committees were required to identify contributors giving over $200 by name, address, occupation, and place of business.

- Public financing of presidential campaigns was instituted, funded by the tax checkoff.

- Regulation of political action committees, campaign expenditures, and reporting requirements was increased.

- The Federal Election Commission was established to regulate the process.

An important Supreme Court decision during this period[6] upheld limits on *contributions* to the campaigns of national parties and federal candidates. However, the Court overturned most limitations on *expenditures* (except where public financing has been accepted) on the ground that they were unconstitutional restrictions on rights of political free speech. Disclosure requirements and public financing were both upheld.

The Supreme Court decision also resulted in major changes in many state campaign finance laws. As a result, individual contributions are limited in about half the states. Disclosure of both contributions and expenditures is required in all states.

Individuals are free to raise money voluntarily in behalf of favored candidates and parties at the federal level, although they must report their expenses if they go over certain limits; there may be state limits as well. In general, companies and other interest groups can also encourage individual contributions to candidates and political committees (including PACs). However, solicitation activities and costs are regulated at the federal level and in some states as well. Contribution limits vary widely.

Direct Mail and Telemarketing

Actually preceding the political reforms was the development of direct mail solicitations to targeted mailing lists. Begun in the 1950s primarily by the Republican Party, direct mail financing was an important factor in Barry Goldwater's 1964 presidential bid. Eight years later, Democrat George McGovern also used direct mail with great financial success, tripling Goldwater's collections.

Over the years, Republican committees and conservative groups were much more attentive to the development of direct mail technology and utilization than their Democratic and liberal counterparts, and invariably raised far more money nationally through this approach. Not until the 1980s, when they had the policies and programs of Ronald Reagan to rail against, did Democratic committees and liberal groups begin to raise significant sums. Although still not extensive below the national level, direct mail appeals are being utilized with increasing frequency and effectiveness in state and local campaigns.

Issues and ideology play a substantial role in persuading individual citizens to mail a check to political causes. Republicans solicitations have relied heavily on strong conservative, anti-government appeals, even during the incumbency of the most conservative president in half a century. Similarly, McGovern's successful financial appeals centered on vehement opposition to the Vietnam War.

Telemarketing for political purposes is a logical outgrowth of direct mail appeals. Using computerized, highly targeted lists, telemarketers aggressively and successfully solicit funds for candidates, parties, and interest groups. Although humans still make many of these calls, a growing number are completely computerized and even interactive, at least to the extent that the recipient of the call is often encouraged to respond orally to simple questions.[7]

The relevance for interest groups is that there are two factors that must be present to achieve substantial fund-raising results from direct mail and telemarketing:

1. A substantial, highly targeted list of individuals likely to be strongly responsive to the cause underlying the fund-raising appeal.

2. A cause (ideology, issue, or candidate) about which people feel quite strongly and emotionally.

"Direct-mail consultants stress the need for a simple, appealing message, and for identification of a monstrous adversary whose allegedly superior resources are arrayed in opposition to the public interest."[8]

Examples of such causes include the abortion and gun control issues (both pro and con), an immensely unpopular war, threatened loss of an important economic benefit (e.g., social security), certain environmental concerns, and so forth. Jesse Jackson, whose 1988 campaign started on the proverbial shoestring, was raising substantial amounts of money through direct mail by the end of his campaign as a result of the strong emotional appeal he was able to generate among certain groups. Such an appeal can also be negative; liberal organizations raised fortunes during the 1980s with President Ronald Reagan serving as the "monstrous adversary," just as conservative groups have over an even longer period with Senator Edward Kennedy in the honored role.

Fund-Raising Events

The political dinner and similar events continue to be tedious but legitimate and very effective fund-raising devices. Inflation of campaign costs has overtaken the $100-a-plate dinner, which may now run as high as $10,000 for the privilege of meeting and greeting the influential, dining on rubber steak, and being entertained by florid oratory. Cocktail parties, sports events, affairs hosted by show business and other celebrities (especially at their homes), and similar activities are all appropriate ways to raise contributions from individuals, subject to pertinent federal and state laws about contribution limits and reporting requirements.

There seems to be no limit on the extravagance of such events. Former Louisiana Governor Edwin Edwards chartered two 747s for a fund-raising junket to Paris at $50,000 per couple to pay off his 1983 campaign debt. (This is the same Edwin Edwards who reportedly once boasted that the voters of his state would never defeat him unless they caught him in bed with a dead girl or a live boy. He was beaten in 1987 without benefit of either.)

Bundling

Some groups desire to show substantial political support for a candidate or party by collecting a number of checks from individuals and presenting them as a package to the recipient. Thus the group might solicit checks for $250 from each of 200 individuals, thereby enabling it to gain credit for $50,000 in contributions, a total that would be illegal if presented as a single PAC contribution.

This process is called "bundling" (with no relationship to the quaint colonial-era courtship practice of the same name). Bundling has been questioned by some critics when used by a political action committee to make contributions in excess of legal totals. Its use by organizations lacking a PAC is probably less questionable if less than fifty individuals give and contributions are made to less than five candidates (the criteria for a federal PAC).

Corporate and Union Contributions

Corporations have been barred from contributing in federal elections since 1907, and labor union contributions have been prohibited since 1943.

State regulation of corporate and union contributions is a mixed picture. Corporate contributions are permitted in twenty-four states and allowed in another seven except for companies in certain industries (such as banks, utilities, and insurance companies). Corporate contributions are barred in the remaining nineteen states, but only ten prohibit union contributions.

Even where permitted, corporate and union contributions are allowable only in state and local contests, not to federal candidates. However, the use of political action committees, soft money, in-kind contributions, and independent expenditures have provided other opportunities for indirect involvement in federal campaigns.

Political Action Committees

No other fund-raising technique has proven as controversial as the political action committee. Invented by organized labor and often the subject of bitter business criticism, the PAC was finally seized on by business groups, greatly expanding its political utilization. Today, it is business-sponsored PACs that receive most criticism. On several occasions during the late 1980s, Congress tried unsuccessfully to curtail federal PACs, and may yet succeed in doing so.

The first PAC, the Committee on Political Education (COPE), was created by the CIO after Congress prohibited direct political contributions by labor unions in federal elections in 1943. The first business-oriented PACs were those sponsored by associations: the American Medical Association's AMPAC and the Business-Industry Political Action Committee (BIPAC), originally sponsored by the National Association of Manufacturers. The mushrooming of corporate PACs has taken place only since 1975 when they were authorized by the Federal Election Commission in its Sun Oil Company decision.

How PACs Operate

Political action committees are voluntary organizations established to collect contributions from classes of individuals for the purpose of making contributions to political parties and candidates, or in other ways to influence elections. PACs are most commonly organized by business companies and labor unions, but also are often sponsored by trade and professional associations, agricultural organizations, and various ideological and "cause" groups. The corporation or organizational sponsor can finance its PAC's administrative expense.

The underlying theory of the political action committee is that by aggregating relatively small donations from a large number of contributors, the sponsor can maximize the political effect of the money. A single contribution of $1,000 has greater impact than 100 donations of $10 each.

PACs seeking to influence elections for President and Congress are regulated by the Federal Election Commission. Federal PACs can take up to $5,000 annually from any individual ($10,000 from a married couple). There is no current limit to total PAC collections (although there is considerable, and growing, sentiment in Congress to put a lid on PAC revenues).

Corporate PACs are largely limited to soliciting management personnel and shareholders and their families, although they can solicit contributions from other employees twice a year. Similarly, labor PACs raise their funds from union members in the main, although they are allowed to solicit corporate managers up to twice annually.

The PACs sponsored by trade associations may solicit only from their members except that, with the member's permission, they can solicit executives, employees, and shareholders once a year. Such PACs are most successful in industries where member-companies do not have their own political action committees, and vice versa, although there are some exceptions. Many companies do not allow their associations to solicit corporate executives. These restrictions are generally less confining at the state level, but as a practical matter no association can solicit corporate personnel if the member-company does not allow it.

In addition to PACs sponsored by business, labor, and associations, there are also so-called unconnected PACs—unaffiliated with a corporation or labor union. These PACs typically promote either a political philosophy (e.g., a liberal or conservative agenda) or are active in such special fields as women's rights, abortion (pro-life or pro-choice), environmentalism, etc. Unconnected PACs can solicit anyone at any time.

Contributions to a PAC must be wholly voluntary: "Contributions may not be secured by the use or threat of physical force, job discrimination or financial reprisal." If the PAC offers contribution guidelines, "no minimum contribution may be specified" and they must state that the "amount of the contribution, or the refusal to contribute, will not benefit or disadvantage the solicitee."[9]

Regardless of sponsorship, PACs may contribute up to $5,000 per election to a candidate, or a total of $10,000 for a typical primary-general election cycle. PACs can give to other PACs (up to $5,000 per year) and to political party committees (up to $15,000 per year). They can also make independent expenditures (those wholly uncoordinated with a candidate or party) without limit. There is also no limit on the total dollars they can contribute, although this is another area Congress may choose to restrain.

What the government giveth with the right hand, it taketh away with the left. Although organizations are permitted to pay the administrative costs of their political action committees, those costs are not tax deductible. Moreover, the tax deductibility of individual political contributions was repealed by the Tax Reform Act of 1986.

Most states permit political action committees. Although there are wide variations in regulations and tax statues, state PACs can generally operate with more flexibility than those involved in federal elections. For example, in states that permit corporate political contributions, companies and unions can usually contribute directly to a state PAC, a process that simplifies both fund-raising and administration.

Notwithstanding the complexities, PACs at all levels provide companies and organizations with the opportunity to become involved in the political process, reward their friends, and work to elect to office candidates sympathetic to their causes and interests.

These are not small advantages for any organization involved in the government relations process. Indeed, for better or worse, it is probably not possible for such organizations to participate effectively without either a PAC or some alternative means. Although they are cumbersome, particularly at the federal level, by their very nature PACs involve their contributors in the political process and thereby provide a useful tie-in and incentive to their grass-roots legislative participation as well.

Guidelines

A number of organizations, both in Washington and the states, provide members and supporters with useful detailed information about how to organize a political action committee. These resource groups can usually provide model or sample letters, brochures, solicitor training manuals, and similar materials (see Information Resources below). In addition, expert legal advice should be obtained to be sure that all requirements are met.

Based on the experiences of a number of organizations, following are some pointers on the process.

PACs have to be *organized from the top down*. Strong endorsements and leadership from the chief executive are critical to success, both in getting started and in maintaining the process. Without that continuing support, the PAC either will not get underway at all, or will falter and fail in a year or two. This is true of both companies and membership organizations.

In the case of the latter, the PAC must be strongly endorsed and backed not only by the chief staff executive but by the chief elected officer and board of directors as well. Chief elected officers generally serve only a year or two and it is important that the PAC have the backing of the group's power elite.

Many corporate chief executives also prefer to start with the endorsement of the company's board.

The first corporate meetings to promote the PAC should be between the C.E.O. and top officers and operating unit executives. He or she should express enthusiastic support for the PAC and ask that they do the same with their subordinates. In the case of unions, associations, and other membership groups, these first meetings should enlist vigorous backing from the board and other large or influential members.

The initial announcement to employees should also come from the chief executive of the corporation or, if more appropriate, the chief executive of the operating unit. In membership groups, this letter should be over the signatures of both the chief staff executive and the chief elected officer, assuming they are not the same individual (as they are in labor unions and a few other groups).

Solicitation, like organization, should begin from the top down. In companies, solicitation of funds should start with senior executives and then, with their support, move down into the ranks of middle management. In membership groups, it is best to begin with the influentials—directors and larger members. (Spouses can also be solicited, thereby doubling the potential revenue base.) Solicitation letters should be separate from but quickly follow the C.E.O.'s letter, and include an informational brochure. Where possible and appropriate, small group meetings should be announced to explain and promote the PAC. Where such meetings are held, they should be opened by a senior executive who, after his introductory remarks, turns the program over to the local solicitor and perhaps even leaves the room to avoid any hint of pressure.

The most effective solicitation efforts are decentralized and localized. Local solicitors should be peers well known and highly regarded: local managers, shop stewards, regional chairmen, etc.

Solicitation appeals should emphasize the importance of political support to legislative goals, and legislative goals to specific economic benefits to the company and employee. (This message should obviously be tailored as appropriate for consumer, environmental, and similar groups.) As in any other sales appeal, personal enthusiasm, commitment, and communications skills are important. Promotional films and video tapes are available from a number of resource groups.

For both legal and public relations reasons, any hint of *coercion is to be avoided* like the plague. It should be made clear that there are no economic rewards for giving, no penalties for not giving. Confidentiality should be assured to the maximum extent possible, consistent with legal reporting requirements and with contribution collection techniques (e.g., payroll deductions). This does not mean, though, that "honor incentives" can't be awarded. Lapel pins, medallions, honorary membership in special clubs, invitations to special PAC dinners or other events are all useful incentives, possibly tied to levels of giving.

General guidelines for contributions should be discussed, perhaps as a percentage of salary, but a minimum contribution may not legally be specified. Payroll deductions are legal and appropriate.

Special PAC fund-raising events can supplement (not substitute for) individual solicitations, e.g., golf or tennis tournaments, picnics or dinners, sports outings, casino nights, and the like.

An *on-going communications program* is important. Contributors should be individually thanked by the solicitor (not their superiors), and special thanks and recognition should be given the solicitors. Contributors should also be kept posted as to fund-raising progress and are entitled to know about disbursement policies and to whom the money is going. Reports (annual or more frequent), newsletters, and C.E.O. letters are possible elements in such a program.

Disbursements should be made by written policy and determined by a steering (or candidate evaluation) committee, which should be broadly representative of contributors, not just senior managers and government relations executives. Contributors should be asked for their suggestions as to recipients; after all, it *is* their money. Some PACs permit contributors to earmark their money for specific candidates (although this does not alter the PAC's legal contribution limits). Others encourage contributors to be part of the check-presentation process.

PAC checks—and indeed any political contribution—should be presented in person if at all possible. Some candidates resent the time, particularly in the middle of a campaign, but a contributor of a substantial sum ($500 or more) certainly should have a chance to chat with the candidate about issues and problems. For legal reasons, contributions should never be made on government property.

Contributions are needed and most appreciated early in the campaign when they can be put to best use. (It is hard to plan for the intelligent use of money that does not arrive until a few weeks prior to the election.) This is not always easy since many PAC contributions do not start coming in until the general election campaign. One solution is to carry over a portion of PAC funds to the next election cycle to facilitate some early giving. However, getting early contributions will not keep candidates from asking again in the fall if they need the money.

PACs can *engage in other activities* besides making direct contributions to candidates and parties. Labor PACs for many years have used their funds to organize voter registration drives, particularly in neighborhoods and communities likely to support labor's favored candidates. Money can also be spent for candidate training, consultant expenses, issue advertising, voter information, and a variety of programs beneficial to the candidates supported by the PAC. PACs can also use their funds for in-kind contributions and to make independent expenditures.

Conduits

Conduits are separate funds partway between individual contributions and political action committees.

A conduit resembles a PAC in that it has an organizational sponsor, usually a company, which sets up separate bank accounts for each individual's contributions. The accounts are generally funded through payroll deductions. Each individual controls his or her own account, determines to whom contributions are made, and writes the checks.

Conduits are useful techniques for the company that seeks to promote and organize individual political giving on the part of managers or employees with few of the legal requirements imposed on PACs. However, the sponsoring firm does not normally get the political benefits of delivering aggregated contributions to candidates, although theoretically they could be bundled.

In-Kind Contributions

Subject to disclosure requirements, corporations and unions can contribute goods and services to political campaigns in those states where these organizations can legally contribute to political candidates and party committees. Of course, even in these states the in-kind contribution cannot be made directly to campaign committees for federal offices but can benefit, say, the Republican or Democratic state committees, thereby freeing up funds that the state parties can then use to help their candidates for president or Congress.

A company or labor union can also use its political action committee to make in-kind contributions. Labor unions in particular have honed this technique to a fine art. For example, telephones and other equipment can be leased to a favored political campaign at cost, generally considerably less than the campaign would have to pay on the commercial market. The company or union would then be reimbursed for these costs by its PAC. Alternatively, the PAC can lease the equipment from its sponsor and sublease it to the candidate. Either way, the PAC has thereby made an in-kind political contribution.

The same process can reimburse an organization that loans an executive or a consultant to a campaign. Loaned executives provide an extra benefit since they establish relationships that can be very useful if the candidate wins.[10]

An attorney knowledgeable about campaign finance law should be consulted about the details of such arrangements.

Independent Expenditures

In its *Buckley v. Valeo* decision, the Supreme Court upheld the right of any group to make unlimited political expenditures so long as they are not coordinated with the political parties or candidates they benefit. Several conservative PACs took advantage of the opportunity in 1980 to mount massive independent campaigns (primarily through negative advertising) against a number of liberal Democratic senators, and have been credited with helping to defeat at least four of them.

With each passing year major donors, both individual and PAC, are spending increasing amounts of money in support of or opposition to certain candidates. Groups can solicit funds and spend the money they receive for advertisements, telephone banks, precinct canvassing, or in almost any other way they wish—all perfectly legal so long as the outlay is genuinely independent and wholly uncoordinated with a campaign.

These activities are not always welcomed by the candidates who ostensibly benefit. Independent groups often siphon off contributions that might otherwise go directly into party or candidate coffers. Fund-raising is an expensive process, and the bulk of the money collected by these groups usually pays for salaries and overhead, with a relatively small percentage actually being spent for the purpose it was raised. This situation has the potential for becoming a scam. In 1988 both the Bush and the Dukakis campaigns publicly requested certain groups to cease their independent activities in behalf of one or the other candidate.

Nonetheless, there are largely unplumbed political opportunities for corporations and labor unions through independent expenditures, as the following model illustrates:

The North American Interstice Corporation wishes to import low-cost components from a supplier in Honduras so that it can sell interstices to consumers at a lower price, and is supporting legislation necessary for it to do so. The United Interstice Workers Union opposes the legislation because many of its workers will lose their jobs. The legislation becomes an issue between opposing candidates in several political campaigns. The company buys advertisements stating its case and urges the voters to support only those political candidates who agree with its position. The union takes out its own ads, urging the opposing view.

So long as the ads do not name the candidates or the offices and are uncoordinated with specific federal campaigns, it may well be that they can be funded as legitimate independent expenditures—not through PACs, but directly out of corporate and union treasuries. This is admittedly a gray and untested area, but it may have considerable potential for direct, independent expenditures by corporations and labor unions.

Soft Money

Interest groups have developed a variety of ways to broaden their involvement in federal elections outside the restrictions of federal regulations. The funds used in this manner are described as "soft money" (as contrasted with "hard money," which Alexander describes as funds "raised, spent and publicly disclosed under federal supervision"[11]). Put somewhat more bluntly, soft money is the indirect use of union or corporate funds for political purposes that would be illegal if contributed directly to federal campaigns.

In 1988 both the Republican and Democratic presidential campaigns raised about $70 million each in soft money, in addition to the $46 million each received in public funds[12]—$1.50 in soft money for each $1 in public money.

For several decades, labor unions have made what amount to indirect contributions to favored political candidates and party committees—generally Democratic. These soft money contributions have financed voter registration and turnout drives, salaries and expenses of union personnel engaged in political activities, voter election information generally with a partisan slant in union publications, and the like. In the 1988 presidential campaign, unions conducted extensive voter registration and turnout drives using videotapes, fliers, telephone banks, direct mail, and other means intended to get 13 million union members to vote for the Dukakis-Bentsen ticket.[13]

At various times, corporations have paid executives' salaries while they raised money and engaged in other political activities, expressed corporate views on partisan issues in advertising, bought ads in political party publications, made a variety of in-kind contributions ranging from office equipment and mailing lists to transportation on company aircraft, and so forth.

Soft money expenditures by companies and trade associations in 1988 helped finance the national party conventions, a variety of state party building activities, and in-kind outlays for a variety of goods and services.

Almost any independent expenditure by a corporation or labor union amounts to the use of soft money if the indirect beneficiary is a candidate for federal office. Soft money contributions also free up party funds that can directly aid both federal and state candidates.

Whether or not it chooses to establish a PAC, there are a number of political activities on which corporations are free to spend their money directly, among them:

- Nonpartisan voter registration and turnout drives, and voter information.

- Partisan information and drives, including candidate endorsements, but only if the audience is limited to shareholders, executives, and their families.

- Allowing candidates and party leaders to speak at corporate functions and make fund-raising appeals, provided the audience is limited as above. (Candidates and party representatives may also speak at corporate events attended by other groups of employees, but only if their opponents are given the same opportunity to appear.)

• Issue or advocacy advertising provided the ads are independent of any particular federal campaign.

As Alexander notes, soft money activities are spreading and, in his opinion, are here to stay.[14] As still another illustration of the principle of unintended consequences, the more one seeks to control political funds, the more likely it is that new and unexpected outlets will be found. Political finance, like water, finds it own level.

Honoraria

Many interest groups invite legislators to speak before their meetings. Such groups include not only trade associations, unions, and various lobbies, but also a number of companies. The lawmaker is typically compensated for the speech by a substantial honorarium.

In a variation on the same soft money theme, the legislator may be asked to write an article for an interest group publication and be paid a fee, generally substantial.

Members of Congress are limited in the amount of honoraria they can accept for speaking engagements, publications writing, and similar activities. (The limits change annually and are different for senators and representatives.) Moreover, they are not supposed to use their official staffs to write the speeches and publications, a practice widely winked at even though it was one of the factors that led to the 1988 House Ethics Committee investigation of Speaker Jim Wright.

Such income is not legally considered a political contribution and is taxable to the legislator. From the standpoint of the paying group, however, the honorarium not only has most of the advantages of the political contribution, but also can produce often quite popular educational benefits for its members or employees.

Sometimes, however, no attempt is made to derive an educational benefit from the legislator's appearance, and the honorarium then becomes a barely disguised political contribution. This misuse of honoraria has led to reform proposals to ban them altogether.

PUBLIC FINANCING

Public funding of elections is a phenomenon that is slowly growing, although in fits and starts. Presidential campaigns have been publicly financed since 1976, on a matching-funds basis prior to the nominating conventions and exclusively in the general election. (Presidential candidates do not have to accept public funds, but those who choose to do so in the fall campaign may not accept private "hard money" contributions from either individuals or PACs.)

Public campaign financing has been adopted in several different forms by some states and localities, beginning in Iowa in 1973. In some instances, funds go directly to candidates; in others, to party committees. Some use a check-off procedure with no increase in personal tax liability (like the presidential check-off); others rely on a tax surcharge or add-on; and still others give the citizen no option by appropriating the money from general revenue.

Public funding of congressional campaigns has long been a heated controversial issue. Many legislators, who would have to vote to approve it, see little reason to provide taxpayer funds for their opponents when, as incumbents, they have ample public and private resources at hand to help them win re-election. Short of a public scandal of Watergate dimensions, it is unlikely that members of Congress will enact legislation to make their seats more competitive.

Less than half the states have adopted public financing of state elections in some form, and several of these have let the system lapse. Beginning with its 1989 municipal elections, New York City's campaigns will be publicly funded. But Californians in 1988 adopted two mutually contradictory referenda:

The most important contradiction relates to the issue of public financing. Proposition 68, which received a 53–47 percent popular vote, provided for a complex system of public funding and expenditure limits on the total amounts candidates for the State Legislature could spend. Proposition 73, which passed by a 58–42 percent margin, prohibits public financing at all levels of government. The passage of Proposition 73, therefore, repealed the heart of, and possibly all, of Proposition 68's provisions.[15]

Public financing has been advocated by many as a device to put campaigns on an equal footing, make it harder for incumbents to become entrenched, and reduce possibilities for corruption in the electoral process. Opponents maintain that it is healthy for citizens to underwrite voluntarily their preferred candidates and parties, and that taxpayers should not be forced to subsidize candidates they oppose. Moreover, blocking the use of hard money in campaigns would only add to the pressures for independent or soft money expenditures to advance political causes and candidates opponents add.

Although there is some growth of public financing, its widespread adoption appears to be many years away, if indeed it ever becomes prevalent.

POLITICAL PARTICIPATION

Antedating the great surge in PACs was the development of programs to involve citizens in politics. Organized labor has had programs to involve its members in political activity since at least the founding of COPE in the 1940s. Business activity came later with the U.S. Chamber of Commerce "Action Course in Practical Politics" and the founding of the Public Affairs Council (originally the Effective Citizens Organization), both in the 1950s; and the establishment of the Business-Industry Political Action Committee (BIPAC) in 1963.

The theory behind these efforts goes to the heart of what government relations is all about. What better way to influence public policy than to have a cadre of members active in the political parties, where they can:

• Be personally influential in the selection of candidates for offices at all levels.
• Be personally involved in the campaigns of the political parties and help shape party platforms and candidate positions on the issues.
• Run for office themselves or become party leaders.

Business as a whole has had a spotty record in actually getting executives and managers directly involved from the precinct up. At least in part, this is because business executives generally find it easier to contribute money (especially since the advent of PACs) than to contribute their time. Related to this point is the claim made by some executives today that corporate "downsizing" has increased managerial workloads, thereby reducing the discretionary time available for politics and other outside activities.

More venerable reasons are (1) a lack of knowledge of how politics is conducted, and (2) personal hesitation or even distaste about consorting with people whose ethics or conduct as a group have never enjoyed high repute. In reality, as anyone who has ever actually participated in political activity knows, the ethics of people in politics are at least as high as those in any other calling, whether vocational or avocational.

Overcoming misconceptions and lack of knowledge about politics was the rationale for the political education and training programs of twenty-five and thirty years ago, and remain the foundation of various programs available today. Such programs are offered by some PACs, associations, unions, and a number of private consultants. Since some are better than others, following is a checklist of topics that a good course should cover.

Federal government:
    Structure and organization.
    Legislative process—how laws are made.
    Executive and regulatory agencies and process.
    Lobbies and lobbying, including trade associations.
State and local governments:
    The same topics should be covered. A test of a good political training course is whether information on state and local governmental processes is specifically tailored to the needs of the audience, or merely generic.
Political process:
    Political party structure—federal, state, and local.
    Presidential nominating and election process.
    How candidates for U.S. Senate & House are nominated and elected in this state.

How state and local candidates are chosen.
Why individual political activity is important and how to begin personally.
Precinct activity and organization.
Political fund-raising.
Campaign management and participation.
Role of the media in campaigns—paid & non-paid.

It is unfortunate that relatively few people, particularly in business, are inclined to become politically active today. Financial political support, whether individually or through a PAC, is important, but there is no substitute for direct personal involvement in partisan politics to establish and maintain a base for political—and ultimately, legislative—influence. Companies, trade associations, and non-business organizations wishing to increase their legislative effectiveness should seriously consider revitalizing political training programs.

INFORMATION RESOURCES

Several organizations and publications provide information or services to groups in need of advice on political action and campaign finance, including data on PACs and candidate information.

Two notable resource groups for companies are:

Public Affairs Council
1255 Twenty-Third Street, NW
Washington, DC 20037

Business-Industry Political Action Committee
1747 Pennsylvania Avenue, NW
Washington, DC 20006

Trade associations can contact:

American Society of Association Executives
1575 Eye Street, NW
Washington, DC 20005

The prime resource for labor and liberal groups is:

AFL-CIO Committee on Political Education
815 Sixteenth Street
Washington, DC 20006

NOTES

1. Interrogation of William Bernstein, a real estate developer, reported in *The New York Times*, March 21, 1988.

2. Quoted in *The New York Times*, March 21, 1988.

3. Ibid.

4. Herbert E. Alexander, *Financing Politics: Money, Elections, and Political Reform* (Washington: CQ Press, 1984), p. 73.

5. Alexander (*Financing Politics*, pp. 59–61) notes that Chicago insurance executive W. Clement Stone gave over $2.8 million in 1968 and $2.1 million in 1972, almost all of it to Richard Nixon's presidential campaigns.

6. *Buckley v. Valeo*, 1976.

7. For a very readable and informative description of the development of direct mail and telemarketing in politics, see Richard Armstrong, *The Next Hurrah: The Communications Revolution in American Politics* (New York: Beech Tree Books/ William Morrow), 1988.

8. Douglas P. Wheeler, "A Political Handbook for the Environmental Movement," *The Washington Post National Weekly Edition*, September 19–25, 1988.

9. Federal Election Commission Regulations, 11 CFR 114.5 (a) (1) and 114.5 (a) (2).

10. John F. Noble, "A New In-Kind Giving Opportunity," *Campaigns & Elections*, Winter 1985.

11. Herbert E. Alexander, *"Soft Money" and Campaign Financing* (Washington: Public Affairs Council), 1986.

12. *The Wall Street Journal*, December 12, 1988.

13. *The Wall Street Journal*, September 20, 1988.

14. Alexander, *Soft Money*, pp. 75–85.

15. Herbert E. Alexander, *California's Mixed Signals on Election Reform* (unpublished paper prepared for the Public Affairs Council), July 1988.

11

The Future of Government
Relations

But my intention being to write something of use to those who understand, it appears to me more proper to go to the real truth of the matter
than to its imagination; and many have imagined republics and princi-
palities which have never been seen or known to exist in reality; for how
we live is so far removed from how we ought to live, that he who abandons
what is done for what ought to be done, will rather bring about his own
ruin than his preservation.

Machiavelli

What good does it do for a man to serve his country when he can't sell
his connections to the highest bidder once his term is over?

Art Buchwald

What will government relations be like in future years? What changes will
technology bring about in the lobbying arts? Will there be a shift away from
firefighting and damage control to more fire prevention and preventive maintenance?

Will society tighten controls on lobbying? Will political action committees
be more restrained and regulated? What about independent expenditures,
soft money, public financing?

Some of these questions are tactical. But others go to the heart of government relations in a democratic society, to the ethical issues, and problems
of whether, or how, to regulate government relations further.

ETHICS AND THE REGULATION OF GOVERNMENT RELATIONS

As discussed in the opening chapter, there are two processes that people in any society use to affect their government:

Politics—the pursuit of *governmental power.*

Lobbying—the pursuit of *public policy.*

The openness of the American political system is one of its greatest strengths. This is a point that needs to be borne prominently in mind as we contemplate the future of lobbying, the ethical issues that constantly surround it, and the proposals being perpetually brought forth to regulate it.

Lobbying in America, like our politics, has had its share of scandal, sometimes because of illegality, sometimes because of ethical impropriety.

It is worth pointing out that the latter two are far from synonymous—some unethical acts are not illegal, and some acts that violate the law may not always be ethical transgressions. Not until 1988 did Congress reluctantly seek to apply the same standards of lobbying ethics to its former members and staff that it has to former high executive branch officials, and even then it applied an easier standard to alumni of the legislative branch. Yet, from an ethical point of view, if it is wrong for former White House aides to lobby their old colleagues, then it must be equally wrong for former legislators to do. It is either wrong for both or right for both.

What is legitimate lobbying activity? The question is slippery because public standards of acceptable and legitimate behavior are continually evolving, generally in a more restrictive direction. Actions that were acceptable in one period of our history become questionable in another era, and sometimes regulated and even illegal in a third.

There are thousands, perhaps tens of thousands, of lobbyists in America, almost all of whom operate in a legal and above-board manner year-in and year-out. But public sensitivity to government relations is apparently so great that even isolated excesses are seized on by critics as justifications for new regulatory controls.

It is hard to think of an area of human endeavor that has not had its excesses. Some we condemn; some we punish; some we glorify; some we ignore.

Yet, there is no movement to reform religion in America because a priest is caught sexually molesting children. There is no movement to reform medicine or the law because a physician or an attorney engages in malpractice. There is no movement to reform the press because a reporter concocts a news story or a television producer pays a group to stage a protest before the cameras.

The story is quite different, though, if a lobbyist engages in a venal action, or an interest group spends more on political contributions then some other interest group thinks it should. Then the cry of widespread corruption is once more heard throughout the land, and the banner of reform is again flown high from ocean to ocean.

Lobbying may be a constitutionally protected right, but not a popular one. Some years ago, the author was asked to speak on the regulation of lobbying, the only spokesman for private-sector advocacy on a six-person panel otherwise comprised of more-or-less harsh critics. One of the other panelists, a public official and ostensibly a liberal, went so far as to indicate that something should really be done to alter the constitutional protection given this pimple on the body politic. There were several nods of agreement among other panelists. Their attitude is deplorable but hardly uncommon.

The Critics' Case

An interesting new magazine, *Ethics: Easier Said Than Done*,[1] contains over 150 pages of articles and essays on the subject of ethics in government, politics, and lobbying. The magazine is a veritable small encyclopedia of differing viewpoints, ranging from the philosophical to the pragmatic. If more of its articles view with alarm than point with pride, that is hardly surprising given the subject matter.

One of the featured articles in the magazine is by Professor Archibald Cox, celebrated by many for his role in the Watergate-related "Saturday night massacre" and currently chairman of Common Cause, the political reform lobby. His article well states the case of the current reform movement. As summarized by the editors of *Ethics*,

Professor Cox believes that the attitudes held by many today in government would depress the Founders of the Constitution. Fundamental to our system are obligations traced to the ancient Greeks—that civilized persons put the law above their own welfare, and that they do not cheat the law for personal advantage. Indeed, these obligations rest more heavily upon those chosen to rule, but compliance is being underminded by the pervasive presence of the dollar in the political system, and the absence of high moral leadership. Professor Cox advocates that Congress put greater restrictions upon post-employment lobbying, strengthen the Office of Government Ethics, radically restructure the method for financing congressional elections, and take a more active leadership role on ethics.[2]

Cox would also ban honoraria for members of Congress and restrain political committee campaign contributions, which like honoraria, "are destroying the institutional integrity of Congress."[3] Although his article does not specifically endorse the idea, Common Cause has long championed public financing of congressional elections.

(A faint whiff of sanctimonious hypocrisy occasionally surrounds such criticisms. The attorney who prosecuted former White House aide Michael Deaver, denouncing him as corrupt because he lobbied his former colleagues after leaving office, then sought to capitalize on his own new prominence by soliciting high-priced speaking engagements to lecture college students on venality in government.)

Reading the reformers' criticisms, one could come to believe that democracy is in mortal peril—that the republic is on the verge of being blown away by the greedy, the unscrupulous, and the corrupt. Yet, anyone who has been a participant and observer of the process knows that our system of contending interests is more open, more competitive, and more vibrant than any in history.

The judgments of the critics suffer from two deficiencies:

1. A fundamental misunderstanding of the proper role of interest groups in the legislative process.
2. A mistaken view about the curative powers of regulation to enhance democracy.

Balance and Accountability

As discussed in Chapter 1, interest groups add value to the legislative process. This added value includes the information and perspectives that these groups provide to lawmakers, thereby expanding their ability to legislate with the fullest possible knowledge of the consequences. No lawmaking body could legislate rationally without the information that only the affected interest groups can provide.

It is the legislator's role, and responsibility, to find the appropriate balance among the competing points of view on any issue.

Elections are the only opportunities that the political process provides citizens to discipline their elected officials. However, the government relations process contributes to the strength of democracy by providing a means through which interest groups can hold government accountable between elections.

How is it possible that such a vital contribution to democratic stability can be made by a process as sleazy as lobbying is often held to be?

Lobbying, it is true, is a messy process. So is legislating. For that matter, so is birth. The messiness, the contentiousness, the struggle to gain and hold political access, the high competition to prevail on the issues—these all combine to contribute to the unsavoriness with which the public at large views the process. Our electoral struggles bear the same characteristics, but in the end, as in lobbying and legislative competitions, a decision is made and accepted, and the system moves ahead. That is no petty achievement.

This contribution to democratic stability seems totally to escape those focused on the peccadillo of the month. If we must endure this democratic perversion, the critics infer, let us at least stringently regulate it and the political fund-raising arrangements that accompany it.

What is forgotten in this impulse to regulate is that people and their interest groups *need* to express their wants and grievances to the government, a need the founders explicitly recognized in the First Amendment. The more we clamp down on the lobbying process and the more fervently we regulate it, the harder it becomes for interests to express themselves—and the smaller the interest, the more difficulty it will have in complying. Regulation is a disincentive to free expression, not an inducement.

Moreover, rights rank higher in our national values than ethics. This does not justify unethical conduct, but it does underscore the difficulty of regulating such behavior. It is one thing to legislate public behavior in defense of constitutional rights; it is quite another when rights will be infringed.

The Regulation of Lobbying

Does the public, then, not have a right to see and know what is going on? Of course, it does. A simple disclosure law is justifiable, limited perhaps to an annual filing by each paid lobbyist or advocacy group setting forth the clients being represented and on which issues. Requiring information on lobbying remuneration is really irrelevant and leads only to evasion, as experience with even the mild federal lobbying law attests. A detailed accounting of the officials and legislators each lobbyist talks to, as some states require, is a travesty of disclosure that benefits no one except the inquisitive and the clerks required to process all the data.

Should ex-legislators or executive branch officials be barred, even temporarily, from lobbying? This has been the trend of legislative ethics legislation, at least at the federal level. Yet, if the information is publicly disclosed, it is hard to discern any real benefit in these restrictions. If something improper is afoot, simple disclosure will enable any enterprising journalist to smoke out a good story—and neither lawmakers nor effective lobbyists like adverse publicity. Legislators will shun a lobbyist who embarrasses them by improper behavior, and the press will ruin a legislator's career if the transgressions are serious enough.

Proposals to rehabilitate campaign financing are even more widespread than lobbying reforms. Critics attack the very presence of private contributions in the political process, urging that election campaigns be financed with public funds. They criticize the growth of political action committees because they "destroy the institutional integrity" (in Professor Cox's words) of our governmental bodies. Honoraria to elected officials are faulted on the same ground. The Supreme Court's protection of independent expenditures and of unlimited privately funded campaign spending remains a topic of considerable grumbling.

Money and Access

Above all, the critics indict the political access that contributors seek through their donations. Seeking, and permitting, access in order to present one's case for changes in public policy is legitimate.

Who gets in the door? Ideally, everyone who wants to. In practice, that is not possible. A congressman represents, on the average, over half a million people—and most U.S. senators vastly more. State legislators in the most populous states may each represent about 100,000 or more. It simply is impossible for lawmakers to see even a tiny fraction of their constituents, let alone interest group representatives who vote in someone else's state or district. Given that legislators' time is necessarily limited, the search for access is competitive.

To paraphrase George Orwell, all constituents are equal but some are more equal than others. Among those who are "more equal" are two groups who helped the legislator or official get elected in the first place: those who worked, and those who gave.

No candidate ever won election without help from many people, from the individual who managed the campaign to those who stuffed envelopes, and everyone in between. Even in an age of declining political patronage, these people feel they are entitled to a bit of special access to those they helped elect—the volunteers particularly but also those who were paid staff.

Campaign contributors feel the same way. They may not have the "sweat equity" that those do who invested hours and weeks in the candidate, but they, too, feel that their contributions have earned them seats in the inner circle of policy advisors—and the larger the contribution, the bigger and better the seat. This is true whether the contributions come from individuals directly or through their interest groups.

It is the nature of the political process, any political process, that leaders will give preferential help to those who aided them in their ascent to power—subject only to the limits of law and current standards of political propriety.

It needs only to be added that if it is legitimate for the elected official to give preferential access to those who participate and contribute to his or her campaign, then surely it is no less legitimate, and ethical, for these participants and contributors to seek that access, whether they be individuals or interest groups.

Political Action Committees

Political action committees permit tens of thousands of citizens to participate financially, significantly and influentially in political campaigns by the aggregation of relatively small donations. Civic involvement of this kind is a public asset, in part because it is good per se, but also because an individual who contributes personal dollars is more likely also to begin investing personal time in political and grass-roots legislative activities.

Nonetheless, business and labor PACs are really a tacit compromise. They exist because their sponsors, corporations and labor unions, are barred from providing direct political support. Those who wish to eliminate these PACs would find that an easy way to do so would be to once again legalize direct political contributions by corporations and unions in federal elections—still permitted in about half the states.

It stands to reason, however, that the group that can contribute both manpower and money will always have a substantial advantage over the group that gives money alone.

COPE and other labor PACs contribute not only money but also campaign managers, workers, and a variety of in-kind services to the candidates they back. With some exceptions, business PACs have not been that sophisticated, largely limiting their support to money. If the political and financial value of unions' intensive in-kind support were to be accurately appraised, the extent of labor's campaign involvement would be recognized as substantially larger than it appears.

Moreover, an individual who has devoted time and effort to a political campaign has a personal relationship with the candidate that is rarely matched by that of the signer of a check, no matter how large. Whether volunteer or paid, the worker has "sweat equity." The contributor is still only a "fat cat."

It would be unjust to restrict PAC activities without recognizing this fact of political life. At the very least, the fair value of in-kind services should be measured and included under any PAC contribution limitations.

Public Financing and Freedom of Speech

It is not the purpose of this book to join in the debate over the philosophic pros and cons of public financing. However, it should be pointed out that to the extent public campaign funding is intended to pre-empt financial participation by private-sector interest groups, it is bound to fail.

If presidential candidates choose to accept public funding in the general election campaign, they are required to forego private contributions. However, nothing currently prohibits national, state, and local party committees from collecting and spending non-public funds to register voters, get out the vote, and utilize literature and advertising to boost the party's candidates. Nor are there many practical ways to restrict the increasingly imaginative use of money by PACs and, where legal, by unions and corporations directly to aid campaigns.

Even if the use of this soft money is curtailed, there is no constitutional way to restrict genuinely independent expenditures in behalf of, or opposition to, any candidate.

Money is as fluid a commodity as there is. The desire to spend it for particular purposes produces a kind of hydraulic pressure in the political system. Just as water under pressure will find even the pinhole leaks, so political money will also find ways to squirt out legally, if not always ethically—as experiences with soft money have repeatedly demonstrated.

This point also illustrates the folly of excessive regulation of First Amendment rights. The Supreme Court has upheld the right of individuals and interest groups to spend whatever they wish in advancing their beliefs and interests, as part of the expression of free speech—just as the Court has defended lobbying against regulatory restrictions.

Restrictions on these rights to spend and to lobby are restrictions on the right of free speech, and should be opposed as much.

Honoraria Programs

The use of honoraria solely as a disguised campaign contribution has to be considered questionable, and is likely to be highly restricted if not banned outright. However, the payment of an honorarium should be considered legitimate when it buys a real educational service.

Some years ago the author helped launch a program at a company that involved bringing members of Congress to corporate headquarters to meet and speak with senior executives and middle managers on a monthly basis. The legislator would address the group, answer questions on topical issues, and often engage in a fairly spirited give-and-take. Attendance was voluntary and after office hours, but the program was always popular and well attended. The guest was usually a U.S. senator or representative, but executive officials, state legislators, and journalists would occasionally appear.

Except to the executive officials who are not allowed to accept honoraria, a fee was generally paid the guest speaker. The company did gain political credits, true, but by far the greater value was the exposure of managers at all levels to political points of view.

Honoraria for purposes like these are completely appropriate and above-board.

THE POLITICAL LOCKS

Horace Busby, a sage among American political analysts, long ago described the "lock" that the Republican Party has developed in presidential elections. Actually, several major elements of the political process have become locked—uncompetitive and apparently invulnerable to electoral change.

The Republican Lock

With the election of George Bush, the Republican Party has now won the White House in seven of the ten presidential elections since mid-century.

Since 1968, Democrats have succeeded only once in six contests and then largely because of Watergate, the most serious political scandal of the modern era.

Busby and other analysts attribute the Republican lock to two factors:

1. The control of the Democratic Party by interests whose support is essential for their party's nomination, but who are consistently unable to muster a majority of the popular vote for their nominees, let alone the state-by-state majorities necessary under the Constitution to win the presidency in the Electoral College.

2. The shifts in population, and hence electoral votes, to the South and West, the most conservative regions of the country. The reapportionment following the 1990 Census will, as a whole, add electoral votes to states that have been consistently voting for Republican presidential nominees, and decrease them in Democratic states.

Barring some national economic crisis or political upheaval, the outlook is for Republican control of the presidency well into the next century.

The Democratic Locks

The Republican lock on the executive branch is matched by the Democrats' own locks:

1. Democrats have controlled the United States Senate for all but eight years since the middle of the century—and the House of Representatives for all but two years. Republicans are still somewhat competitive in the Senate since they had a majority there in six years of the 1980s, and it is easier for well-financed Senate challengers to gain the paid and free media time needed to oust incumbents. The House, however, is likely to remain under Democratic control for many years to come— in part because incumbency breeds more incumbency, but also because Democrats are largely in control of the machinery that draws the boundaries of congressional districts.

2. The shape of congressional districts, and state legislative districts, is determined by state legislatures. Democrats control these legislatures in almost three-fifths of the states, with split control in another dozen. Less than ten have Republican majorities in both houses. Over the past two decades, Republicans have never controlled both legislative houses in more than twenty states; Democrats have controlled as many as thirty. A majority of the governorships have also been held by Democrats in most recent years. Although there have been shifts in power from state to state, the overall pattern of Democratic dominance has remained consistent. Unless there are major power changes in the 1990 elections (the last election of state legislators before the post-Census redistrictings take place), the Democratic lock on state government is likely to continue for many years to come.

The voters seem to like this twist on the checks-and-balances principle. In 1988, George Bush won 54 percent of the major-party presidential popular vote at the same time that Republican House candidates were garnering only

47 percent nationally. One-fourth of Bush's supporters cast ballots for Democratic House candidates, according to election exit polls.

In one sense, locks have an advantage for lobbyists. Considerable predictability about political situations and personalities makes it easier to plan relationships if there is little likelihood of change. But there are severe drawbacks. The need to be responsive to constituencies and diverse interest groups inevitably diminishes if elected officials are no longer seriously threatened by competitive pressures and fears of defeat and loss of power.

These major trends are truly locking up the democratic process for the foreseeable future. The system would be much healthier and more responsive if there were genuine two-party competition throughout national and state elections.

The Incumbency Lock

Although it is a question of strategy rather than legitimacy, it is hard to defend the growing tendency of most business PACs to throw the overwhelming bulk of their support to incumbents. The chief justification of giving almost exclusively to incumbents is that groups donate to gain and maintain legislative access and incumbents are almost always re-elected today (at a rate of 95–98 percent in the U.S. House of Representatives and most state legislatures). This is less true of the very conspicuous public offices like governorships and U.S. Senate seats—probably because serious challengers can still often raise and spend enough money to buy political visibility through media advertising.

Giving preponderantly to incumbents, however, often means giving substantial aid to legislators who may frequently oppose the very causes the contributors espouse—and writes off any real hope of replacing those people with friendlier lawmakers. (As one executive said, "We spit on the check but give it to them anyhow.")

For a number of their earlier campaigns, business PACs tended to be more balanced between incumbents and challengers and between Republicans and Democrats; the stampede toward incumbent support is a more recent development. Unions have always been more inclined to help those who help labor, and have done so both in periods of its political ascendancy and in times of diminished influence. It is a strategy that builds for the long term, rather than just for the next legislative session.

In 1988, PACs gave House Democratic incumbents $2 for every $1 to Republicans. Democratic candidates for House seats with no incumbent were favored by the same margin. Democratic challengers, as a group, were given four times as much PAC support as Republican challengers.

These imbalances may prove self-defeating. It is not a partisan comment to note that supporting only incumbents means perpetuating Democratic majorities in Congress and most state legislatures. Yet, it is the Democrats in the main who have worked to curtail PACs and Republicans who have blocked congressional PAC restrictions. The PACs' tightfistedness toward Republican challengers and contenders for open seats in the 1988 campaign led GOP leaders to warn corporate political action committees that they need not rely further on Republicans to deter future reforms. It would be an unfortunate irony if the PAC bias toward incumbents led to their own ruination.

More serious than PAC behavior, though, is the growing virtual invulnerability of incumbents who, for all practical purposes, are no longer accountable to the electorate. There are a number of reasons for this trend:

- *Incumbent protection programs* have been developed by party campaign committees for their legislators "to wed their office operations with their political needs by adroitly using mail, media and scheduling to beam a consistent message to their districts."[4] Highly targeted computerized mail and newsletters (distributed at public expense at an estimated value of about $1 million per House incumbent), plus the incumbents' ability to command year-round media coverage, are factors of increasing importance.

- *Name familiarity.* Although few citizens can identify their legislators, incumbents' names are still much more likely to be familiar than those of challengers. Without a compelling reason to unseat incumbents, voters tend strongly to support re-election bids. In fact, they may do so *even if* they are given good reasons to oust them. In the 1988 primary election in New York City (where Democratic nomination is almost always tantamount to election), several congressional and state legislative incumbents who had been indicted or even convicted, actively sought renomination. All won by large margins.

- *Political careerism.* There is a growing tendency of many lawmakers to see their offices as full-time careers. Supporting this have been the development and growth of year-round professional legislative staffs, the steady increase in state and local legislative pay, and the increasing acceptance of honoraria to supplement federal salaries.

- *Redistricting.* Gerrymandering, the practice of drawing legislative district boundaries in a way that favors one party over another, increasingly protects incumbents. Legislative majority parties almost invariably redraw district lines to take care of their own. In New York, for example, where Republicans have long controlled the Senate and Democrats the Assembly, legislative and congressional districts after the 1980 reapportionment were redrawn to protect each party's majority largely by incumbent protection. The 1988 result was that Democrats were able to win 60 percent of U.S. House seats with only 53 percent of the national vote.

The Supreme Court has been willing to consider the constitutionality of partisan gerrymandering in recent years, but its refusal in 1989 to overturn California's flagrant redistricting indicates that partisan remapping will have to be extreme before court relief can be obtained.

Redistricting of congressional and state legislative districts will occur again after the 1990 Population Census and in time for the 1992 elections. This will be the last opportunity in this century to realign districts fairly and without regard to the desires of entrenched incumbents. In most states, however, it is the state legislatures that redraw these boundaries, and for the most part the decisions will be made by the lawmaking bodies elected in 1990 (a few will be elected in 1989). Only if public and interest group pressures are great enough will the nation avoid still another round of gerrymandering and incumbent protection.

Representative democracy hardly benefits when lawmakers are routinely re-elected, facing progressively weaker opponents in each campaign. If the political process continues to fail in this way, it may be only the interest groups (along with the press) that are in a position to hold elected officials accountable. And even they will fail if their financial support goes only to those already in office.

NEW FORCES AND ISSUES

As the twentieth century moves into its final decade, several forces will shape the issues on which government relations practitioners will focus. These include:

1. The dual deficits of fiscal and international trade policy that threaten potentially deep recession and a resurgence of inflation.
2. The probability of mandatory transfer to the private sector of responsibility for many social and economic issues likely to result from the fiscal deficit and shortage of adequate federal revenues.
3. Growing assertiveness, experimentation, and regulation by state and local governments, continuing the trend begun as the federal government emphasized deregulation. As this trend continues, companies seeking pre-emptive federal legislation are unlikely to succeed, while finding themselves compelled at the same time to assume certain kinds of social costs that state governments had previously borne.
4. Movement toward at least partial re-regulation of certain industries where increased costs or decreased service have produced growing public dissatisfaction. This could well be accompanied by a return to more stringent federal and state antitrust policies.
5. The pressure of social and economic concerns that built up during the 1980s, including:

   - *Environmental and energy problems*, including coastal pollution, national energy policy, the ozone "hole", nuclear power, solid waste disposal and resource conservation.
   - *Personal and family issues* ranging from parental leave and child day care to universal private pension systems, escalating medical costs, and the growing unaffordability of home ownership for young families in many parts of the country.
   - *Social problems* like drug control, the plight of the homeless, educational needs, and health services for the aged and the poor.

- *Ideological issues* including school prayer and abortions.
- *Public investment needs* like increasingly dilapidated bridges and highway systems, and the costly delays in restoring or replacing them because of environmental concerns.

THE CHANGING SHAPE OF GOVERNMENT RELATIONS

Interest groups of all kinds will meet this new wave of challenges with government relations techniques of ever-increasing sophistication.

To explore the technologies lobbyists will use tomorrow, we need only see what innovations marketers developed yesterday—and what politicians are doing today.[5]

All areas of government relations are likely to be altered by new technologies, but the greatest impacts will be felt in increasing capabilities to identify, reach, and motivate grass-roots legislative communications. Technology can not only get more people involved; it also has the ability to get them more *intensely* involved. Sheer numbers can be an overwhelming influence as the senior citizens' lobby frequently illustrates on Social Security and other issues of the aged. But one need look no further than the National Rifle Association to see how intensity of member attitudes can transcend mere volume in grass-roots effectiveness.

Following is a sampling of some of the changes likely to occur in government relations in the 1990s.

1. *Computerization* will be increasingly employed—in issues research and tracking, grass-roots programs, communications, political action, and legislative redistricting. Applications, ease of use and access, and processing speed will increase; costs and equipment size will decrease.

2. *Issues research and strategic planning* will get more sophisticated, partly because of the steady growth in availability of data bases, partly because of new kinds of information correlations that computerization increasingly facilitates, and partly because of increases in personal imagination and creativity that these new tools will stimulate.

Public opinion surveys should become more widely used in developing issue positions and strategies. Many groups establish their positions based almost totally on their own internal needs, with insufficient attention to what will "sell" politically. Sometimes this is necessary, but often alternatives are available that are not adequately considered. Opinion polls can help direct strategies in directions that legislators may find more palatable politically, or indicate to the company or organization areas in which better public communications are needed. *Statistical modeling* of survey data can help pinpoint strategies that may sway significant population subgroups.

Focus groups (small panels of people chosen to approximate the characteristics of the population at large) can provide opportunities for in-depth discussion of these same topics at less cost than polls, although also with somewhat less accuracy. An advantage of focus groups is that they can be used cost effectively to get the thinking of constituents in the home districts of key legislators, and thereby provide guides to issue communications targeted to altering public opinion in those districts.

Vote predictor models, still largely in developmental stages, hold considerable promise of being able to forecast the outcome of legislative votes through sophisticated analysis of significant political, social, economic, and demographic variables. This may open the door toward highly targeted information addressed, and deliverable, to those specific legislative constituencies whose attitude shifts could sway the votes of their elected representatives.

3. *Grass-roots and political programs* will involve both more managers and retirees, plus greater political skill on their part as they develop experience and comfort with legislative activity. Individual membership organizations will experience the same phenomenon, but trade association programs may be at least partially pre-empted by those of increasingly active member-companies. Individual shareholders can become a particular strength for business if more companies overcome their reluctance to involve them in legislative and political activity. PACs, if reforms do not cripple them, will find it easier to raise more money from all these increasingly involved groups.

Direct mail is a highly sophisticated tool today in the hands of marketers, political and "cause" group fund-raisers, and campaign managers. Its use in grass-roots lobbying, however, still largely stresses volume rather than personalization. The technology exists for personalization of an almost intimate nature, as everybody from magazine sales companies to fund-raisers for the Home for Aged Ox-Cart Drivers prove every day.

For example, a company that wants its stockholders to write their legislators on an issue could enclose the actual letter it wishes sent. Computers can generate not only letters that vary in language and content (so that legislators are not clued into the organized origin of the mail) but, thanks to laser printers, even produce personal-appearing letterhead and envelops. With first-class stamps already attached, all the recipients have to do is sign the letters and mail them; they wouldn't even have to do that much if they give permission for the computer's laser printer to sign their names. The same technology can even produce what appears to be a completely hand-written letter and envelope. *Electronic mail* can be combined with these computerized techniques to produce overnight, or even instantaneous, delivery of communications to both grass-roots participants and their legislators.

4. *Communications* technologies provide an enormous number and variety of ways to reach highly specific population subgroups, including individual communities and neighborhoods. Some of the techniques that government relations will utilize in the future—and that, in a few cases, are being used now—include telemarketing, cable TV, and communications satellite technology.

Telemarketing—the telephone version of direct mail—is already widely used for a variety of purposes ranging from fund-raising and association membership solicitation to convention attendance promotion and legislative mobilization. Automated telemarketing will permit calls to grass-roots members with computerized recordings alerting them to the need for specific legislative actions. For instance, suppose a key vote on a top priority issue is suddenly scheduled on 24 hours notice. Computers, armed with a quickly recorded set of messages, can call designated members of the grass-roots network, giving them the critical details and arguments, along with the urgent message that they call their legislators immediately; the computer will be able to give them their lawmakers' names and telephone numbers as well. If feedback is needed for direct lobbying purposes, the computer can supply an 800 number to be called after the constituent has reached the legislator. The toll-free 800 number may even have an interactive capability so that specific questions can be asked and answered.

For the grass-roots member who wants updated information on the status of issues, a toll-charge 900 number can be supplied. Recorded issue updates are not new, of course, but by using an interactive computer the caller will be able to obtain answers to specific, though limited kinds of questions: "If you wish information in Issue X, press 1 on your button phone; for Issue Y, press 2; to learn how your legislator voted this morning on Issue Z, press 7 followed by the legislator's previously supplied code number."

Cable television will provide government relations professionals with a whole new quiver of highly targetable communications arrows for influencing public opinion on their issues. Inexpensive advertising time is available on many local cable channels, enabling interest groups to reach people in specific legislative districts. Because there are so many special channels, it is also possible to get the message to the particular demographic groups those channels appeal to in just those districts, a capability that will grow as cable channels proliferate and specialize.

Let's take a bottle bill as an example. Having identified a group of swing legislators on the issue, the bill's opponents could run targeted advertising on cable channels in the districts of those lawmakers. One ad, aimed at suburban homemakers, could run on a daytime channel carrying programming geared to that audience. Another ad, run in the evening, would be aimed at busy, urban working parents showing long, slow-moving lines of consumers waiting to return their empties at the supermarket—perhaps with special versions on channels featuring programming for blacks, Hispanics, and other ethnic groups. A third ad, keyed to the aged, might show an elderly woman struggling with a bag of empties on her way back to the store. A fourth, aimed at blue-collar families, could show closed packaging plants and laid-off workers lined up at the unemployment office. Each ad, of course, would urge viewers to write or call their legislator, Senator Barbara Beverage, and tell them just how to do it.

Communications satellites can be used for a variety of government relations purposes, ranging from teleconferencing to propagandizing. Satellite technology can be used to direct press releases, interviews, and features to local cable or broadcast television news departments anywhere. The Chamber of Commerce of the United States has had its own network, BizNet, for several years, using satellites to feed programming to stations. The AFL-CIO and other labor groups have used satellite communications for political and legislative objectives. Programs can be broad-scale or highly targeted, and can range from straight news to subtly angled features, from issue updates to ideological messages.

Coupled with cable, satellite communications can be used to get across any kind of message to any group—employees, members, or specifically targeted demographic and geographic subgroups. Says Richard Armstrong: "When it comes to reaching out to a broad constituency, inculcating them with a system of values and beliefs, encouraging them to give their time and money, building a corps of activists and volunteers, creating a sense of shared interests and culture, satellite technology is without peer."[6]

5. *Direct lobbying* will benefit from all these improvements although individual personal contact with legislators and their staffs will necessarily remain the primary medium of persuasion. *Video cassettes* provide an alternative to position papers for direct lobbying use. Instead of reading a written document, legislators and their staffs can watch a spokesman make the case on the issues. An environmental group can show visually the threat to an endangered species; manufacturers can dramatize how a bill will affect plant operations; consumer organizations can demonstrate "live" an objectionable retail practice. The lobbying impacts of such messages will be much more dramatic than any written statement.

Unless more resources are made available than government relations departments have traditionally been able to tap, the basic direct lobbying strategy will continue to be firefighting and damage control. However, more marketing- and opportunity-oriented issue strategies will develop, particularly as a greater number of chief executives become politically comfortable and legislatively involved.

Comprehensive *issue management* programs are unlikely to become prominent without increased departmental budgets. However, a consequence of increased political sophistication among top executives will be corporate sensitivity to broad emerging issues early enough to implement strategies that can deflect the worst legislative proposals. Proactive strategies that apply business technology and expertise in attacking public problems can do much to alleviate the reactive, and reactionary, image companies have too often developed.

Although there are not as many illustrations of the value of this principle as one might like, an excellent one occurred about a decade ago with the rise of the corporate governance issue. Ralph Nader and his allies began an attack on the structure of corporate decision making by boards of directors comprised almost exclusively of business executives. Nader said that many consumer and environmental problems arose because of corporate isolation from public concerns and a lack of corporate accountability to the public sector. His proposal was to require corporations to obtain federal charters that would be granted and renewed only if companies showed themselves sufficiently responsive to public concerns.

Business responded by pre-empting the issue: Corporate boards were expanded, more outsiders (particularly including blacks and women) were added as directors, and board-level public affairs committees were created to audit corporate performance in such areas as employment of minorities and investment in South Africa. Through a strategy that might be called "proactive pre-emption," pressures for corporate governance legislation were completely dissipated. As an individual active on the issue later put it, "Nader never knew what hit him."

Another opportunity for proactive pre-emption may flow out of the risk of an increased "greenhouse effect" and the dangers associated with a rise in global temperatures. The ozone problem is a contributory factor, but so is the increase in carbon dioxide produced by petro-fuels. There is really only one practicable alternative to continued reliance on coal, oil, and natural gas: nuclear power which, however, has had its own share of environmental problems. Power from nuclear *fusion* (the principle of the hydrogen bomb) holds promise, though, of being both safer and more efficient than the old uranium fission process. The business community could take the lead in solving two enormous problems with a single solution by actively promoting the development of fusion power.

6. *Congressional and legislative redistricting* have always been important to interest groups that want as many of their own people and other friendly candidates elected as possible. New technologies now will enable these groups to become far more involved than ever before. Street-by-street computer maps, for example, are now available from the Census Bureau. Commercially available software allows lobbies, political parties, and legislators to integrate political and demographic data with computer graphics. Users can thus adjust district lines on computerized maps and see instantly what the effects would be on voting behavior and population characteristics.

Interest groups can not only develop their own redistricting proposals, and analyze the schemes of others, but also will be better equipped than ever before to challenge in court the constitutionality of redistricting plans. If the technicalities of the redistricting process will be streamlined, the politics are likely to become more complicated. As one expert said, "What's to stop the left-handed, red-headed Estonian Democrats from coming up with a targeted plan for their district?"[7]

Two factors will determine the utilization and limitations of the new technologies: economic feasibility and government relations effectiveness. Some techniques are more expensive than others—just as some tactics will be more effective than others. For a number of interest groups, cost alone will be a limiting factor (although some technologies, like cable TV, may not be all that expensive). For others, the question will be not cost as such but cost-effectiveness. If the issue is important enough and the stakes large enough, both companies and membership organizations of all kinds will find available a steadily widening array of new tactical instruments with which to accomplish their legislative aims.

Some of these techniques are fully developed and available now. Others are still being refined. Many of them will seem exotic, but what is outlandish today may be commonplace within a few years.

Government relations has made do up to now with a relatively primitive kit of tools and instruments. That period in its development is coming to an end. By the dawn of the next century, the revolutions in computer and communications technology will remake government relations into a medium hardly recognizable to the lobbyists of today.

A CONCLUDING WORD

Whatever the changes in the art and technology of lobbying, the very nature and sensitivity of government relations will always subject it to close scrutiny, high criticism, and repeated calls for reform.

Yet, there is a principle here akin to Adam Smith's "invisible hand" of economics: Individuals, corporations, membership organizations, and crusaders of all kinds will continue to pursue their own causes, seeking private benefits from change in public policy wherever they can. Some will win, most will not. All will claim to serve the public interest, although in reality that is never more than pure lip service.

Ironically, though, the *net sum* of their efforts does contribute to the public interest, and indeed arguably *is* the public interest. In the aggregate pursuit of each interest group's objectives, an ever-shifting balance of power is maintained. In the process, through the same dynamic of checks and balances, the lobbies will continue to hold government accountable, and the stability of the democratic system will continue to be preserved—provided only that our citizens remain vigilant against those who would restrict their First Amendment rights in the name of reform.

The American public may never come to love either the lobbies or the lobbyists. Nonetheless, they are, however unwittingly, democracy's true defenders.

NOTES

1. Spring/Summer 1988. Published quarterly by the Josephson Institute for the Advancement of Ethics, Marina del Rey, California. Ethical considerations compel the

author to disclose that his article, "Ethics, Lobbying and Political Money," appeared (without remuneration) in this issue of *Ethics*.

2. *Ethics*, p. 53.

3. Ibid., p. 55.

4. Tom Kenworthy, "The Hardest House to Break Into," in *The Washington Post National Weekly Edition*, September 5–11, 1988.

5. Richard Armstrong, *The Next Hurrah: The Communications Revolution in American Politics* (New York: Morrow/Beech Tree Books), 1988. A useful and very readable survey of new developments in political technology, with considerable emphasis on the uses of direct mail.

6. Ibid., p. 205.

7. Quoted in *The New York Times*, January 10, 1989.

Sources and Resources

ISSUES TRACKING AND INFORMATION

National Newspapers

Several newspapers with national circulations are sources of information about issues in different regions of the country, in addition to their national and local coverage:

- *Christian Science Monitor*
- *Los Angeles Times*
- *The New York Times*
- *The Wall Street Journal*
- *The Washington Post*

Note that *The Washington Post* publishes a national weekly edition, available by mail subscription, which covers political and governmental news stories and analyses nationwide.

Periodicals on Federal Issues

Amid the slew of Washington information services, a few are pre-eminent:

Congressional Quarterly Weekly Report: *CQ*, as it is universally known, publishes a large number of Washington information sources. Its weekly magazine is a highly respected and authoritative guide to developments in Congress and politics. It is the publication of record on congressional decisions, legislative voting records, and both current and historical election statistics. Published by Congressional Quarterly, Inc., 1414 22nd Street NW, Washington, DC 20037.

National Journal: This weekly publication is the other indispensable guide to major federal policy-making. Although there is some overlap, *National Journal* focuses more on developments in the executive and regulatory agencies than *CQ* does, and tends to emphasize the political and lobbying aspects of issues. Emerging trends and issues are well covered. Published by National Journal, Inc., 1730 M Street NW, Washington, DC 20036.

Daily Report for Executives: About as readable as a legal brief, this newsletter provides authoritative coverage of legislative, regulatory, and judicial developments on business and economic subjects, often including full texts of key documents and reports. DRE is issued each business day by a house that also offers a wide range of other publications and periodicals on regulatory topics. Published by Bureau of National Affairs, 1231 25th Street NW, Washington, DC 20037.

Periodicals on State and Local Issues

- *Governing*: General issues in state and local government. Published by Congressional Quarterly, Inc., 1414 22nd Street NW, Washington, DC 20037. Monthly.

- *Initiative and Referendum Report*: Authoritative and informative newsletter reporting on current issues in direct democracy. Edited by Patrick B. McGuigan. Published by Institute for Government and Politics, 721 Second Street NE, Washington, DC 20002. Monthly.

- *Journal of State Government*: Scholarly analyses of state policy developments. Published by Council of State Governments, P.O. Box 11910, Lexington, KY 40578. Bi-monthly.

- *State Government News*: Information on state policies and programs. Published by Council of State Governments, P.O. Box 11910, Lexington, KY 40578. Monthly.

- *State Legislatures*: Topics of broad interest on state legislation and government. Published by the National Conference of State Legislatures, 1050 17th Street, Denver, CO 80265. 10 issues per year.

- *State Policy Reports*: Analyses of state activities by topic. Published by State Policy Research, Inc., 7706 Lookout Court, Alexandria, VA 22306. Semi-monthly.

Electronic Issues Tracking

Issues tracking is highly computerized today. There are a large number of firms offering public affairs and government relations professionals on-line tracking, database libraries, and management software services. As in any new industry, firms arise and disappear with great frequency. In addition to the data base and software service, there are several offerers of on-line tracking of federal issues that appear relatively stable as of mid–1988. (On-line services provide customers with direct computer-to-computer telephone line linkages so that legislative status and information can be instantly accessed.)

As much as federal issues research has gained from computerization, state government relations has benefited even more. Tracking issues was formerly difficult at best even intra-state, and slow and sometimes impossible on a multi-state basis. Today, tracking of both legislative and regulatory issues has improved enormously. The information available is comprehensive and accessible relatively quickly—indeed, in some states immediately. There are only two fifty-state tracking systems at this writing, down from four several years ago, both of which also track federal issues:

Electronic Legislative Search System: ELSS is an on-line service that tracks both legislative and regulatory developments in both Washington and the fifty state capitals. SLRS, the *State Legislative Reporting Service*, is the printed version of ELSS. Both are published by Commerce Clearing House, Inc., 2700 Lake Cook Road, Riverwoods, IL 60015.

Legi-Slate: On-line congressional issues tracking. Published by Legi-Slate, a subsidiary of The Washington Post Co.; 111 Massachusetts Avenue NW, Washington, DC 20001.

State Net: Legislative and regulatory tracking, covering federal and fifty state governments. Published by Information for Public Affairs, 1900 14th Street, Sacramento, CA 95814.

Washington Alert Service: On-line congressional issues tracking. Published by Congressional Quarterly, Inc.

Washington On-Line: On-line congressional issues tracking. Published by Washington On-Line, 507 Eighth Street SE, Washington, DC 20003.

Comprehensive tracking services are also available in a growing number of individual states, including Alaska, California, Florida, Iowa, Maryland, Michigan, Nebraska, North Dakota, New York, Ohio, Oregon, and Texas. Some of these provide access to the state legislature's own tracking system; others are commercial services. (Access to more limited official services can be obtained in several other states.) The number of states in which either official or commercial tracking services are available is growing and is up-dated in the annual editions of *State Legislative Sourcebook* (see Almanacs and Directories below). Up-dated information on official state systems is also available from the National Conference of State Legislatures. The Public Affairs Council has information on commercial systems.

Many other publications and computerized services offer a variety of information about federal and state governments, including regulatory tracking, legislative analyses, voting records, district profiles and descriptions including streets and zip codes, political contribution sources, and the like. There is also a variety of software and data base services to aid in the management of this information and, generally, of government relations and public affairs programs, including legislation redistricting. The Public Affairs Council and its Foundation for Public Affairs are a good source of current information on these services.

ALMANACS AND DIRECTORIES

Federal Government

- *Almanac of American Politics*: Detailed political profiles of senators, representatives, and governors, and their constituencies. By Michael Barone and Grant Ujifusa. Washington: National Journal. Biannual.
- *Almanac of the Unelected*: Political and biographic profiles of 800 key congressional staffers. Washington: Almanac of the Unelected. Biannual.

- *Braddock's Federal-State-Local Government Directory*: Comprehensive information on Congress. Selected data on federal agencies, state legislators and officials, local officials, political committees, trade associations, labor unions, media, and "think tanks." Washington: Braddock Communications. Annual.

- *The Capital Source*: Comprehensive congressional lists, selected data on federal departments and agencies, and selected information on trade associations, labor unions, political groups, and the media. Washington: National Journal, Inc.

- *Congressional Quarterly's Green Guide*: Selected information on Congress. Washington: CQ. Biannual.

- *Congressional Staff Directory*: Comprehensive list of congressional staff aides. Selected data on other federal officials. Mt. Vernon, VA: Congressional Staff Directory, Ltd. Annual.

- *Congressional Yellow Book*: Comprehensive lists of members of Congress and their staffs, up-dated often. Washington: Monitor Publishing Co. Quarterly.

- *Federal Executive Staff Directory*: Comprehensive lists of executive and regulatory officials, regularly up-dated. Washington: Carroll Publishing Co. Bi-monthly.

- *Federal Regulatory Directory:* Comprehensive descriptions of regulatory agencies, the laws they enforce, and the officials who enforce them. Washington: CQ. Biannual.

- *Federal Staff Directory*: Comprehensive list of executive and regulatory officials. Mt. Vernon, VA: Congressional Staff Directory, Ltd. Annual.

- *Federal Yellow Book*: Comprehensive lists of executive and regulatory agency officials, up-dated often. Washington: Monitor Publishing Co. Quarterly.

- *Judicial Staff Directory*: Judges and officials of the federal courts. Mt. Vernon, VA: Congressional Staff Directory, Ltd. Annual.

- *National Directory of Corporate Public Affairs:* Lists 11,500 public affairs executives in 1,600 companies. Washington: Columbia Books. Annual.

- *National Trade and Professional Associations of the U.S.*: List of 6,000 associations (including labor unions), their C.E.O.s, budget data, etc. Washington: Columbia Books. Annual.

- *Politics in America*: In-depth profiles of each senator and representative. Washington: CQ. Biannual.

- *Public Interest Profiles*: Comprehensive descriptions of about 250 public interest and public policy groups from far right to far left and everything in between. Provides information on each organization relating to scope and interests, political orientation, funding sources, effectiveness, staff, budget, board of directors, etc. Compiled by Foundation for Public Affairs. Washington: CQ. Biannual.

- *Washington '88*: Comprehensive list of 15,000 key figures in 3,400 governmental and private organizations, by subject. Washington: Columbia Books. Annual.

- *Washington Information Directory*: Names, addresses, and telephone numbers for the federal government and private groups, by subject. Washington: CQ. Biannual.

- *Washington Representatives*: Directory of 11,000 executives representing their companies and organizations in Washington, together with officials of trade associations and other Washington-based interest groups. Washington: Columbia Books. Annual.

State Government

- *Book of the States*: An exhaustive and authoritative statistical compendium on numerous aspects of state government. Published by Council of State Governments. Biannual.
- *Campaign Finance, Ethics & Lobby Law Blue Book*: Summaries of laws and pertinent data for the fifty states, and the U.S. and Canadian federal governments. Published by Council of State Governments for an affiliate, the Council on Governmental Ethics Laws. Biannual.
- *The National Directory of State Agencies*: Fifty-state directory of all elected officials, agencies classified by function, and telephone numbers for 13,000 state officials and staff aides. Published by Cambridge Information Group, 7200 Wisconsin Avenue, Bethesda, MD 20814. Annual.
- *State Administrative Officials Classified by Function*. Published by Council of State Governments. Biannual.
- *State Elective Officials and Legislators*. Published by Council of State Governments. Biannual.
- *State Legislative Leadership, Committees and Staffs*. Published by Council of State Governments. Biannual.
- *State Legislative Sourcebook*, by Lynn Hellebust. A thorough and apparently complete resource guide to the legislatures of each of the fifty states. The book lists copious references to legislators, lobbying, and legislative process and schedule, with much additional information. Telephone numbers for obtaining legislative status data and copies of bills are provided for every state. The book also includes an excellent annotated bibliography on state legislatures and lobbying. Published by Government Research Service, 701 Jackson, Topeka, KS 66603. Annual.
- *State Lobbying Laws* is a compendium of information on state lobbying requirements, official interpretations, and sample registration forms; updated as changes occur. Published by State and Federal Associates, Inc., 1101 King Street, Alexandria, VA 22314.
- *State and Regional Associations of the U.S.* Directory of about 5000 groups, their C.E.O.s, budgets, etc., indexed by state. Washington: Columbia Books. Annual.

NEWSLETTERS ON POLITICS

Government floats on a sea of politics—partisan and personal, ideological and institutional. Newsletters on politics abound, almost totally in Washington. Many pontificate, a few are insightful and occasionally even profound. All claim to offer an insider's analysis, and some do.

- *The American Political Report*: National and state political trends and developments. Kevin Phillips, editor. Published by American Political Research Corp., 7316 Wisconsin Avenue, Bethesda, MD 20814. Biweekly.
- *Business & Public Affairs Fortnightly*: Business and politics, social issues, lobbying, public opinion, etc. Kevin Phillips, editor. Published by American Political Research Corp., 7316 Wisconsin Avenue, Bethesda, MD 20814. Biweekly.

- *The Busby Papers*: Thoughtful analyses, trends, and perspectives on politics and government by a long-time observer. Horace Busby, publisher. Published by Horace Busby & Associates, 1280 21st Street NW, Washington, DC 20036. 32-plus issues annually.

- *Congressional Insight*: Commentary on the legislative and political scene. Published by CQ. Weekly.

- *The Evans-Novak Political Report*: Keyhole commentary on politics by the syndicated columnists. Published by Evans-Novak Reports, 1750 Pennsylvania Avenue NW, Washington, DC 20006. Weekly.

- *The GRC Cook Political Report*: The nuts and bolts of Senate and House election campaigns, reported in depth. Charles Cook, editor. Also includes a column by Alan Baron who formerly edited his own well-regarded newsletter. Government Research Corp., 1250 Connecticut Avenue NW, Washington, DC 20036. Issued approximately every six weeks.

- *The Southern Political Report*: Political trends, developments and issues in the twelve states from Virginia to Texas. Hastings Wyman, Jr., editor. Published by Southern Political Report, P.O.B. 15507, Washington, DC 20003–5507. Bi-weekly.

OTHER PUBLICATIONS

- *Campaigns and Elections*: Magazine of news and analysis on management, techniques, and regulation of the political wars. Published by Campaigns and Elections, 1331 Pennsylvania Avenue NW, Washington, DC 20004. Quarterly.

- *Corporate Public Issues and Their Management*: Newsletter on issues management. Edited by Teresa Yancey Crane. Published by Issue Action Publications, 219 South Street SE, Leesburg, VA 22075.

RESOURCE ORGANIZATIONS

National Resource Groups

Many national organizations, all with a point of view, provide information on issues. Others are sources of information on governmental, political, or lobbying processes. Listed here are some of the more significant groups. (For an excellent directory of some 250 "cause" groups, see Public Interest Profiles, listed above under *Almanacs and Directories*.)

All those shown below put out newsletters or other publications that may or may not be restricted to members. Those marked "R" compile and publish ratings of congressional voting records on the issues that concern them. (See Chapter 2 for information on interest group ratings.) All addresses are in Washington, DC, except where otherwise noted.

AFL-CIO Committee on Political Education (labor)   R
    815 Sixteenth Street NW, 20006

American Business Conference (CEOs of entrepreneurial companies)   –
    1730 K Street NW, 20006

American Civil Liberties Union (liberal)   R
  600 Pennsylvania Avenue SW, 20003

American League of Lobbyists (lobbyists of all philosophic persuasions)   –
  P.O. Box 20450, Alexandria, VA 22320

American Security Council (national defense)   R
  499 South Capitol Street SW, 20003

Americans for Constitutional Action (conservative)   R
  955 L'Enfant Plaza North SW, 20024

Americans for Democratic Action (liberal)   R
  1411 K Street NW, 20005

American Society of Association Executives (the trade associations' trade   –
  association)
  1575 Eye Street NW, 20005

Business-Industry Political Action Committee   R
  1747 Pennsylvania Avenue NW, 20006

Business Roundtable (corporate CEOs)   –
  200 Park Avenue, New York, NY 10166

Chamber of Commerce of the United States (business)   R
  1615 H Street NW, 20062

Committee for Survival of a Free Congress (liberal)   R
  721 Second Street NE, 20002

Common Cause (liberal; political and governmental reform)   –
  2030 M Street NW, 20036

Consumer Federation of America   R
  1424 Sixteenth Street NW, 20036

League of Conservation Voters (environmental)   R
  317 Pennsylvania Avenue SE, 20003

League of Women Voters of the U.S. (liberal, civic)   R
  1730 M Street NW, 20036

National Association of Manufacturers   –
  1331 Pennsylvania Avenue NW, 20004

National Federation of Independent Business (small businesses)   –
  150 West 20th Avenue, San Mateo, CA 94403

National Taxpayers Union (government spending)   R
  713 Maryland Avenue NE, 20002

Public Affairs Council (corporate public affairs/government relations profes-   –
  sional group)
  1255 23rd Street NW, 20037

Resource Groups on State and Local Government

State and local lawmakers and officials are great joiners. There are associations of
lieutenant governors and attorneys general, as well as the better known organizations

of legislators and governors, among many others. These organizations exist to provide their members with opportunities to exchange information and ideas with peers from other states and localities concerning potential new policies, programs, and operations. If a state or local government develops new programs on AIDS, solid waste management, or budge controls, these organizations are the media by which counterparts across the country are kept posted, often through vast publications programs. These groups sometimes coordinate multi-state projects including, for example, an investigation of nutrition claims in advertising by the attorneys general.

Many of these groups maintain corporate support programs and other channels to the private sector, as sources of both revenue and ideas. They are valuable resource groups because they provide opportunities both to influence public policy concepts on almost a wholesale level and also to develop contacts among state and local legislators and officials nationwide. Among the more significant associations are:

Council of State Governments
P.O. Box 11910, Lexington, KY 40578

International City Management Association (professional municipal administrators
1120 G Street NW, Washington, DC 20005

National Association of Attorneys General
444 North Capitol Street NW, Washington, DC 20001

National Association of Counties
440 First Street NW, Washington, DC 20001

National Association of Towns and Townships (small communities)
1522 K Street NW, Washington, DC 20005

National Conference of State Legislators
1050 17th Street, Denver, CO 80265

National Governors Association
444 North Capitol Street NW, Washington, DC 20001

National League of Cities (most populous cities)
1301 Pennsylvania Avenue NW, Washington, DC 20004

State Governmental Affairs Council. (Private-sector association of over 100 companies and trade associations that maintains liaison between its members and some of the above state public-sector groups. Membership is open to organizations doing business in four or more states with full-time state government relations programs.)
1001 Connecticut Avenue NW, Washington, DC 20036

U.S. Conference of Mayors (large and medium-sized cities)
1620 Eye Street NW, Washington, DC 20006

Selected Bibliography

The following publications deal with particular aspects of government relations for those interested in additional reading. Lists of periodicals, reference works, tracking services, resource groups, and related materials are found under Sources and Resources.

BOOKS

Alexander, Herbert E. *The Case for PACs*. Washington: Public Affairs Council, 1983.

———*Financing Politics: Money, Elections, and Political Reform*, 3rd ed. Washington: CQ Press, 1984.

———*"Soft Money" and Campaign Financing*. Washington: Public Affairs Council, 1986.

Armstrong, Richard. *The Next Hurrah: The Communications Revolution in American Politics*. New York: Morrow Beech Tree Books, 1988.

Berry, Jeffrey M. *The Interest Group Society*. Glenview, IL: Scott Foresman, 1984.

———*Lobbying for the People: The Political Behavior of Public Interest Groups*. Princeton, NJ: Princeton University Press, 1977.

Broder, David S. *Changing of the Guard: Power and Leadership in America*. New York: Penguin Books, 1981.

Caplan, Marc. *Ralph Nader Presents a Citizens' Guide to Lobbying*. New York: Dembner Books, 1983.

Chase, W. Howard. *Issue Management: Origins of the Future*. Stamford: Issue Action Publications, 1984.

Ciglar, Allan J., and Burdett A. Loomis. *Interest Group Politics*, 2nd ed. Washington: CQ Press, 1986.

Davies, Jack. *Legislative Law and Process*, 2nd ed. St. Paul: West Publishing Co., 1986.

Deakin, James. *The Lobbyists*. Washington: Public Affairs Press, 1966.

Dominguez, George S. *Government Relations: A Handbook for Developing and Conducting the Company Program*. New York: John Wiley, 1982.

Eastman, Hope. *Lobbying: A Constitutionally Protected Right*. Washington: American Enterprise Institute for Public Policy Research, 1977.

Epstein, Edwin M. *The Corporation in American Politics*. Englewood Cliffs, NJ: Prentice-Hall, 1969.

Ewing, Raymond P. *Managing the New Bottom Line: Issues Management for Senior Executives*. Homewood, IL: Dow Jones-Irwin, 1987.

Grefe, Edward A. *Fighting to Win: Business Political Power*. New York: Harcourt Brace Jovanovich, 1981.

Harris, Fred R., and Paul L. Hain. *America's Legislative Processes: Congress and the States*. Glenview, IL: Scott, Foresman, 1983.

Heath, Robert L., and Richard Alan Nelson. *Issues Management: Corporate Public Policymaking in an Information Society*. Beverly Hills: SAGE Publications, 1986.

Heath, Robert L., and Associates. *Strategic Issues Management: How Organizations Influence and Respond to Public Interests and Policies*. San Francisco: Jossey-Bass, Inc., 1988.

Hrebenar, Ronald J., and Ruth K. Scott. *Interest Group Politics in America*. Englewood Cliffs, NJ: Prentice-Hall, 1982.

Jewell, Malcolm E. *Representation in State Legislatures*. Lexington: University Press of Kentucky, 1982.

———, and Samuel C. Patterson. *The Legislative Process in the United States*, 4th ed. New York: Random House, 1985.

Key, V. O. *Politics, Parties, and Pressure Groups*. New York: Thomas Y. Crowell, 1964.

Kingdon, John W. *Agenda, Alternatives, and Public Policies*. Glenview, IL: Scott Foresman, 1984.

Lustberg, Arch. *Testifying with Impact*. Washington: Chamber of Commerce of the U.S., 1982.

Lusterman, Seymour. *The Organization & Staffing of Corporate Public Affairs*. New York: The Conference Board, 1987.

———. *Managing Federal Government Relations*. New York: The Conference Board, 1988.

Magleby, David B. *Direct Legislation: Voting on Ballot Propositions in the United States*. Baltimore: Johns Hopkins University Press, 1984.

Malbin, Michael J. *Parties, Interest Groups, and Campaign Finance Laws*. Washington: American Enterprise Institute for Public Policy Research, 1980.

Matasar, Ann B. *Corporate PACs and Federal Campaign Financing Laws: Use or Abuse of Power?* Westport, CT: Quorum Books, 1986.

Mater, Jean. *Public Hearings, Procedures and Strategies: A Guide to Influencing Public Decisions*. Englewood Cliffs, NJ: Prentice-Hall, 1984.

McFarland, Andrew S. *Common Cause: Lobbying in the Public Interest*. Chatham, NJ: Chatham House, 1984.

McGuigan, Patrick B. *The Politics of Direct Democracy in the 1980s: Case Studies in Popular Decision Making*. Washington: The Institute for Government and Politics of the Free Congress Research and Education Foundation, 1985.

Nagelschmidt, Joseph S., ed. *The Public Affairs Handbook*. New York: American Management Associations, 1982.

Nowlan, Stephen E., and Diana R. Shayon. *Leveraging the Impact of Public Affairs: A Guidebook Based on Practical Experience for Corporate Public Affairs Executives*. Philadelphia: HRN, 1984.

Ornstein, Norman J., and Shirley Elder. *Interest Groups, Lobbying, and Policymaking*. Washington: CQ Press, 1978.

Peirce, Neal R., and Jerry Hagstrom. *The Book of America: Inside 50 States Today*. New York: W. W. Norton, 1983.

Ritchie, James I. *How to Work Effectively with State Legislatures*. Washington: American Society of Association Executives, 1969.

Rosenthal, Alan. *Legislative Life: People, Process, and Performance in the States*. New York: Harper & Row, 1981.

Sethi, S. Prakash. *Handbook of Advocacy Advertising: Concepts, Strategies and Applications*. Cambridge, MA: Ballinger, 1987.

Sorauf, Frank J. *Money in American Elections*. Glenview, IL: Scott, Foresman, 1988.

Stanley, Guy D. D. *Managing External Issues: Theory and Practice*. Greenwich: JAI Press, 1985.

Truman, David B. *The Governmental Process*. New York: Alfred A. Knopf, 1964.

The Washington Lobby, 5th ed. Washington: Congressional Quarterly, 1987.

Webster, George D., and Frederick J. Krebs. *Associations and Lobbying Regulation: A Guide for Non-Profit Organizations*. Washington: Chamber of Commerce of the U.S., 1985.

Webster, George D. *The Law of Associations*. New York: Matthew Bender, 1986.

What Price PACs? New York: The Twentieth Century Fund, 1984.

ARTICLES

Barry, John M. "Business Lobbyists Battle Each Other," *Dun's Business Month*, January 1987.

Baysinger, Barry D., and Richard W. Woodman. "Dimensions of the Public Affairs/Government Relations Function in Major American Corporations," *Strategic Management Journal*, 3: 27–41 (1982).

Boyle, Larry, and John Hysom. "Independent Expenditures: Cutting through Barriers," *District Lawyer*, May/June 1986.

Crandall, Derrick A. "Working with Congressional Staffs," *Association Management*, June 1988.

Frammolino, Ralph. "Big Business Taps Its Own for Lobbyists," *Los Angeles Times*, April 4, 1988.

Garbett, Thomas F. "When to Advertise Your Company," *Harvard Business Review*, March-April 1982.

Haley, Martin Ryan, and James M. Kiss. "Larger Stakes in Statehouse Lobbying," *Harvard Business Review*, January-February 1974.

Keim, Gerald, Carl Zeithaml, and Barry Baysinger. "New Directions for Corporate Political Strategy," *Sloan Management Review*, Spring 1984.

Keim, Gerry. "Corporate Grassroots Programs in the 1980s," *California Management Review*, Fall 1985.

Keller, Morton. "State Power Needn't Be Resurrected Because It Never Died," *Governing*, October 1988.

Kelley, David. "Critical Issues for Issue Ads," *Harvard Business Review*, July-August 1982.

Komisarjevsky, Christopher P. A. "Communications Strategy: Fighting Your Way Out of the Fishbowl," *Journal of Business Strategy*, Winter 1982.

Marchand, Roland. "The Fitful Career of Advocacy Advertising: Political Protection, Client Cultivation, and Corporate Morale," *California Management Review*, Winter 1987.

Melloan, George. "What to Do When Your Own Lobby is Against You," *Wall Street Journal*, February 16, 1988.

Molitor, Graham T. T. "Plotting the Patterns of Change," *Enterprise*, March 1984.

Moore, W. John. "Dear Feds—Help!" [re federal preemption of state regulation], *National Journal*, July 9, 1988.

Moore, W. John. "Have Smarts, Will Travel," [re growth of state government relations], *National Journal*, November 28, 1987.

Nathan, Richard P., and Martha Derthick. "Reagan's Legacy: A New Liberalism Among the States," *New York Times*, December 18, 1987.

Noble, John F. "A New In-Kind Giving Opportunity," *Campaigns & Elections*, Winter 1985.

Nolan, Joseph T. "Political Surfing When Issues Break," *Harvard Business Review*, January-February 1985.

Post, James E., et al. "The Public Affairs Function," *California Management Review*, Fall 1983.

Solomon, Burt. "Measuring Clout," *National Journal*, July 4, 1987.

Tierney, John. "Old Money, New Power" [profile of the American Association of Retired People]. *New York Times Magazine*, October 23, 1988.

Victor, Kirk. "Being Here" [re Washington corporate offices], *National Journal*, August 6, 1988.

Wheeler, Douglas P. "A Political Handbook for the Environmental Movement," *Washington Post National Weekly Edition*, September 19–25, 1988.

"Why the Democratic Process Cannot Function without Lobbying," *Journal of American Insurance*, vol. 60, no. 3 (1984).

GOVERNMENT PUBLICATIONS

Campaign Guide for Corporations and Labor Unions. Washington: Federal Election Commission, 1986.

Campaign Guide for Nonconnected Committees. Washington: Federal Election Commission, 1985.

Supporting Federal Candidates: A Guide for Citizens. Washington: Federal Election Commission, 1987.

APPENDICES

Appendix A

A Statement of Ethical Guidelines for Business Public Affairs Professionals

Public Affairs Council

A. The Public Affairs Professional maintains professional relationships based on honesty and reliable information, and therefore:
1. Represents accurately his or her organization's policies on economic and political matters to government, employees, shareholders, community interests, and others.
2. Serves always as a source of reliable information, discussing the varied aspects of complex public issues within the context and constraints of the advocacy role.
3. Recognizes diverse viewpoints within the public policy process, knowing that disagreement on issues is both inevitable and healthy.

B. The Public Affairs Professional seeks to protect the integrity of the public policy process and the political system, and therefore:
1. Publicly acknowledges his or her role as a legitimate participant in the public policy process and discloses whatever work-related information the law requires.
2. Knows, respects and abides by federal and state laws that apply to lobbying and related public affairs activities.
3. Knows and respects the laws governing campaign finance and other political activities, and abides by the letter and intent of those laws.

C. The Public Affairs Professional understands the interrelation of business interests with the larger public interests, and therefore:
1. Endeavors to ensure that responsible and diverse external interests and views concerning the needs of society are considered within the corporate decision-making process.
2. Bears the responsibility for management review of public policies which may bring corporate interests into conflict with other interests.
3. Acknowledges dual obligations—to advocate the interests of his or her employer, and to preserve the openness and integrity of the democratic process.
4. Presents to his or her employer an accurate assessment of the political and social realities that may affect corporate operations.

May 1979

Appendix B

Guidelines for the Operation of a Business-Employee Political Action Committee

Public Affairs Council

THE BASIC PREMISES

In our free society, citizens have the inherent right to join together to protect their interests, be they philosophical or economic, and to assert a joint point of view. Moreover, they have the right to pool their resources to assist in the election of public officials who they feel share their attitudes and aspirations about the conduct of government.

Present laws governing contributions to political campaigns, while not perfect are indisputably a vast improvement over previous laws and practices. Based on the key principles of volunteerism and disclosure, enacted by Congress and endorsed by the Supreme Court, they have demonstrably increased the involvement of the citizenry in our political processes. They have provided a much-needed balance in interest-group participation, and have expanded and augmented our democratic processes through the establishment of Political Action Committees.

Political Action Committees (PACs) are diverse in membership, interests and political goals. They are a legitimate reflection of myriad cultural, social, ideological, labor, and private economic interest groups found throughout this vast and complex nation. Consequently, PACs as a group do not constitute a monolithic influence. Environmentalist and conservationist PACs do not speak with one voice or support the same legislators. PACs concerned with the well-being of various foreign nations do not speak with one voice. Labor PACs do not speak with one voice. And certainly the economic and business-oriented PACs do not speak with one voice.

No two people are the same. As individuals we differ in an almost infinite variety of ways. The same is true of American business. No two are identical in size, organizational structure, operating area, management style, and especially internal operating policies and procedures. So it is with the PACs that businesses have sponsored. Laws establishing PACs place primary emphasis on disclosure and contribution levels. Very prudently they provide wide latitude and discretion as to how PACs should be structured and operated internally.

Intensive research, studies, and conferences conducted by the Public Affairs Council verify that, as a consequence of the varied nature of individual businesses, as well as the laws regulating PACs, no two business-sponsored PACs are structured or operate in exactly the same manner. There simply is no uniformity. Even those businesses which consider their PACs to be operating successfully are continually fine-tuning them and changing their procedures and systems—largely in response to the wishes of the contributing employee members. There is no such thing as a "model" PAC, nor can any single business be singled out as having the "best" PAC.

It appears inevitable that additional business-employee PACs will be established. Americans, taking an ever-increasing interest in political affairs, want options in the way they can express themselves, and PACs have proven to be a remarkably beneficial and popular option.

The Public Affairs Council cannot and indeed should not define a "model" business-employee PAC. In its years of working with corporate Public Affairs Directors and their organizations, the Council has, however, acquired vast amounts of knowledge and information about the operation of all types of PACs. It feels an obligation and responsibility to share with businesses and their employees what the Council considers to be guidelines essential to the operation of a successful and effective federal PAC.

GUIDELINES

1. Compliance with all Federal and State laws and regulations is essential. This extends beyond merely filing prompt and accurate reports. The spirit and intent of the laws, while not always easy to discern, must be upheld. The spirit of volunteerism should be authentic in practice—no career rewards for contributing, no stigma for not contributing. All PAC contribution records should be confidential to the extent possible under provisions of the law. No PAC should seek, request, or expect any specific benefits from any incumbent or challenging candidate as a reward for a contribution. Nor should a PAC do anything in substance, or even in appearance, to circumvent legal giving limits.

2. The business-employee PAC should be more than merely a system for people with common interests to pool their resources to assist in the election of, or defeat of, a holder of public office. It should encourage its contributing members to involve themselves in a broad range of voluntary political activities at all levels of government. If conditions permit, it should provide opportunities for personal contact between the PAC members and the political decision-makers who receive, or perhaps wish to receive, the PAC's contributions.

3. The business-employee PAC should keep its contributing members well informed on the activities of the PAC—the contributions it has made, the recipients, and the criteria under which those recipients were selected. No PAC member should ever have to resort to newspaper or TV news to learn what his PAC governing board has done—or why. Every business has its own system for communicating with employees; these resources should be utilized to the fullest to keep PAC members continually conversant with the activities of their PAC.

4. The business-employee PAC should, to the fullest extent possible, envision itself as a mini-political entity, separate from and independent of corporate management. Broad participation should be sought. PAC members should be encouraged through a variety of means to recommend support for various candidates of their choice

in either major political party or in independent parties. They should also be encouraged to make suggestions for improving our political processes. Suggestions should include the criteria the PAC uses for determining the recipients of its contribution.

5. In considering the making of political contributions, the following factors, among others, should be weighed by the business-employee PAC:

   a. The degree of opposition faced by the candidate;
   b. the appropriateness of giving to more than one candidate in any single primary or general election;
   c. the financial need of the candidate;
   d. whether or not the person is a candidate in the current election cycle; and
   e. whether or not the funds will be distributed by the candidate to others.

September 1986

Appendix C

Guidelines for Professional Conduct

American League of Lobbyists

The American League of Lobbyists believes that effective government depends on the greatest possible participation of those being governed. At the federal level, such participation focuses on the legislative and executive branches where professional and citizen lobbyists drawn from every major discipline represent literally every segment of society and every sector of the economy.

The League further believes that the heavy responsibility of the professional lobbyist, functioning in the eye of public opinion, requires standards of ethical behavior beyond those generally accepted by a free and moral society.

The League, therefore, offers the following guidelines which it urges be observed by its members and all those whose professional objectives are to influence national public policy decisions:

- The professional lobbyist accepts the fact that it is the system of representative government we enjoy that makes possible the practice of lobbying and, while keeping the interest of employer or client in a position of primacy, will temper the advocacy role with proper consideration for the general public interest.

- The professional lobbyist will protect confidences, not only those of the employer or client but those of elected and appointed officials of government and professional colleagues.

- The professional lobbyist will always deal in accurate, current and factual information, whether it is being reported to the employer or client, government officials, the media or professional colleagues, and will not engage in misrepresentation of any nature.

- The professional lobbyist will acquire enough knowledge of public policy issues to be able to fairly present all points of view.

- The professional lobbyist will avoid conflicts of interest, not only conflict with the interests of the employer or client, but also those of colleagues pursuing the same or similar objectives, and where conflict is unavoidable will communicate the facts fully and freely to those affected.

- The professional lobbyist will comply with the laws and regulations governing lobbying as well as the standards of conduct applying to officials and staff of the Congress and the Executive Branch and will strive to go one step further and function in a manner that goes beyond these official enactments and promulgations.

- The personal conduct of the professional lobbyist should not bring discredit to the profession, government or individual colleagues.

- The professional lobbyist will refrain from any form of discrimination which is legally proscribed or simply generally recognized as such.

- A priority goal of the professional lobbyist should be to increase public understanding of the process and this objective should be pursued in every possible way— public appearances, media contacts, articles in company and other publications, and contacts in the normal course of everyday life.

- The professional lobbyist should constantly strive to upgrade the necessary skills by every means available, continuing formal education, attendance at meetings and seminars, and participation in ad hoc groups with like-minded colleagues.

September 1987

Index

About the Author

CHARLES S. MACK is a management consultant with more than a quarter-century of experience in corporate government relations, trade association management and politics—at both federal and state levels. He was president and chief executive officer of the New York State Food Merchants Association, and earlier director of public and government affairs for CPC International Inc. Previously, he directed the consumer affairs program of the Chamber of Commerce of the U.S. and spent five years on the staff of the Republican National Committee. He ran successfully for political office in Maryland and later chaired a victorious Congressional campaign in New Jersey. He has taught, spoken, and written widely on government relations.